Debating the Presidency

Debating the Presidency

CONFLICTING PERSPECTIVES ON THE AMERICAN EXECUTIVE

SECOND EDITION

EDITED BY

RICHARD J. ELLIS
Willamette University

AND

MICHAEL NELSON
Rhodes College

CQ PRESS

A Division of SAGE
Washington, D.C.

CQ Press
2300 N Street, NW, Suite 800
Washington, DC 20037

Phone: 202-729-1900; toll-free, 1-866-4CQ-PRESS (1-866-427-7737)
Web: www.cqpress.com

Cover design: Matthew Simmons, Myself Included Design
Cover photo: © Brooks Kraft/Corbis
Typesetting: C&M Digitals (P) Ltd.

⊖ The paper used in this publication exceeds the requirements of the American
National Standard for Information Sciences—Permanence of Paper for Printed
Library Materials, ANSI Z39.48-1992.

Printed and bound in the United States of America

13   12   11   10   09   1   2   3   4   5

Library of Congress Cataloging-in-Publication Data
Debating the Presidency : conflicting perspectives on the American executive / edited
by Richard J. Ellis and Michael Nelson. — 2nd ed.
     p. cm.
  Includes bibliographical references.
  ISBN 978-1-60426-565-1 (pbk. : alk. paper) 1. Executive power—United States.
2. Presidents—United States. I. Ellis, Richard (Richard J.) II. Nelson, Michael,
III. Title.

  JK516.D43 2010
  352.230973—dc22

                                                                        2009028520

To the memory of Francis E. Rourke,
professor of political science,
Johns Hopkins University

CONTENTS

PREFACE

In 1969 the political scientist Aaron Wildavsky published a hefty reader on the American presidency. He prefaced it with the observation that "the presidency is the most important political institution in American life" and then noted the paradox that an institution of such overwhelming importance had been studied so little. "The eminence of the institution," Wildavsky wrote, "is matched only by the extraordinary neglect shown to it by political scientists. Compared to the hordes of researchers who regularly descend on Congress, local communities, and the most remote foreign principalities, there is an extraordinary dearth of students of the presidency, although scholars ritually swear that the presidency is where the action is before they go somewhere else to do their research."[1]

Political scientists have come a long way since 1969. The presidency remains as central to national life as it was then, and perhaps even more so. The state of scholarly research on the presidency today is unrecognizable compared with what it was forty years ago. A rich array of new studies has reshaped our understanding of presidential history, presidential character, the executive office, and the presidency's relationship with the public, interest groups, parties, Congress, and the executive branch. Neglect is no longer a problem in the study of the presidency.

In addition, those who teach about the presidency no longer lack for good textbooks on the subject. A number of terrific books explain how the office has developed and how it works. Although students gain a great deal from reading these texts, even the best of them can inadvertently promote a passive learning experience. Textbooks convey what political scientists know, but the balance and impartiality that mark a good text can obscure the contentious nature of the scholarly enterprise. Sharp disagreements are often smoothed over in the writing.

The primary purpose of *Debating the Presidency* is to allow students to participate directly in the ongoing real-world controversies swirling around the presidency and to judge for themselves which side is right. It is premised philosophically on our view of students as active learners to be engaged rather than as passive receptacles to be filled. The book is designed to promote a classroom experience in which students debate and discuss issues rather than simply listen to lectures.

Some issues, of course, lend themselves more readily to this kind of classroom debate. In our judgment, questions of a normative nature—asking not just what is, but what ought to be—are likely to foster the most interesting and engaging classroom discussions. So in selecting topics for debate, we generally eschewed narrow but important empirical questions of political science—such as whether the president receives greater support from Congress on foreign policy than on domestic issues—for broader questions that include empirical as well as normative components—such as whether the president has usurped the war power that rightfully belongs to Congress. We aim not only to teach students to think like political scientists, but also to encourage them to think like democratic citizens.

Each of the thirteen issues selected for debate in this book's second edition poses questions on which thoughtful people differ. These include whether the president should be elected directly by the people, whether the media are too hard on presidents, and whether the president has too much power in the selection of judges. Scholars are trained to see both sides of an argument, but we invited our contributors to choose one side and defend it vigorously. Rather than provide balanced scholarly essays impartially presenting the strengths and weaknesses of each position, *Debating the Presidency* leaves the balancing and weighing of arguments and evidence to the reader.

The essays contained in the first edition of this book were written near the end of President George W. Bush's fifth year in office; this second edition was assembled during and after Barack Obama's first 100 days as president. The new edition includes four new debate resolutions that should spark spirited classroom discussion about the legitimacy of signing statements, the war on terror, the role of the vice presidency, and the Twenty-second Amendment. Nine debate resolutions have been retained from the first edition and, wherever appropriate, the essays have been revised to reflect recent scholarship or events. For this edition we welcome David Karol, Tom Cronin, John Yoo, Lou Fisher, Peter Shane, Nelson Lund, Doug Kriner, and Joel Goldstein, as well as Fred Greenstein, who joins the debate with Stephen Skowronek over the importance of individual attributes in accounting for presidential success.

In deciding which debate resolutions to retain from the first edition and which ones to add, we were greatly assisted by advice we received from many professors who adopted the first edition of this book. Particularly helpful were the reviewers commissioned by CQ Press: Craig Goodman of Texas Tech University, Delbert J. Ringquist of Central Michigan University, Brooks D. Simpson of Arizona State University, and Ronald W. Vardy of the University of Houston. We are also deeply grateful to chief acquisitions editor Charisse Kiino for her continuing encouragement and guidance in developing this volume. Among the others who helped make the project a success were editorial assistants Jason McMann and Christina Mueller, copy editor Mary Marik, and the book's production editor, Gwenda Larsen. Our deepest thanks go to the contributors, not just for their essays, but also for their excellent scholarship on the presidency.

—Richard J. Ellis and Michael Nelson

CONTRIBUTORS

Terri Bimes is the director of the Center for the Study of Representation and a lecturer in the department of political science at the University of California, Berkeley. Her book manuscript, *The Metamorphosis of Presidential Populism,* examines the evolution of presidential rhetoric from Andrew Jackson through Barack Obama.

Andrew E. Busch is professor of government at Claremont McKenna College, where he teaches courses on American politics and government. He is the author or coauthor of eleven books, including *Horses in Midstream: U.S. Midterm Elections and Their Consequences, 1894–1998* (1999); *Ronald Reagan and the Politics of Freedom* (2001); *The Front-Loading Problem in Presidential Nominations* (2004); *The Constitution on the Campaign Trail: The Surprising Political Career of America's Founding Document* (2007); and, most recently, *Epic Journey: The 2008 Elections and American Politics* (2009). He received his doctorate from the University of Virginia.

Thomas E. Cronin is the McHugh Professor of American Institutions and Leadership at Colorado College and president emeritus at Whitman College. He is author, coauthor, or editor of more than a dozen books on American politics, including, as author, *On the Presidency* (2009) and, as coauthor, *The Paradoxes of the American Presidency* (3rd ed., 2010). He is a past president of both the Presidency Research Group and the Western Political Science Association.

Richard J. Ellis is the Mark O. Hatfield Professor of Politics at Willamette University. Among his recent books are *To the Flag: The Unlikely History of the Pledge of Allegiance* (2005) and *Presidential Travel: The Journey from George Washington to George W. Bush* (2008). In 2008 he was named the Carnegie Foundation for Advancement of Teaching Oregon Professor of the Year.

Louis Fisher is specialist in constitutional law with the Law Library of the Library of Congress. Earlier in his career at the Library of Congress, from 1970 to 2006, he worked for the Congressional Research Service. During his service with CRS he was senior specialist in separation of powers, and in 1987 he was research director of the House Iran-Contra Committee, writing major sections of the final report. He is the author of numerous books, including *Presidential War Power* (2nd ed., 2004), *Constitutional Conflicts between Congress and the President* (5th ed., 2005), *Military Tribunals and Presidential*

Power: American Revolution to the War on Terrorism (2006), and *The Constitution and 9/11: Recurring Threats to America's Freedoms* (2008). He testifies frequently before congressional committees on such issues as war powers, state secrets, national security whistleblowing, covert spending, and National Security Agency surveillance. He received his doctorate in political science from the New School for Social Research and has taught in a number of universities and law schools. The views expressed in his essay are personal, not institutional.

Joel K. Goldstein is the Vincent C. Immel Professor of Law at Saint Louis University School of Law where he teaches courses on constitutional law. He is the author of *The Modern American Vice Presidency: The Transformation of a Political Institution* (1982) and of numerous other books and articles about the vice presidency, the presidency, and constitutional law. He is currently at work on a new book on the vice presidency as well as on projects dealing with the political career of Senator Edmund S. Muskie and the work of Justice Louis D. Brandeis. He received his doctorate of philosophy in politics from Oxford University, which he attended as a Rhodes Scholar, and his law degree from Harvard Law School.

Fred I. Greenstein is professor of politics emeritus at Princeton University. His books include *Children and Politics* (1965), *Personality and Politics* (1969), *The Hidden-Hand Presidency: Eisenhower as Leader* (1982), *How Presidents Test Reality* (with John P. Burke, 1989), *The Presidential Difference: Leadership Style from FDR to Barack Obama* (2009), and *Inventing the Job of President: Leadership Style from George Washington to Andrew Jackson* (2009). He is a fellow of the American Academy of Arts and Sciences and past president of the International Society for Political Psychology. He received his doctorate from Yale University in 1960.

Marc J. Hetherington is professor of political science at Vanderbilt University. He is the coauthor of *Authoritarianism and Polarization in American Politics* (with Jonathan Weiler, 2009) and the author of *Why Trust Matters: Declining Political Trust and the Demise of American Liberalism* (2006). He has also published numerous articles on political trust, party polarization, and other topics in *American Political Science Review, American Journal of Political Science, Journal of Politics,* and *British Journal of Political Science.* In 2004, he won the Emerging Scholar Award from the Elections, Public Opinion, and Voting Behavior section of the American Political Science Association as the top scholar in the field within ten years of earning a doctorate.

David Karol is an assistant professor of political science at the University of California, Berkeley. His interests include parties, institutions, interest groups, and American political development. He was a visiting scholar at the Center for the Study of Democratic Politics at Princeton University in 2002–2003. Karol is the author of *Party Position Change in American Politics: Coalition Management* (2009), coauthor of *The Party Decides: Presidential Nominations before and after Reform* (with Marty Cohen, Hans Noel, and John Zaller, 2008), and coeditor of *Nominating the President: Evolution and Revolution in 2008 and Beyond* (with Jack Citrin, 2009). His work has appeared in *International Organization, Journal of Politics, Studies in American Political Development, Brookings Review, The Forum,* and edited volumes. His current research focuses on the role of elite opinion in American politics.

Nancy Kassop is professor and chair of the department of political science and international relations at the State University of New York at New Paltz. She writes on issues of the presidency and law. Her most recent articles are "The White House Counsel's Office" (coauthored with Mary Anne Borrelli and Karen Hult), in *The White House World: Transitions, Organization, and Office Operations* (edited by Martha J. Kumar and Terry Sullivan, 2003); "When Law and Politics Collide: Presidents and the Use of the Twenty-Fifth Amendment," in *Presidential Studies Quarterly* (March 2005); and "A Political Question by Any Other Name: Government Litigation Strategy in the Enemy Combatant Cases of *Hamdi* and *Padilla,*" in *The Political Question Doctrine and the Supreme Court of the United States* (edited by Nada Mourtada-Sabbah and Bruce E. Cain, 2007).

Matthew R. Kerbel is professor of political science at Villanova University and author or editor of seven books and multiple scholarly articles on American politics, the mass media, and the presidency, including *Netroots: Online Progressives and the Transformation of American Politics* (2009), which details the effectiveness of online progressive activists in achieving political outcomes, shaping media narratives, and building virtual and real communities. His earlier writings addressed television's often detrimental role in the political process, and derived in part from his experiences working as a radio and television news writer for various outlets including the Public Broadcasting Service in New York City.

Douglas L. Kriner is assistant professor of political science at Boston University. His research examines American political institutions and the importance of inter-institutional dynamics in shaping political strategies and policy outcomes. His work has recently appeared in the *Journal of Politics, British Journal of Political Science, Presidential Studies Quarterly,* and *Legislative Studies Quarterly.* He is coauthor (with Francis Shen) of *The Casualty Gap: The Causes and Consequences of American Wartime Inequalities* (forthcoming). He is also completing a book manuscript that examines how congressional constraints have shaped presidential conduct of major military actions from the end of Reconstruction to the war in Iraq.

Marc Landy is professor of political science at Boston College. He and Sidney Milkis wrote *Presidential Greatness* (2000) and *American Government: Balancing Democracy and Rights* (2008). Their essay, "The Presidency in the Eye of the Storm," appears in the current edition of *The Presidency and the Political System* (edited by Michael Nelson, 9th ed., 2010). In addition to writing about the presidency, he also writes about federalism, public policy, and the environment. His article, "Mega-Disasters and Federalism," was published in October 2008 in *Public Administration Review*. He is an author of *The Environmental Protection Agency: Asking the Wrong Questions: From Nixon to Clinton* (1994) and an editor of *The New Politics of Public Policy* (1995), *Seeking the Center: Politics and Policymaking at the New Century* (2001), and *Creating Competitive Markets: The Politics of Regulatory Reform* (2007).

Burdett Loomis is professor of political science at the University of Kansas. He received his doctorate from the University of Wisconsin–Madison in 1974 and served as an American Political Science Association congressional fellow in 1975–1976 in the office of the then-representative Paul Simon, D-Ill. He was a guest scholar at the Brookings Institution in Washington, D.C., in 1984 and 2000 and was named a Fulbright Senior Scholar in 2006 (Argentina). He has written or edited more than twenty-five books in various editions. His scholarship focuses on legislatures, interest groups, and policy making. Among his books are *The New American Politician* (1990), *Time, Politics, and Policy: A Legislative Year* (1994), and *The Sound of Money* (coauthor, 1998). In addition, he has coedited seven editions of *Interest Group Politics*. He won a Kemper Teaching Award in 1996 and has lectured for the State Department in Brazil, the West Indies, Mexico, Malaysia, Singapore, China, Iraq, Nepal, and Bangladesh. His current work focuses on political change in Kansas in the 1960s and 1970s as well as editing *A Guide to Interest Groups*, an extensive set of original essays.

Nelson Lund is the Patrick Henry Professor of Constitutional Law and the Second Amendment at George Mason University School of Law, where he has served as vice dean and as coeditor of the *Supreme Court Economic Review*. Professor Lund served as law clerk for Judge Patrick E. Higginbotham of the U.S. Court of Appeals for the Fifth Circuit (1985–1986) and for Supreme Court justice Sandra Day O'Connor (October Term 1987). In addition to experience in the U.S. Department of Justice at the Office of the Solicitor General and at the Office of Legal Counsel, Lund served in the White House as associate counsel to the president from 1989 to 1992. He holds a doctorate from Harvard University and a law degree from the University of Chicago, where he was executive editor of the *University of Chicago Law Review.*

John Anthony Maltese is the Albert Berry Saye Professor of American Government and Constitutional Law and head of the political science department at the University of Georgia. His books include *Spin Control: The White House Office of Communications and the Management of Presidential News* (1994), *The Selling of Supreme Court Nominees* (1998), and *The Politics of the Presidency,* currently in its 7th revised edition (with Joseph A. Pika, 2010). He was named Georgia Professor of the Year by the Carnegie Foundation for the Advancement of Teaching and the Council for the Advancement and Support of Education in 2004 and is a Josiah Meigs Distinguished Teaching Professor, the University of Georgia's highest teaching honor.

Bruce Miroff is professor of political science at the State University of New York, Albany, and a former president of the Presidency Research Group. His most recent books are *Icons of Democracy: American Leaders as Heroes, Aristocrats, Dissenters, and Democrats* (2000), *The Liberals' Moment: The McGovern Insurgency and the Identity Crisis of the Democratic Party* (2007), and *The Democratic Debate: American Politics in an Age of Change* (5th ed., 2010).

Michael Nelson is the Fulmer Professor of Political Science at Rhodes College, where he teaches courses on U.S. politics, the presidency, and southern politics. He is also a senior fellow of the Miller Center of Public Affairs at the University of Virginia and a former editor of the *Washington Monthly.* His recent books include *The American Presidency: Origins and Development, 1776–2007* (with Sidney M. Milkis, 5th ed., 2008), *How the South Joined the Gambling Nation: The Politics of State Policy Innovation* (with John Mason, 2008), which won the Southern Political Science Association's V. O. Key Award for the outstanding book on southern politics, *The Elections of 2008* (2010), and *The Presidency and the Political System* (9th ed., 2010).

David Nichols is associate professor in the department of political science at Baylor University and is a senior fellow of the Alexander Hamilton Institute for the Study of Western Civilization. He is the author of *The Myth of the Modern Presidency* (1994) as well as numerous articles on American politics, constitutional law, and politics and literature. He is currently completing a book on responsible government and the separation of powers.

Richard M. Pious is the Adolph and Effie Ochs Professor at Barnard College and professor at the Graduate School of Arts and Sciences at Columbia University. His scholarly books include *The American Presidency* (1979), *The President, Congress, and the Constitution* (1984), *Why Presidents Fail* (2008), and a book of cases and materials, *The War on Terrorism and the Rule of Law* (2006). He has coauthored a widely used print and online reference work, *The Oxford Guide to the United States Government* (2001). Pious has lectured on war powers at the United States Military Academy at West Point, at universities in the United States and Canada, and at seminars in the Far East organized by the government of Taiwan; he has lectured on presidential power and the war on terrorism at Oxford University and the British Library. He has served as a consultant to the Foreign Ministry of Japan since 1994. Pious is on the editorial advisory board of *Presidential Studies Quarterly* and served on the foreign experts panel of the *Journal des Élections.*

Byron E. Shafer is the Glenn B. and Cleone Orr Hawkins Chair of Political Science at the University of Wisconsin–Madison. For many years before that, he was Andrew W. Mellon Professor of American Government at Oxford University. He is the author, most recently, of *The American Public Mind: The Issue Structure of Mass Politics in the Postwar United States,* with William J. M. Claggett (forthcoming) and of *The End of Southern Exceptionalism: Class, Race, and Partisan Change in the Postwar South,* with Richard Johnston (2006), winner of the V. O. Key Prize of the Southern Political Science Association and the Race and Ethnicity Prize of the American Political Science Association. Many of his recent article-length pieces are collected in *The Two Majorities and the Puzzle of Modern American Politics* (2003).

Peter M. Shane is the Jacob E. Davis and Jacob E. Davis II Chair in Law at the Ohio State University's Moritz College of Law and author of *Madison's Nightmare: Unchecked Executive Power and the Threat to American Democracy* (2009), among many other works. A graduate of Harvard College and Yale Law School, Shane clerked for Judge Alvin B. Rubin of the U.S. Court of Appeals for the Fifth Circuit. He served in the Justice Department's Office of Legal Counsel and as an assistant general counsel in the Office of Management and Budget before entering full-time teaching in 1981. He is an internationally recognized authority on constitutional and administrative law, with research interests in law and the American presidency; democratic theory; and cyberdemocracy— the use of new information technologies to expand public opportunities to participate meaningfully in government policy making.

Stephen Skowronek is the Pelatiah Perit Professor of Political Science at Yale University. He has written extensively about American political development and the American presidency, and his works include *The Politics Presidents Make: Leadership from John Adams to Bill Clinton* (1997) and *Presidential Leadership in Political Time: Reprise and Reappraisal* (2008).

Bartholomew H. Sparrow is professor of government at the University of Texas at Austin. He is the author of *Uncertain Guardians: The News Media as a Political Institution* (1999), the coeditor of *Politics, Discourse, and American Society: New Agendas* (with Roderick Hart, 2001), and a contributor to *American Political Science Review, Political Communication, Presidential Studies Quarterly,* and other journals as well as of chapters in edited volumes. He is also the author of *From the Outside In: World War II and the American State* (1996), *The* Insular Cases *and the Emergence of American Empire* (2006), and, with Thomas R. Dye, *Politics in America* (8th ed., 2009). He is currently writing a biography of former U.S. national security adviser Brent Scowcroft.

David A. Yalof is associate professor of political science at the University of Connecticut. His first book, *Pursuit of Justices: Presidential Politics and the Selection of Supreme Court Nominees,* won the 1999 Richard E. Neustadt Award as the best book on the presidency from the American Political Science Association's presidency research group. He is coauthor of *The First Amendment and the Media in the Court of Public Opinion* (2002) and *The Future of the First Amendment* (2008). His articles on connections between the branches of government have appeared in, among other publications, *Political Research Quarterly, Judicature,* and *Constitutional Commentary.* He is currently completing a book examining how and why the Supreme Court overrules its own precedents.

John Yoo is a professor of law at the University of California at Berkeley. He has published more than seventy scholarly articles on foreign affairs, national security, and constitutional law and is the author of *The Powers of War and Peace* (2005) and *War by Other Means* (2006). He also contributes to the *Wall Street Journal, New York Times, Washington Post, Los Angeles Times,* and the *Philadelphia Inquirer.* Professor Yoo was a deputy assistant attorney general in the Office of Legal Counsel of the U.S. Department of Justice, where he worked on issues of national security and terrorism after the September 11, 2001, attacks. He also served as general counsel of the Senate Judiciary Committee and as a law clerk for Judge Laurence Silberman of the D.C. Circuit and Justice Clarence Thomas of the U.S. Supreme Court. Professor Yoo graduated from Yale Law School, where he was an articles editor of the *Yale Law Journal,* and summa cum laude from Harvard College with a degree in American history.

RESOLVED, the framers of the Constitution would approve of the modern presidency

PRO: David Nichols

CON: Terri Bimes

Americans are supposedly a forward-looking people, devotees of progress who have scant respect for traditions or customs. But, at least when it comes to politics and government, Americans are, arguably, the most backward-looking people on the face of the earth. What other nation spends so much time trying to decipher the intentions of people who lived more than two centuries ago? Few people in Great Britain, France, or Germany care about what politicians of the far distant past would say about today's political debates. Nobody in England asks, "What would Pitt the Younger say?" Even fewer care what George III would say. But Americans care a great deal about what James Madison, Alexander Hamilton, and the other "founders" would say about the ways in which Americans order their political lives.

One reason Americans care is that the United States, unlike Britain, has a written constitution that is a touchstone for how it resolves legal and political disputes. In deciding constitutional questions, federal and state judges regularly rely on the words of the framers to decipher the meaning of the Constitution. Politicians, too, frequently appeal to the framers to support their interpretations of what is and is not constitutional. Those who wish to defend or indict a contemporary practice, whether it be the Senate's filibuster or prayer in public schools, reach for the framers.

The Constitutional Convention was conducted in the summer of 1787 behind closed doors—no cameras, no reporters, no observers. The fifty-five delegates were sworn to secrecy. One might think this secrecy would make it difficult for anyone to say today what the framers had in mind when they were creating the Constitution. But, fortunately, the convention was blessed with an energetic young member who was determined to leave a detailed record of the proceedings. Every day that the convention was in session, Virginia's James Madison sat directly below the president's chair, facing the delegates and taking detailed notes of what they said. Every evening, he would write out the notes he had scribbled down during the day. It was a labor, he said, that almost killed him; yet it was also a labor that succeeded in bringing the framers' deliberations to life for subsequent generations.

Even with Madison's heroic labors, the task of determining what the framers intended remains difficult. To begin with, "the framers" were hardly a unified group. They were a diverse collection of individuals with many different ideas and interests. Some were slaveholders; some abhorred slavery. Some were wealthy; some were of modest means. Some favored democracy; others feared the masses. Moreover, whose intent matters the most? Is it the intent of the fifty-five men who attended the convention or only of the thirty-nine who signed the document? Should the intent of the hundreds of delegates at the state ratifying conventions matter the most? Or should the intent as interpreted by the most articulate or the most prolific of the framers be accorded special importance? New York's Alexander Hamilton, who penned the essays in *The Federalist Papers* that focus on the presidency, is often read as the authoritative framer, but he missed well over half of the convention's proceedings.[1]

Complicating matters still further, the decisions reached in the convention often were not what any delegate or group of delegates intended. Many decisions were the product of compromise and bargaining. Such decisions might be defended and rationalized after the fact, but, as the political theorist Michael Walzer points out, they reflected, as political decisions often do, "the balance of forces, not the weight of arguments."[2]

David Nichols and Terri Bimes are well aware of the difficulties in ascertaining a single intent, but in their pro and con arguments they gamely try to reconstruct what the framers believed about the presidency. According to Nichols, the framers envisioned a strong and democratic executive. Although he does not ignore the undeniable differences between the presidency of 1787 and the presidency of today, Nichols argues that today's presidency is a natural outgrowth of the presidency created by the framers. Bimes's understanding of the framers' intent is diametrically opposed. In crucial respects, she argues, the modern presidency is unrecognizable from the relatively weak office intended by the framers. They would neither recognize nor approve of the office that exists today. Short of bringing Madison, Hamilton, and the rest of framers back from the grave, this is not a question that can be answered definitively. But it is a question that Americans will certainly continue to ask.

PRO: David Nichols

The framers of the Constitution would approve of the modern presidency, because to a great extent they created it. The essential elements of that presidency—executive discretion, legislative leadership, a substantial administrative apparatus directed by the president, and the president's role as popular leader[1]—originated in the institutional arrangements and incentives the framers established in Article II of the Constitution. Important changes in society and technology, as well as in the size, scope, and purpose of government, have occurred since the time of the founders, but these changes only accentuate the importance of a powerful popular president to the successful operation of the U.S. constitutional system.

A common assumption among presidential scholars is that the Constitution, reflecting the founders' fear of monarchy, created a relatively weak chief executive or, at most, provided a vague outline of the office that would only be filled in by history. The debates that surrounded the creation of the presidency reveal, however, a different and more complex picture.

The men who gathered in Philadelphia in the summer of 1787 had learned much about the problems of democratic government in the eleven years since the signing of the Declaration of Independence. Among other things, they had learned that overthrowing British rule was only the first step toward establishing a free and independent nation. Such a nation required a competent government, and the Articles of Confederation were inadequate to the task. The equal representation of the states in the Continental Congress, the requirement that major structural changes receive unanimous approval, and the inability of Congress to levy taxes were all important defects of the Articles, but perhaps their most fundamental flaw was the absence of a mechanism to enforce decisions of the national government. There was no national executive authority under the Articles, and from the beginning of the Constitutional Convention most delegates agreed that an independent executive was essential to the success of a new constitution.

None of the delegates entered the convention with a definite plan for accomplishing this goal. Many were not fully aware of the enormity of the task, and even by the end of the convention most did not appreciate the originality and scope of their invention. The presidency evolved gradually over the course of three months of debate. This debate focused on specific practical problems involving the structure of the executive, and it occurred in the context of a host of other debates, not the least of which were states' rights and slavery. The creation of the presidency required compromise and improvisation. Through this process, however, a deeper and more complex understanding of executive power emerged, so that by the end of the process the framers were able to deliver a new institution to the world—the popular modern presidency.

The Virginia Plan provided the starting point for the debate on the executive. It called for the creation of a national executive that would be elected by the legislature for an undetermined number of years. The executive would receive a fixed salary, would be ineligible for reelection, would possess a general authority to execute the national laws, would enjoy the executive rights vested in Congress by the Articles of Confederation, and, together with "a convenient number" of the national judiciary, would form a council of revision with the power to veto all laws subject to override by a vote of the legislature.[2]

This plan was only an outline—it did not even specify the number of executives. Edmund Randolph of Virginia wanted a plural executive, claiming that a unitary executive would be the "fetus of monarchy." Roger Sherman of Connecticut argued that because the executive was to be a servant of the legislature, the legislature should be free to determine the number of executives it desired at any time. No other delegate, however, agreed with Sherman. Even Randolph stressed that the executive must be independent of the legislature.[3]

What powers would this independent executive possess? Article II does not present an extensive list of specific powers, but this has more to do with the framers' understanding of the character of executive power than with any desire to create a weak presidency. Article I begins, "All legislative Powers *herein granted* shall be vested in a Congress…" (emphasis added), whereas Article II begins, "The executive Power shall be vested in a President…." Legislative powers could be enumerated in the Constitution, but the executive power could not be so easily delineated. The legislature makes laws, or general rules, but the executive must implement these laws in an infinite number of possible circumstances. No rule can cover all cases, the framers realized. That is why an independent executive was needed.

The framers did, however, recognize that the president would need assistance. Some delegates suggested that the Constitution include a list of officers who would help the president to carry out the law. They wanted there to be no doubt but that the president was to be the head of the administrative offices of the government.[4] But their proposal was rejected because it might interfere with executive independence. It was feared that constitutionally created offices would undermine the unity of the executive branch. The president was to be the only constitutional officer responsible for the execution of the laws. The framers, then, created the structure of an executive branch under the direction of a president, leaving later presidents to expand it as the times required.

The framers' understanding of executive power is most apparent in two of the powers listed at the beginning of Article II, Section 2: the commander in chief power and the pardoning power. The commander in chief power involves the use of force, and the pardoning power involves the need for discretion. Together, these two provisions are a good description of executive power. Because of its many members, Congress is not suited to quick action, and because it makes laws that must apply to all citizens, it does not have the discretion to deal with particular circumstances. Force and discretion are the essence of executive power. Congress has often complained about the executive's unilateral use of force or discretion, but when President George Washington issued a Proclamation of Neutrality during the war between Great Britain and France in 1793, he understood the place of executive discretion in the Constitution, and when he led the militia in 1794 against an uprising by farmers in western Pennsylvania against a federal tax on liquor and distilled drinks (it was known as the Whiskey Rebellion), he understood the need for forceful action. The framers did not want the president to be a servant of Congress.

The framers also wanted the president to play an independent role in the legislative process. The Virginia Plan had called for the executive to share the veto power with the judiciary, but the convention delegates excluded judges because they feared such a scheme would undercut executive responsibility and independence. They wanted a president who could stand up to Congress and thereby play an active role in the legislative process.

The framers also specified that the president "shall from time to time give to the Congress Information of the State of the Union, and recommend to their Consideration such Measures as he shall judge necessary and expedient." The initial version of this provision began with the word *may* rather than *shall*. The change was made at the suggestion of Gouverneur Morris, a delegate from Pennsylvania who wanted to ensure that the president would play an active role in the legislative process. If recommending legislation was merely an option, a president might be reluctant to do so for fear of arousing the jealousy of the legislature. By making it mandatory, the framers enabled presidents to defend their actions as an obligation of their office.

Their constitutionally prescribed authority to help to set the agenda at the beginning of the legislative process and their right to cast a veto at the end of that process have enabled presidents to exert tremendous legislative influence. Not all presidents have taken full advantage of this potential, but it exists because of the efforts of the framers.

Although they concede that the framers wanted an independent president, most scholars have concluded that the framers did not want a popularly elected one. Early in the Constitutional Convention, James Wilson of Pennsylvania called for the popular election of the president, claiming that it was necessary to guarantee executive independence from the legislature.[5] But during most of the convention, a majority of the delegates supported legislative election. Political scientist Charles Thach has argued that the preference for legislative election was based more on the fears of the small states than on any theory of executive power. The small states supported legislative selection, because they thought it would give them more power than they would have in a direct popular election. They hoped to use their control of the Senate to veto any candidate of whom they disapproved. However, when the delegates turned their attention to the specific mechanism for legislative election of the president, it became clear that a majority supported a joint vote of the House and the Senate. Because the influence of the small states would be greatly diminished in such an election, the small states became open to a compromise.[6]

The compromise was, of course, the electoral college. The idea of an electoral college was first introduced by James Wilson on June 2, who saw it as only a minor modification of his plan for a direct popular election. Recent commentators, however, often portray the electoral college as a product of the framers' distrust of democracy. They go on to argue that if the framers distrusted democracy, they certainly would not approve of what is arguably the most important element of the modern presidency—popular leadership.

To be sure, some convention delegates did speak disparagingly of popular election. George Mason of Virginia said, "It would be as unnatural to refer the choice of a proper character for chief magistrate to the people, as it would be to refer a trial of colors to a blind man."[7] Roger Sherman of Connecticut said the people would be ill-informed, and South Carolinian Charles Cotesworth Pinckney complained that the people would be led by a few "active and designing men."[8] None of these delegates, however, supported the electoral college; they were all proponents of legislative election. It was the delegates who defended the principle of popular election, such as James Madison, James Wilson, and Gouverneur Morris, who were the prime supporters of the electoral college.

If these framers supported popular election, then why (apart from Wilson) did they not favor direct popular election? The reason was the need for compromise on two issues not directly related to executive power: federalism and slavery. Because the number of electors each state received in the electoral college would be based on the number of representatives and senators from a state, the small states would have a little more weight in the electoral college than they would in a direct popular election. The desire to protect the interests of their states, not distrust of democracy, motivated these delegates.

Madison also argued that the different election laws in the states made direct popular election virtually impossible.[9] Madison was gently reminding the delegates that direct popular election would reopen the question of slavery and potentially rip the convention apart.[10] The South wanted its entire slave population to count in apportioning seats in the House of Representatives, whereas the northern states argued that because the South did not recognize the rights of slaves as human beings slaves should not count for purposes of apportionment. The Three-Fifths Compromise allowed the South to gain some representation in Congress based on its slave population, but no such compromise would be possible in a direct popular election of the president. Either the South would lose a substantial part of its power in the election because its slaves could not vote, or it would have to allow its slaves to vote. Neither option was acceptable to the South. The electoral college, however, incorporated the Three-Fifths Compromise into the selection of the president, because it based the number of electors for each state on the size of its congressional delegation.

One can debate the merits of the Three-Fifths Compromise, but its importance to the creation of the electoral college cannot be ignored. The electoral college represented the best approximation of direct popular election the framers could achieve considering the political realties they faced. The framers who were the most influential in creating the electoral college wanted a popular election, and, in practice, that is what they got. Presidential electors have seldom exercised any independent judgment—and never in a way that affected the outcome of an election. The electors have been a conduit for, not a filter of, popular opinion.

The most far-sighted of the founders, Gouverneur Morris, understood the potential for popular leadership inherent in the constitutional presidency: "The Executive Magistrate should be the guardian of the people, even the lower classes, against Legislative tyranny, against the great and the wealthy who in the course of things will necessarily compose—the Legislative body.... The Executive therefore ought to be constituted as to be the great protector of the mass of the people."[11]

Morris also predicted the rise of political parties, explaining that two parties would soon form, one in support of the president and one in opposition. Not all of the framers were as prescient as Morris, and even he undoubtedly would find many aspects of modern American politics strange and disagreeable. But the framers were the first to see the need for a powerful, popularly elected executive in a modern republic, and they would certainly approve of the modern presidency they did so much to create.

CON: Terri Bimes

The job description of the modern president revolves around three central domestic roles: chief legislator, popular leader, and chief executive of the federal bureaucracy. Today, presidents are expected to offer extensive domestic legislative programs, which then become the basis for Congress's agenda. When President Dwight D. Eisenhower decided not to propose a legislative package in 1953, he was broadly criticized for falling short of the standard set by Presidents Franklin D. Roosevelt and Harry S. Truman. In pursuit of their programs, presidents now routinely barnstorm the country, delivering speeches to all manner of audiences. Indeed, "going public"—the strategy of rousing the people to put pressure on Congress to enact the president's priorities—has become a routine feature of the modern presidency.[1] Finally, modern presidents lead the immense federal bureaucracy, which provides the substantial resources needed to launch presidential initiatives independent of Congress. Within that bureaucracy, a "presidential branch" has emerged that is especially responsive to an administration's priorities. Signing statements, executive orders, and other mechanisms are increasingly being used to shape bureaucratic decision making. None of these three central roles of the modern presidency is spelled out in the Constitution. The framers would certainly be surprised at what they have wrought.

In fact, the Constitution says very little about executive power. The "vesting clause" of Article II states that "the executive Power shall be vested in a President of the United States of America." It is followed by a list of specific presidential powers. In the domestic policy realm, the most important are the duty to report on the state of the Union to Congress from time to time, to recommend "necessary and expedient" legislation to Congress, and to nominate officers to the various departments with the approval of the Senate. As spelled out in Article I, the president also is empowered to veto legislation, subject to override by a two-thirds majority of each chamber. This terse description of executive power constitutes the extent to which the Constitution gave the nation's first presidents formal guidance on domestic policy making.

This scarcity of guidance is not surprising, however. The debates at the Constitutional Convention focused more on how presidents would be selected than on the proper scope of presidential power. This emphasis likely reflected the delegates' view that the legislature would be the most powerful branch of government, at least in domestic policy making. As noted in *Federalist* No. 51 by James Madison, "the legislative authority necessarily predominates" in a republic.[2] The legislative branch enjoyed two critical advantages: its close ties to the people and its authority to make laws. Thus the most important question of executive design was how to provide a mode of election that ensured some independence from Congress, while still leaving the president accountable to the public. The obvious answer—popular election—was advocated by a handful of the founders—notably James Wilson and Gouverneur Morris—but it was widely regarded as impractical. In the view of most of the founders, the people would be unable to judge candidates for the presidency and would have trouble agreeing on a single candidate. Election of the president by the legislature was repeatedly, if controversially, approved by the Constitutional Convention, but this plan foundered upon a basic dilemma: unless the president was ineligible for reelection, legislative selection would give presidents a strong incentive to defer to congressional whims in the hope of securing another term. Yet limiting each president to a single term was inadvisable, because reelection was regarded as a vital incentive for good behavior by the president.

The electoral college emerged as the solution: it gave the president a power base independent of Congress, while providing a measure of accountability. Although several of the founders expected the ultimate selection of the president to often end up in the hands of the House of Representatives (the Constitution-mandated solution when a single candidate failed to obtain a majority in the electoral college), this mode of election afforded at least a partial barrier to legislative domination of the president. The electoral college also solved the dispute between large and small states by granting each state a number of electors equal to its representatives and senators.

The president's role as popular leader was not at stake in these debates. By delegating the decision on how electors would be chosen to each state legislature, the framers neither precluded nor required a substantial role for ordinary voters in selecting the president. In the first presidential election in 1788, the state legislatures divided equally on the issue of how popular the presidential vote should be. Six states (Delaware, Maryland, Massachusetts, New Hampshire, Pennsylvania, and Virginia) opted for various sorts of direct popular election of electors, and five states (Connecticut, Georgia, New Jersey, New York, and South Carolina) opted for legislative appointment of electors.[3] Thus the framers' endorsement of the electoral college cannot be interpreted as a stamp of approval for modern popular presidential leadership.

It is highly unlikely that even the two main supporters of popular election, Gouverneur Morris and James Wilson, envisioned the president going out on the hustings to rally voter support. Instead, Morris and Wilson conceived of the president as a "patriot king"—that is, as a leader who would rise above politics and not engage in aggressive popular leadership appeals. Morris described the president as the "guardian of the people" and the "great protector of the people" against legislative tyranny.[4] Wilson, in his defense of the executive at the Pennsylvania convention held to consider ratification of the Constitution, contended that the president would "watch over the whole with paternal care and affection."[5] Meanwhile, throughout *The Federalist Papers* Hamilton and Madison described campaigning as the "art" of flattering prejudice and distracting people from their true interests.[6] In *Federalist* No. 10, for example, Madison argued that a large republic would make it more difficult for "unworthy candidates to practice with success the vicious arts by which elections are too often carried."[7] In *Federalist* No. 71, Hamilton lamented that, although "the arts of men" can delude the people, the executive would be their "guardian," rescuing them from the "fatal consequences of their own mistakes."[8] The president would not respond to "every sudden breeze of passion," but instead would take a more reflective view of the public good. In short, these framers portrayed the executive as a trustee who exercises his own judgment rather than as a delegate who slavishly follows the opinions of the people.

Most of the framers supported a more limited conception of executive power than Morris, Wilson, and Hamilton. Certainly many of the convention delegates would have been uncomfortable with the notion of the president as a guardian protecting the public interest against legislative excesses. Distrust of executive power still ran deep in a nation that had only recently fought a war against the British king. But there was no disagreement among the framers that the role of Congress was to initiate legislation and that presidents would not actively cultivate mass support in order to pressure Congress to cater to their priorities. The supporters and opponents of a strong executive agreed on this much.

Although the framers anticipated a more direct role for the president in leading the executive branch, their conception of presidential administrative leadership was limited when judged by the standards of the modern presidency. At first, convention delegates granted the power to make appointments, one of the president's most important tools in controlling the bureaucracy, to the Senate. But toward the end of the convention that idea fell by the wayside, in part because the Senate now represented states rather than population. The convention voted instead to give the power of appointment to the president, preserving an important role for the Senate in providing "advice and consent." As historian Jack N. Rakove has noted, "The growth of the presidency owed more to doubts about the Senate than to the enthusiasm with which Hamilton, Morris, and Wilson endorsed the virtues of energetic administration."[9] In *Federalist* No. 51, Madison clarified why the president and the Senate were linked in this manner, explaining that the "qualified connection between this weaker department [the executive] and the weaker branch of the stronger department [the Senate]" would enable "the latter … to support the constitutional rights of the former, without being too much detached from the rights of its own department."[10] The presidency needed the support of the Senate, because otherwise it would lack the firmness to withstand the initiatives of the House, the more popular legislative branch.[11]

In summary, the framers anticipated a division of powers in which Congress would be the leading legislative force and the president would provide a limited check. The House would be the branch closest to the people, and as such would have a critical advantage in battles with the president. As a trustee for the nation, the president would not be entirely divorced from the people, nor would he wield public opinion as a weapon in institutional or policy battles. Even in the area of administration, where the president had the appointment power, the framers expected close consultation and cooperation with the Senate to be the norm.

The modern presidency has overturned each of these expectations. Strains in the founders' model could be seen even in the conduct of the first presidents, but for the most part George Washington and his immediate successors sought to abide by the model of the restrained patriot king.[12] Washington played a vital role in defining appropriate presidential behavior, helping to resolve some of the ambiguities left by the framers. In many ways, Washington was the republican embodiment of a "patriot king." His two tours of the country as president were not the modern-day campaign swings in which presidents kiss babies and shake hands.[13] Rather, great formality and aloofness marked these affairs. Washington also stuck to a script devoid of comment on public policy issues, and his remarks were strictly ceremonial. The most common criticism of the tours was that they were "monarchical" in nature—more befitting a king than an elected president. Partly as a result of such criticism, Washington's successors generally did not go out on tour and assiduously avoided monarchical gestures. Above all, the first generation of presidents generally steered clear of explicit appeals to the public to support their policies.

In the capital, Washington often entertained public visitors, but these events, or levees as they were called, resembled his tours of the country. Washington stood at the fireplace and greeted each visitor with a bow. After making some brief remarks, he then resumed his place in front of the fireplace and each visitor then bowed to the president as he or she left the room.[14] By holding these levees, Washington acknowledged that it was important for the president to be accessible to the public. At the same time, the regal choreography of the event imposed a respectful distance between the president and the people.

Even Washington's one bold public appeal, which appeared in his Farewell Address, showed the vitality of the patriot leadership model. In the address,

Washington dealt with the rise of political parties—entities that are crucial to the operation of the modern presidency but were disparaged by the framers. Even though by the end of his administration Washington had cast his lot with the Hamiltonian Federalists and against the Jeffersonian Republicans, he used this stance of nonpartisanship to attack those who opposed his administration's foreign policy. He warned Americans about a "small but artful and enterprising minority of the community" who sought to replace the "delegated will of the nation" with the "will of party."[15] The fact that Washington attacked the Jeffersonian Republicans in the language of nonpartisanship reveals the power of the patriot king model in the early republic. It is also noteworthy that Washington waited until he was leaving office to launch an explicitly political attack in an address that is now widely regarded as a "campaign document."[16] Only then could he offer such criticisms without appearing to promote his own self-interest.[17]

The early presidents were also circumscribed in how they practiced legislative leadership. The president was expected to leave most of the initiative and maneuvering of the legislative process to Congress. Even when the president and his allies lobbied for legislation, they used "hidden-hand" leadership techniques that were consistent with the norm that made it unacceptable for the president to aggressively push his program through Congress.[18] Thomas Jefferson, for example, drafted bills behind the scenes and had members of Congress introduce them as their own. He also quietly appointed floor leaders to be his personal lieutenants in Congress, directed cabinet members to act as political liaisons with Congress, lobbied members of both parties at White House dinners, and anonymously penned editorials supporting his administration's policies in the official government newspaper.[19] The Federalists attacked Jefferson for his backstage dominance of Congress, but Jefferson's public deference to the legislature limited the damage.

Finally, in part because the federal bureaucracy was so small, the president's administrative role was limited in the early Republic. The general expectation was that departments would be staffed by people chosen for their good character and that they would serve during good behavior. Even Jefferson, who took office after the acrimonious election of 1800, did not purge many Federalists from the bureaucracy. John Quincy Adams, one of the last presidents to adhere to this character-based norm when staffing the bureaucracy, promised in his inaugural address to base his appointments on "talent and virtue alone."[20] With the election of Andrew Jackson in 1828 came an avowedly partisan approach to administration. Bureaucratic appointments would now be distributed on the basis of party loyalty and service. But this partisan approach did not necessarily empower the White House. Instead, presidents became brokers, forced to respond to the aggressive patronage demands of state and local party organizations. Not until the twentieth century did presidents begin to build an extensive bureaucratic apparatus that they could control, the Executive Office of the President. The rise of presidential administration has been a relatively recent process, not something foreordained by the Constitution.[21]

In general, then, the most important features of the modern presidency were neither anticipated nor desired by the founders. They did not want or expect the president to become the chief legislator, setting much of Congress's agenda. Nor did they want or expect the president to be a public opinion leader, aggressively rallying the people to the administration's side in battles with the legislative branch. Nor, finally, did they desire or anticipate that the president would become the leader of an extensive administrative apparatus. These elements of the modern presidency, which took shape over many decades, have created an office that neither the founders nor early presidents would recognize, let alone embrace.

2

RESOLVED, political parties should nominate candidates for the presidency through a national primary

PRO: Michael Nelson

CON: Andrew E. Busch

Americans celebrate that the United States has had the same constitution for nearly its entire history: more than two centuries and counting. No other democracy in the world can make the same claim. But constitutional stability does not mean the nation has undergone no fundamental institutional changes. Indeed, some American institutions have been characterized by almost perpetual change. Nowhere is that truer than elections—specifically, the ways in which political parties nominate presidential candidates.

The framers were smart men, but they did not foresee the rise of political parties. They anticipated that the electoral college would both nominate and select presidential candidates. Yet almost as soon as the Constitution went into effect, it became clear that this system would not work. Groups with common interests and values must be able to come together and agree on a candidate. If they were unable to do so, their votes would be spread among too many candidates, and they would lose the election to those groups that had agreed to direct all their votes toward a single candidate.

The first nominating process centered in Congress. Each party's members of Congress got together and decided who would be their party's nominee. But almost as soon as the congressional caucus system emerged, it began to attract criticism. That criticism intensified when the Federalist Party went into decline, leaving the Jeffersonian Republicans as the only national party. Nomination became equivalent to election. Critics complained that "King Caucus" was undemocratic, because it was conducted by just a few individuals behind closed doors. Moreover, they argued that legislators had no business nominating presidential candidates.

In 1824 the congressional caucus system fell apart. Dissatisfaction with the caucus's choice, Secretary of the Treasury William H. Crawford, propelled state legislatures to nominate their own favorite son candidates, including John Quincy Adams of Massachusetts, Henry Clay of Kentucky, and Andrew Jackson of Tennessee—all Democratic-Republicans. The result was a fractured general election in which the winner of the popular vote—Jackson—failed to receive a majority of the electoral vote and the election was sent to the House of Representatives. Clay then threw his support to Adams, and Adams prevailed on the first ballot. Three days later, Adams chose Clay to be his secretary of state, igniting charges that the new president had made a "corrupt bargain" with Clay. The outrage was aimed not only at Adams and Clay but also at the nominating system that had made the election of Adams possible.

The congressional caucus system was soon replaced by national nominating conventions. In 1831 and 1832, the National Republicans (soon to become the Whigs) and the Democrats followed the lead of the Anti-Masons in holding national nominating conventions made up of delegates from every state. Although more inclusive than the congressional caucus system, the conventions were made up of delegates selected by the state parties, not by popular vote. The conventions were often long, contentious affairs, especially those in the Democratic Party, which required its presidential nominee to receive at least a two-thirds vote of the delegates (this requirement remained in place until 1936). In 1924 the Democrats met for eighteen days and endured 103 ballots before nominating John W. Davis, who was promptly thrashed in the general election by the Republican nominee, Calvin Coolidge.

In the early twentieth century, the national convention system came under attack for being undemocratic and corrupt. Reform was in the air again— this time in the call for presidential primaries that would enable voters to have a direct say in selecting the parties' nominees. In the 1912 election, twelve states, including California, Illinois, Massachusetts, New Jersey, Ohio, and Pennsylvania, held primaries. Former president Theodore Roosevelt's challenge of President William Howard Taft for the Republican nomination generated intense excitement. In virtually every primary state, Roosevelt defeated Taft, including Taft's home state of Ohio. Although Taft won the nomination anyway because his allies controlled the convention, his victory was an empty one. In the general election, Taft received only 23 percent of the popular vote and 1.5 percent of the electoral vote. He finished a distant third behind the winner, Democrat Woodrow Wilson, and Roosevelt, who ran at the head of the Progressive Party.

Unlike the 1824 election, the 1912 election did not transform the way presidential elections were conducted. Despite calls by prominent national figures, including President Wilson, for a national primary, the parties decided to retain the national nominating convention. Primaries were still held, but as late as the 1960s they remained a subordinate part of the nominating process. A primary occasionally played an important role in demonstrating a candidate's strength—in 1948, for example, Thomas E. Dewey's victory over Harold E. Stassen in the Oregon primary helped to secure Dewey the Republican nomination. Still, winning primaries was no guarantee of victory. In 1952, for example, Adlai E. Stevenson II did not enter a single primary, and yet he secured the Democratic Party's nomination anyway, besting Estes Kefauver, who had received two-thirds of the votes cast in Democratic primaries.

Not until 1972 did primaries become the linchpin of the nominating process. As primary voters displaced party officials in selecting the parties' presidential nominees, the national convention ceased to be the theater in which the nominating process played itself out. This transformation led to yet more change. After the triumph of the largely unknown Democratic nominee, former governor Jimmy Carter, in 1976 and his defeat by another former governor, Republican Ronald Reagan, in 1980, Democrats changed their rules to ensure that around one-seventh of convention delegates (dubbed "superdelegates") would be state governors and members of Congress and the Democratic National Committee.

A more consequential change has been that states, jockeying for advantage in the selection process, have advanced the dates of their primaries and caucuses to earlier in the election year, creating the "front-loading" that Michael Nelson and Andrew E. Busch discuss. Both Nelson and Busch agree that front-loading is a problem. They disagree, however, about what should be done about it. Nelson favors a national primary; Busch opposes such a plan. It is difficult to say whether a national primary is in the nation's future, but one thing is certain: the nominating process will continue to change, sometimes dramatically and often unexpectedly.

PRO: Michael Nelson

How about this for an idea? Because we Americans have to elect a president every fourth November, let's choose the Democratic and Republican nominees eight or nine months earlier, in February or March, when most voters aren't paying much attention. Let's start the process in two small, rural, nearly all-white states—Iowa and New Hampshire would be perfect—and give them the power to weed out all but a couple candidates from each party. Then, before we've had a chance to learn much about even these few candidates, let's get as many other states into the game as we can in the shortest time possible. And because there's no real way to keep score in such an accelerated and far-flung contest, let's trust the news media to decide who's winning, who's losing, and who isn't even worth paying attention to. Then, after we know who the nominees are, let's sit back and relax for half a year, until September when the final campaign begins. If during that time we learn things about one or both major-party candidates that make us want to change our minds and nominate someone else, let's stick with them anyway.

Bad idea, right? Considering the stakes—the choice of the two finalists for the most powerful job in the world—no one ever would adopt such an approach if given the choice. And, the truth is, no one ever did. The current system for nominating presidential candidates is one that the United States stumbled into blindly.

It happened like this. In the early 1970s, both parties decided that every state's delegates to the presidential nominating conventions should be chosen through a process in which the rank-and-file members of each party can participate. In practice, that meant choosing the delegates through either primaries or caucuses. (In a primary, one votes by secret ballot; in a caucus, one attends a meeting and votes openly.) New Hampshire, which began holding the first primary of the election year in 1952, when primaries were unimportant, now found itself in the privileged position of holding the first primary when primaries were very important. Iowa quickly jumped to the head of a different line, becoming the earliest caucus state and voting even before New Hampshire.

Both states have reaped the harvest of going first ever since. Nearly all the candidates campaign endlessly in Iowa and New Hampshire, promising their voters the moon (or in cornfield-laden Iowa's case, ethanol subsidies) and infusing their economies with huge doses of campaign spending. The news media also camp out for months in Iowa and New Hampshire and, depending on how scholars do the counting, devote between one-fourth and three-fourths of their coverage of the entire nominating process to these two small states.[1] A candidate who does not win Iowa or New Hampshire has hardly any chance of being nominated, and candidates who do not finish in the top three are finished, regardless of how popular they may be elsewhere in the country.

Iowa and New Hampshire deserve credit for quickly figuring out what most other states realized only slowly: the earlier a state votes, the more influence it has in the nominating process and the more benefits it derives.[2] For a time, California and New Jersey held their primaries in June, at the very end of the process, thinking that going last would make them the decisive states. Instead, it usually made them irrelevant, because the winners were determined weeks or even months before. Eventually, succumbing to "New Hampshire envy,"[3] nearly every state advanced its primary or caucus to as close to the start of the year as possible, a process called "front-loading." In the 1976 election, the second held under the reformed nominating system, only 10 percent of delegates were chosen by March 2. In the 2008 election, 70 percent were.[4] Indeed, on February 6, 2008, alone, nearly half the states held their primaries or caucuses.

Faced with the current mess, some thoughtful observers want to try to undo the reforms of the early 1970s and revive the nominating process that existed during most of the nineteenth and twentieth centuries. "Under the old system," writes *Washington Post* columnist David Broder, "running for president involved taking a few months off from your public office in the election year to present your credentials largely to political peers—other officeholders, party leaders, leaders of allied interest groups—and then persuade them that you were best qualified to carry the party banner." As it happened, argues political scientist Jeane Kirkpatrick, the qualities those "political peers" were looking for were the very qualities that made for good presidents: "the ability to deal with diverse groups, ability to work out compromises and develop consensus, and the ability to impress people who have watched a candidate over many years."[5]

All this may sound good, but, unfortunately, nostalgia more than history marks these and similar accounts of the prereform system. Writing in the late nineteenth century, James Bryce noted in his classic book *The American Commonwealth* that party professionals indeed had a talent for choosing electable candidates. But he also felt compelled to explain "Why Great Men Are Not Chosen President" in terms of that very talent: "It must be remembered that the merits of a President are one thing and those of a candidate another thing.... It will be a misfortune to the party, as well as to the country, if the candidate elected should prove a bad President. But it is a greater misfortune to the party that it should be beaten in the impending election, for the evil of losing national patronage will have come four years sooner."[6]

The indifference of party professionals to nominating good presidents extended to an occasional inability to weed out dangerous ones. Of the presidents beginning with William Howard Taft who were analyzed by James David Barber in his 1972 study *The Presidential Character,* four of the eleven who were nominated under the old rules (Woodrow Wilson, Herbert C. Hoover, Lyndon B. Johnson, and Richard Nixon) fell into the category of "active-negatives"—that is, persons who tended to turn political crises into personal crises and "persevere in a disastrous policy." Only three of the eleven—Franklin D. Roosevelt, Harry S. Truman, and John F. Kennedy— qualified as "active-positives," or leaders with "personal strengths specially attuned to the presidency." The other four presidents were mediocre—or, in Barber's terminology, "passive"—presidents.[7] So much for the party professionals' much-vaunted talent for peer review.

Even the party pros' ability to choose electable candidates may have been overstated. Bryce wrote at a time of unusually close electoral competition. But in the twentieth century, twelve of the eighteen presidential elections held before the reforms of the early 1970s were landslides in which the loser won less than half as many electoral votes as the winner. At least one set of party pros in each of these elections must have poorly judged their candidate's electability. In all, then, the good old days of the past were no better than the bad new days of the present, at least when it comes to nominating candidates for president.

Fortunately, Americans are not bound by either the past or the present— they can shape the future. In designing a new presidential nominating process, two criteria should be foremost in our thinking: simplicity and clarity.

To be sure, complexity in a political system need not mean that it is undemocratic, just as simplicity and clarity alone do not guarantee a democratic process. For example, a lottery drawing would be a clear, simple—and awful— method for nominating a presidential candidate. The Constitution, by contrast, is a complex system of "separated institutions sharing powers," in which citizens exercise limited authority, chiefly by voting in elections.[8]

In the design of the presidential nominating process, however, Americans are squarely in the center of that domain in which citizens get to exercise their limited authority, and that is where simplicity and clarity come in. As Henry Mayo argues in *Introduction to Democratic Theory,* "If [the] purpose of the election is to be carried out—to enable the voter to share in political power— the voter's job must not be made difficult and confusing for him. It ought, on the contrary, to be made as simple as the electoral machinery can be devised to make it."[9] In other words, whenever the Constitution opens the door to citizens, walking through it should be a clear and simple process.

Federalism, like complexity, is another vital constitutional principle that is irrelevant to the presidential nominating process. The states not only are constitutionally sovereign in their own domain, but also are embedded in Congress, where the people are represented according to where they live. Although the president, uniquely among elected officials, is meant to represent the entire country, federalism is even woven into the electoral college, in which presidential candidates seek electoral votes state by state. Federalism does not need to be entrenched in the nominating process as well.

The best way to remedy the problems with the current nominating process and replace it with one that is clear and simple (as well as democratic and practical) is to create a national primary.

Here is how a national primary could work. Any candidate trying to get on the Republican or Democratic national primary ballot would have until June of the election year to round up valid signatures equal in number to 1 percent of the turnout in the most recent presidential election (around 1.3 million in 2012). Each party's rank-and-file supporters would be eligible to vote for their party's nominee. The primary itself would be held on the first Tuesday in August—that is, voters across the country would all go to the polls on the same day. If none of a party's candidates receives 50 percent of the vote, a runoff election between the top two candidates would be held three weeks later. The national party conventions would meet soon afterward to approve the vice-presidential candidates, write party rules, adopt their platforms, and hear the nominees' acceptance speeches.

Most of the specific elements of this proposal are subject to tinkering. Perhaps independent voters could be eligible to vote in the primary of their choice. The 1 percent requirement could be a little higher or lower, so long as it is high enough to screen out frivolous candidates but not so high as to screen out serious ones. A further variation could make the 1 percent rule mandatory in a minimum number of states as well as nationwide. The date of the primary could be a little earlier than August. Forty percent could be defined as sufficient for victory. The conventions could take a different form. Because none of these variations would alter the essential nature of the national primary, any or all of them would be fine.

The national primary is not a far-fetched idea. It has a distinguished pedigree: both Theodore Roosevelt and Woodrow Wilson promoted it a century ago. Since then, through reforms of state election laws, direct primaries have become the way Americans nominate virtually every candidate for elective office in the country except president. Virtually every U.S. senator, every member of the House of Representatives, and every governor had to win a primary election to become the nominee of his or her party. It is hard to imagine an idea riper for extension to the presidency, or more thoroughly road-tested at the federal, state, and local levels, than the national primary.

Apart from its intrinsic democratic virtues and its deep resonance in the American experience, what beneficial effects would flow from the adoption of a national primary? First and foremost, every vote would count equally. No longer would the ballots of a relatively few New Hampshirites, now so crucial in determining who can be president, count infinitely more than the votes of the millions of people in states whose primaries are held after the race is essentially over. As a consequence, voter turnout would rise substantially. In recent elections, the turnout rate in the New Hampshire primary has been double that in the rest of the country.[10] Why the disparity? Because the people of New Hampshire know that their votes will directly affect the choice of the major-party nominees for president, and in most years the people of most other states know that their votes will not. If everyone is allowed to vote on the same day, everyone will feel the same connection between their vote and the outcome that New Hampshirites do now. Moving the date of the national primary to August, several months closer to the November election than is the current round of crucial primaries, would mean that people would be asked to vote when they are paying attention to the election, not before—another spur not just to higher turnout, but also to a more informed electorate.

An additional beneficial effect of the national primary is that it would reduce the scorekeeping role of the news media. The national primary is its own scoreboard: when the votes are counted on primary night, everyone can see who won. Public opinion polls would continue to measure how the candidates are doing before primary day, but journalists no longer would be called on to determine, as well as to report on, the status of the race—a role journalists themselves are uncomfortable performing.

Yet another benefit of the national primary would be a shift in the candidates' focus from the local issues that preoccupy Iowa and New Hampshire to the national issues that presidents must confront. Today, candidates for president have little incentive to address, for example, the concerns of racial minorities or the residents of big cities (neither of whom are found in Iowa and New Hampshire) and lots of incentive to defend agricultural subsidies in rural Iowa and the deductibility of property taxes in high-property-tax New Hampshire. If presidential candidates are forced to compete nationwide, then national—that is, presidential—issues will rise to the fore, as they should.

Finally, adopting the national primary would mean that the American people would have the presidential nominating process they want. Since the Gallup Poll began asking voters in 1952 what they think of the national primary, they have endorsed it every time by margins ranging from two to one to six to one. Democrats, Republicans, and independents consistently support the idea, as do the people of every age, income, race, sex, region, religion, and educational level.[11] The national primary would not have to prove itself to voters, because its legitimacy has been preapproved.

The case for a national primary is strong, but what about the case against? One common objection is that only established political figures would have a chance of being nominated, because only they would be able to raise the vast amounts of money needed to wage a nationwide campaign. To the extent that this is true, would it be any different than the current system? After all, for more than a quarter century every major-party nominee for president has begun the election year as either the front-runner or a top-tier candidate.[12] But *is* this still true? As the once little-known former governor of Vermont, Howard Dean, showed in 2003, it is now possible for a political outsider to raise tremendous sums of money through the Internet, as long as he or she is saying things that strike a powerful chord with a great many people. Barack Obama enjoyed even greater online success in 2008 even though he had been in the Senate only two years when he announced his candidacy for president.

Another objection is that by making Iowa and New Hampshire no more influential than their combined 1.4 percent of the nation's population warrants, a national primary would remove from the nominating process the kind of face-to-face scrutiny by voters (so-called retail politics) that presidential candidates must now undergo to compete successfully in those two states. That is a reasonable objection if one believes that Iowans and New Hampshirites are uniquely qualified to serve as the screening and selection committee for the rest of the country. There is good reason to doubt that they are, however, especially considering that these states do not represent the country in anything close to its variety and also that they have a record of imposing locally major but nationally minor policy litmus tests on candidates.

A final objection to the national primary is that it would undermine the political parties. This tired wheeze was raised by defenders of the old nominating process when the reforms of the 1970s mandated that delegates be chosen through state caucuses and primaries—in complete disregard of the fact that the strongest party organizations in the country (for example, the Daley machine in Chicago, the Crump machine in Memphis, and the Byrd machine in Virginia) had happily coexisted with primary elections for decades. Since the 1970s, the two major parties, which had been in steep decline during the 1960s, have grown stronger in government, in the electorate, and as organizations. The historical record is clear: parties and primaries coexist happily.

In summary, the front-loaded Iowa and New Hampshire–centric presidential nominating process is broken. Either the federal government, through simple legislation, or the two national parties, by requiring states to participate in the national primary or forfeit their say in the choice of the nominees, has the power to fix it.[13] Other proposed remedies—regional primaries, for example, in which the states of each region would vote on a different first Tuesday between February and June—are inadequate. Whichever region got to go first would have the same distorting power in the choice of presidential nominees as Iowa and New Hampshire do now. The truth is that because more and more states are cramming their primaries into the same few early weeks of the election year, the country has already drifted into a kind of de facto national primary, but a lousy one. It is time to have a good one.

CON: Andrew E. Busch

The idea of a national primary election to choose presidential party nominees is almost as old as the primary itself. The 1912 Progressive Party platform demanded "nation-wide preferential primaries for candidates for the presidency."[1] One year later, President Woodrow Wilson endorsed the idea in his first State of the Union message to Congress.[2]

Since then, the national primary has garnered considerable support, chiefly because of its appeal as a simpler form of democracy. It is clean, straightforward, and majoritarian—or so it would seem. In more recent years, some have also advocated a national primary as a means of combating the flaws in the modern "front-loaded" primary system—that is, one in which the state primaries and caucuses are disproportionately crammed together early in the primary season. In national opinion polls, at least two-thirds of Americans typically say they would prefer a national primary to the current system.

Yet despite its seductive appeal, the national primary is a bad idea. Upon closer examination, its supposed advantages prove to be largely illusory, and its disadvantages are serious indeed.

THE VIRTUE OF SIMPLICITY?

Much of the argument for a national primary lies in its alleged simplicity, but should simplicity be the driving motivation behind reform of the nominating system?

The genius of the American political system lies in its complexity. Separation of powers, checks and balances, bicameralism, and federalism all represent a deliberate embrace of complexity, as does the very idea, outlined in *Federalist* No. 10, of a large republic filled with contending and balancing "factions." When it comes to presidential selection, the electoral college was adopted by the framers, and is defended today by its supporters, precisely because its complexity allows for a tempered democracy and a balance between large and small states. It is, as such, emblematic of the "Compound Republic" extolled by James Madison in *Federalist* No. 39, a republic whose complicated structure does not fit neatly into the category of a unitary national government or of a confederation of states, but does succeed in meeting the needs of a diverse nation.

America's previous experiments with simplicity in presidential nominations have not turned out well. By far the most straightforward system for party nomination was the congressional caucus, in which congressional members of each party met to select their presidential nominee. From 1800 to 1824, the congressional caucus was a model of simplicity, but that benefit was rapidly outweighed by various defects, including insufficient representation of party voters in the caucus and the potential for a breakdown in separation of powers brought on by Congress's involvement in selecting presidential nominees. In 1824 the system collapsed amid the conflicts among political factions that shattered its simple frame.

The congressional caucus was quickly replaced by the national convention system, a nominating mechanism that relied on local and state party meetings to supply, through a circuitous route, delegates to the convention. It was highly decentralized, depending on the actions and calculations of dozens of local party leaders and hundreds of delegates. This complex system served the nation well for the better part of a century before progressive reformers inadvertently added even more complexity by superimposing primaries in some states on top of the traditional convention system. The convention system and the "mixed" system that supplanted it were both more complicated than the congressional caucus system and more democratic. Thus there is no evidence that simplicity is inherently better.

Just as the congressional caucus threatened separation of powers, the national primary threatens to undermine central features of the complex and balanced American political system. It would weaken federalism by reducing the importance of states in the selection process, reduce deliberation within the nominating process, and strengthen the presidency by adding power to the president's claim of possessing an unmediated popular mandate. Moreover, the national primary can prevail only if the public is persuaded that simplicity is preferable to subtlety—a success that could have the side effect of lowering Americans' resistance to other reforms that seek to dismantle other, more central manifestations of the complex American system (such as the electoral college). As French political observer Alexis de Tocqueville argued long ago in *Democracy in America,* the seeking of simplicity and uniformity often drives a political centralization that, over time, can unbalance and degrade America's polity and even threaten its liberty.

NOT AS SIMPLE AS IT SEEMS

In addition to the symbolic damage it might do to federalism, the notion of limited presidential power, and popular respect for the nuances of the American system, a national primary would probably not deliver on its promise to simplify American democracy. Instead, in the name of simplicity, the nation would just trade one set of complexities for another—and it is hardly obvious that the trade would be a good one.

For example, there is a potential conflict between the simplicity of the plan and its democratic nature. Nomination races often feature more than two candidates, and so the winners of early primaries frequently finish with less than 50 percent of the primary votes. In a national primary, should a plurality (more votes than those won by any of the opponents) be enough for a candidate to be declared a victor? Or must the winner win an outright majority (more than half of the votes)? A plurality rule diminishes the democratic element of the plan, making it possible for an extreme candidate who has intense but narrow support to win the nomination in a multicandidate field. But a runoff between the top two candidates, which would guarantee that someone wins a majority, would introduce a second election, thereby diminishing the plan's simplicity. Experience has shown that runoff elections almost invariably draw fewer voters.[3] Moreover, even a runoff does not guarantee that the winner will be broadly acceptable to the party. There is the possibility in a multicandidate race that two fringe candidates will finish first and second in the initial round of voting.

To avoid the problems inherent in multicandidate fields, some students of the electoral process have suggested introducing novel and complicated forms of voting, such as approval voting or cumulative voting. In such schemes, voters would vote for all the candidates they find acceptable, indicate their preferred ordering of all candidates, or allocate multiple votes in whatever proportions they wish. None of these experimental voting methods has ever been tried on a national scale in the United States, and they are certainly not simple.

There is also the question of whether the "national primary" would really be a single, unified national election, or whether it would consist of fifty-one separate primaries held on the same day. Most national primary proposals follow the first course, but in the latter case there would still be delegates and a convention. And there would be little opportunity, as there is now, for a multicandidate field to "shake out," increasing the likelihood that a convention would be split and deadlocked among numerous contenders and dominated by unseemly deal making. Although many political scientists and news correspondents might welcome the return of the brokered convention, it is not clear who in the modern era of fractured parties would have the power to broker it. More to the point, however interesting the spectacle might prove, it is the last thing that supporters of the national primary have in mind.

FRONT-LOADING REDUX

Proponents of a national primary have recently argued that such a reform is needed because of the front-loading of the contemporary primary process. However, the nation's experience with front-loading actually supplies some of the strongest arguments against the national primary.

Front-loading is a phenomenon that has been driven predominantly by the independent decisions of a large number of states to move their primary elections forward in the primary calendar. "Meaningful" primaries—primaries whose results could actually have an impact on the outcome of the nomination race—were once spread out over three months or more. By contrast, in 2004 the meaningful primary season began in Iowa on January 19 and ended on March 7, only six weeks later; the decisive portion of the 2008 Republican nominating contest lasted from January 3 through February 5, a period of only five weeks.

The front-loading of presidential primaries has been almost universally decried, including by the officials who pushed their states' primaries up. Critics have focused on four central shortcomings of the front-loaded system.[4] First, it is clear that front-loading has enhanced the importance of the so-called invisible primary—that is, the jockeying among candidates and the preparatory work that takes place in the year or more before the real primaries begin. Many analysts judge that a serious candidate must raise an "entry fee" of at least $20 million before the primaries begin; in 2008, only one candidate in either party who won even one primary had raised less than $37 million by January 1. In most years, this has meant that political insiders have regained most of the advantage that they allegedly had before the Democratic Party undertook reforms in 1970 that sought to open up and democratize the nominating process.

Second, because the meaningful primary season ends so soon after it begins, voters have fewer opportunities for second thoughts or careful deliberation. In the aftermath of the 2004 general election, some Democrats argued that the front-loaded system that sped John Kerry's nomination failed to allow sufficient examination of Kerry's strengths and weaknesses as a nominee.[5] Likewise, John McCain's 2008 victory in all but name by February 5 left Republican voters little opportunity for rethinking their choice.

Third, as the state primaries begin to come fast and furious, candidates no longer have time for the "retail" (face-to-face) politicking they cultivated in small states like Iowa and New Hampshire. Instead, they engage in a wholesale "tarmac campaign" in which they flit from one big-city airport to another, while relying mostly on expensive and superficial television ads to reach mass audiences.

Finally, once one candidate has amassed enough convention delegate votes to capture the nomination (or to drive serious opponents from the field), all later presidential primaries are rendered moot. Thus roughly half of the states often have no meaningful participation in the presidential nominating process, and the contests in those states, compared with those held earlier, see a marked decline in voter turnout. If the later primaries do not matter, why vote?

The national primary would worsen all but one of these problems. The irrelevance of later primaries would end, because everyone would vote at once. Modest Iowa and tiny New Hampshire could not start a stampede toward a candidate, and no state would be left out of the decision. In every other respect, a national primary—no matter how it is arranged—is sure to drastically worsen the problems that most analysts associate with front-loading. Indeed, the national primary would represent, in essence, front-loading taken to its extreme.

If there is a high entry fee for the invisible primary now, that fee will only go up in a national primary. As the stakes of primary day rise, the price of playing will rise, too. To participate in a one-day national election, candidates will have to run national campaigns from the beginning. They will have to raise more money, and all of it up front. And candidates will not be able to take advantage of an early surprise win in a small state to raise more money via the Internet, as John McCain did in the 2000 Republican primaries. The higher campaign costs will discourage some potential candidates from running, and more of those who do enter the race will withdraw before the primary voters have a chance to render a verdict. Long-shot candidates will have even less chance of overtaking the leader than they do in the current system. If there is a runoff provision, fund raising will become even more important, because candidates who advance will have to finance not one but two hugely expensive national primary campaigns.

If there is too little retail politicking in the front-loaded system after Iowa and New Hampshire, there would be virtually *no* retail politicking in a national primary system. The entire race would revolve around a costly and impersonal mass media effort, with little chance for the candidates to come face-to-face with the voters. No state would vote after the nominees have been selected, but many states and regions would be ignored in the rush of wholesale politics. Many issues of local significance that now receive at least some attention may be shunted to the side entirely.

Finally, if voters in today's front-loaded system often have little opportunity to change their minds or to gather and reflect on new information produced in earlier primaries, a national primary decided by a plurality vote would allow for no second thoughts at all. A national primary with a runoff would be a bit better, but the second thoughts would be limited to the top two candidates.

In short, if front-loading is the problem, a national primary is most definitely not the solution. Indeed, a national primary will only exacerbate the pathologies of the current front-loaded system. In contrast, the extended 2008 Democratic nomination contest, in which Barack Obama fought Hillary Rodham Clinton tooth and nail for five months before prevailing in early June, demonstrated that the current system is capable of breaking out of some of the problems associated with front-loading, albeit under unusual circumstances.

THE PROBLEM OF ENACTMENT

A final reason to oppose a national primary is the difficulty of establishing it through legitimate means. Almost all supporters of a national primary seem to assume that such a reform could be implemented by federal legislation. However, there are ample reasons to doubt this assumption.

The Constitution gives no outright authority to the federal government to intervene in the presidential nominating process. Only three provisions of the Constitution deal explicitly with elections for federal office. Two of the three (in Article II, Section 1) allocate between the states and Congress the powers related to the selection of presidential electors; Congress is given only the right to determine the "time" of such selections. The third (in Article I, Section 4) provides that "[t]he Times, Places, and Manner of holding Elections for Senators and Representatives, shall be prescribed in each State by the legislature thereof; but the Congress may at any time by Law make or alter such regulations, except as to the Places of chusing Senators."

Strictly speaking, then, the presidential nominating process for the parties is outside the Constitution—that is, in literal terms no constitutional provision touches nominations. Less strictly speaking, in "spirit" the Constitution treats congressional control of congressional elections more favorably than it does congressional control over presidential selection processes, which are mostly directed to state governments.

A handful of Supreme Court cases have permitted federal legislation affecting presidential elections beyond what a strict reading of the Constitution would seem to allow—for example, some rulings have upheld campaign finance regulations for both presidential and congressional elections. Some would go even further. Justice Hugo Black's opinion in *Oregon v. Mitchell*

(1970) argued that the power of Congress to regulate presidential elections was equal to its power to regulate congressional elections. The Court, however, has never concurred with Black's solitary view.

Indeed, two recent lines of Supreme Court interpretation have moved in the opposite direction. In one of these strands, the Court has increasingly held over the last three decades that the political parties are substantially private associations with considerable power to set their own nomination procedures.[6] This line of reasoning would limit both federal and state legislative interference in party affairs, at least in theory; all actual cases have involved state legislation. The second strand, evident especially since the mid-1990s, has reasserted the rights of the states against federal domination on the basis of the Tenth Amendment and a narrower reading of the enumerated powers of Congress.[7] Both strands have worked to limit, not expand, federal legislative powers that might be used to impose a national primary. Thus both the text of the Constitution and recent judicial interpretations of that text give little reason to assume that the federal government possesses the authority to pass legislation establishing a national primary.[8] A constitutional amendment could solve this problem, but amendments are not easily ratified.

The national parties would seem to possess the legal authority to seek such a reform, but primaries are actually established by state law. The national parties can refuse to seat delegates selected in a manner contrary to party rules, but they cannot force state legislatures to change primary dates. Although there were exceptions in both parties in 2008, the parties are typically reluctant to follow through on threats to deny seating to state delegations.[9] Refusing to seat state delegations is one of only a very few enforcement tools available to the parties, but it is too blunt an instrument to be used frequently. The more radical a proposed change—and a national primary is radical—the more unlikely it is that the national parties will be able to compel compliance. They may possess the authority, but they may not possess the power.

MITIGATING THE PRIMARY PROBLEM

The national primary, then, is in most respects inferior to a problematic status quo. However, a variety of measures currently available might at least mitigate the problems of front-loading. The goal should not be to collapse all primaries into a single election, but rather to spread out primaries and extend the meaningful nomination race. The place to start is reform of the campaign finance rules, which have made it difficult for all but the best-endowed candidates to raise sufficient funds to enter and continue in the race. A substantial increase (or perhaps even elimination) of the $2,000 limit on individual contributions would make it possible for more candidates to run and would extend the viability of candidates who do not win the first contests. Other steps aiming to spread out rather than consolidate primary dates could also extend the race. The national parties could mandate proportional representation in early primaries and could negotiate and encourage moderate calendar adjustments.

CONCLUSION

In summary, the national primary should be rejected. It offers a simplicity that is both illusory and undesirable. Although it would solve one problem associated with primary front-loading—the loss of meaningful participation by states that vote too late in the primary calendar—it would exacerbate the other problems. Indeed, a national primary would produce the most front-loaded schedule imaginable, with everything riding on a single day's contest. And there is no obvious way to bring about the reform: the federal government likely does not have the authority to impose it, whereas the parties have the authority but probably not the power. Despite the good intentions of the proponents of the national primary, the nation can do better.

RESOLVED, the president should be elected directly by the people

PRO: Burdett Loomis

CON: Byron E. Shafer

No issue vexed the delegates to the Constitutional Convention more than how the president should be chosen. A few wanted the president to be elected directly by the people. Quite a few more (but, in the end, not a majority) preferred that Congress elect the president. Other ideas included having the governors of the states or a small group of randomly selected members of Congress make the choice. After going around and around on this question for nearly the entire length of the convention, the delegates created a committee to come up with a solution that all of them could live with. The committee's proposal—the electoral college—accomplished that goal admirably. Offered to the convention on September 4, it was adopted with only minor modifications two days later.

Further tinkering took place in 1804, when the Twelfth Amendment stipulated that each elector must vote separately for president and vice president instead of voting (as the Constitution originally provided) for two candidates for president. Since then, more amendments have been introduced in Congress to replace or overhaul the electoral college than to change any other feature of the Constitution—about five hundred. But the only one to be enacted was the Twenty-third Amendment, which left the electoral college intact but enfranchised voters in the District of Columbia to participate in the election.

How does the electoral college work? To begin with, each state is assigned a number of electors equal to its number of representatives and senators in Congress. Currently, for example, California has fifty-five electoral votes, and several small states have the minimum number of three, corresponding to the one representative and two senators that a state gets no matter how few people live there. With the adoption of the Twenty-third Amendment in 1961, the District of Columbia received three electors. The Constitution leaves it up to each state to decide how its electors will be chosen and its electoral votes allocated. In practice, all of the states entrust this decision to the people. Except in Maine and Nebraska where each congressional district chooses an elector, the candidate who receives the most popular votes in the state wins all of its electors, a system known as winner-take-all.

To be elected president or vice president, a candidate must receive more than half of all the electoral votes in the country—currently, at least 270 out of 538. If no candidate does so, the House of Representatives elects the president from the top three electoral vote recipients, with each state delegation in the House casting a single vote until one of the candidates receives a majority. Meanwhile, the Senate chooses the vice president from the top two vice presidential candidates, with each senator assigned one vote. The House has been called on to elect the president twice: in 1800, when it chose Thomas Jefferson over Aaron Burr, and in 1824, when it chose John Quincy Adams over Andrew Jackson. The latter was a highly controversial decision, because Jackson had outpaced Adams in both the popular vote and the electoral vote. Although it has been a long time since the House has had to act, every time a serious third party candidate enters the race against the Republican and Democratic nominees, the possibility arises that none of them will secure an electoral vote majority and the House will once again be called on to elect the president.

A more frequent occurrence, although still a relatively rare one, is for the candidate who receives the most votes from the people to lose the election because the other candidate receives a majority of electoral votes. This is what happened in 1876, in 1888, and most recently in 2000, when Democrat Al Gore received a half million more popular votes than his Republican rival, George W. Bush, but Bush bested him in the electoral college by a vote of 271–266. By contrast, in every election from 1892 to 1996 (and again in 2004 and 2008) the electoral college "magnified" the victory of the popular vote winner—that is, he received a larger percentage of electoral votes than of popular votes.

The electoral college has ardent defenders, including Byron E. Shafer. But as the many attempts to repeal it indicate, the electoral college also has its critics. In the early 1950s, Congress seriously considered modifying the electoral college by adopting a proportional system in which each state's electoral votes would be awarded in proportion to the popular vote each candidate received in the state. More recently, the leading alternative to the electoral college has been direct election by the people. This is the idea championed by Burdett Loomis.

PRO: Burdett Loomis

I live in Lawrence, Kansas, home of the University of Kansas and part of the last "blue" county for well over five hundred miles for anyone headed west. More prosaically, Kansas is a Republican state; in fact, it is so Republican that the party's two major factions energize state politics with their bloody feuds. When presidential elections roll around, however, Kansans are reliably "red," voting by large margins for every Republican nominee in the past forty years (57 percent for John McCain in 2008).

In 1979 I moved to Kansas from Illinois. Earlier, I had lived in Wisconsin and Pennsylvania, where the race for president meant candidate visits, lots of advertising, and a real sense of competition. But not here, where both the Democratic and Republican presidential campaigns studiously avoid the state, knowing full well that Kansas's six electoral votes will almost certainly end up in the Republican column. On occasion, a vice-presidential candidate might stop by, as Democrat John Edwards and Republican Dick Cheney did in 2004, but that's about it.

Since 1980 I have cast a Kansas ballot in each election for the Democratic presidential candidate. For all the difference it has made, I may as well have voted for the Libertarian candidate, the Socialist Workers' nominee, or the Man in the Moon. In this country's most important election, my vote, along with those of my fellow Kansas Democrats, counts for nothing.

The contrast with Missouri, just forty miles away, is stark, because of that state's highly competitive partisan makeup. Living forty miles from Missouri, within the media market for three major Kansas City television stations, I do get to *watch* an actual presidential election take place. It's great. Candidates fly in, have press conferences, and tend to any number of local Missouri issues. They raise money and spend lots of it on television advertising. Both parties seek to win every possible vote in Missouri, and its citizens benefit from a vigorous campaign, fought in every corner of the state. In 2008 the contrast with Kansas was especially sharp, with McCain's Missouri margin of 3,903 votes (0.14 percent) requiring several days to sort out.

Even Kansas Republicans are not part of the presidential campaign. Their job is merely to deliver the expected six electoral votes and contribute some money to a candidate whose campaign will never visit the state. All of this would be bad enough if Kansas were somehow an oddity in presidential politics. But it is not; in fact, Kansas is closer to the norm than is Missouri, because most states are not competitive and are thus ignored by presidential campaigns.

To summarize, because of the nature of contemporary presidential politics under the rules of the electoral college, millions of Americans are effectively disenfranchised in choosing the president, whose actions affect all of them. Simply put, that is just not fair.

As a student of American politics, I certainly understand, and even celebrate, the importance of the nation's political institutions. Moreover, as a political scientist I recognize that institutions affect elections and policy decisions and that institutional rules are never neutral. But I have a hard time appreciating a system in which the cards are stacked, over and over again, so that my vote for president does not count.

Although I am a Democrat in a GOP stronghold, this is no partisan argument. Indeed, a Massachusetts Republican might well offer the same complaint. But my argument is both personal and general, lodged on behalf of the minority-party voters in the thirty or so states that are uncompetitive in any given presidential election. Unlike any other statewide electoral contest in Kansas, the presidential race is finished before it even starts. Writing in 2009, I will venture to guess that all sides already consider it to be over for the 2012 presidential campaign.

So what? Should Americans condemn the electoral college because most state races are not competitive? After all, presidential elections have been vigorously contested and competitive at the national level for more than two centuries. Even if every voter is not treated equally or fairly, the system has worked reasonably well, producing legitimate winners for two hundred years, despite disagreements that once rose to the level of a civil war. It is an argument worth addressing, and so I will now abandon, for the time being at least, the frustrating stories of Kansas and other similarly situated states. But I will return to them later, because in the end the most profound critique of the electoral college rests on its failure to give each citizen an equal voice in selecting the nation's president.

THE ELECTORAL COLLEGE AS A CONTINUING POLITICAL EXPERIMENT

The electoral college is the institutional mechanism used to select the president of the United States. Like the legislative branch and the judicial branch, the executive branch was conceived by the framers in their dual roles as political philosophers and practicing politicians. Although the framers' debates about the nature of the Constitution and the subsequent debates over its ratification reveal many of the core theoretical underpinnings of the American system, the framers were political reformers who were seeking institutional solutions to actual problems of governance.[1]

Although the framers seriously considered allowing the legislative branch to select the president, they decided that any such process would have given lawmakers too much power, while rendering the executive less strong and independent. At the same time, direct election of the chief executive was rejected, but largely for practical reasons rather than because of an aversion to direct democracy. To be sure, some delegates to the Constitutional Convention rejected the idea of direct election because they feared placing too much power in citizens' hands. More of the framers, however, found direct election impractical because of the difficulties of communicating effectively and knowledgeably across the entire nation.[2]

As for the electoral college, during the battle over ratifying the Constitution New York delegate Alexander Hamilton argued that it had escaped serious scrutiny at the convention.[3] In fact, it was an amalgam of various compromises, including the number of electors to be assigned to each state, the counting of slaves as three-fifths of a person for the purpose of calculating voting population, and the mediation of direct elections through the state-by-state selection of electors. The electoral college, then, is more a product of political necessity than of overriding principle. The framers also proved to be poor prognosticators when it came to the electoral college. They anticipated that electors would exercise judgment in voting for candidates, and they gave no consideration to the possibility that political parties—specifically two parties—would come to dominate the process. Rather, the framers foresaw eminent men being chosen as electors and then selecting a highly qualified president.

But their expectations about the electoral college proved wrong on almost every count. Political parties, both in their emerging form of the early 1800s and in their more mature manifestations that appeared in the Jacksonian era, proved capable of holding electors to their pledges to support the parties' choices for president and vice president. The role of electors as independent intermediaries vanished almost as soon as the first real contest for the presidency was waged, in 1796.

By 1836 the role of the electoral college had become well defined. Voters selected electors pledged to candidates who ran for president under party labels. In large part because each state adopted a "winner-take-all" rule for presidential (and most other) elections, only two major parties emerged.

Although the politics of presidential nominations and campaigns has changed greatly since the early 1800s, the basic features of the electoral college have not. So there the electoral college sits, an eighteenth-century institution, conceived in political compromise and essentially unchanged for two hundred years. Yet during those many years Congress has evolved, as has the presidency and the Supreme Court. Why then do Americans return every four years to a jury-rigged system that discriminates against millions of American voters and raises profound questions over the legitimacy of its results?

THE ELECTORAL COLLEGE: A SUCCESSFUL FAILURE

If twenty-first-century Americans designed a system to select their chief executive, two values would likely emerge as especially important: equality and transparency. Each vote should count the same, and all citizens should understand easily how the process works. Over the course of U.S. history, those values have become part of the fabric of the democratic process. Today, almost no one is denied access to the polls, and in almost all elections—whether for governor or school board or on referenda—each vote counts the same. Likewise, the reforms of the twentieth century, from the Australian ballot to primary elections to campaign finance reporting rules, increased the transparency of the electoral process. Irregularities may remain, but the values of equality and transparency are essentially honored in how Americans conduct their elections—with one major exception: the electoral college. In the electoral college, the votes of individual citizens in different states do not count the same. And despite legions of newspaper stories that purport to explain the electoral college every four years, it remains notoriously misunderstood, in large part because Americans vote simultaneously for a presidential candidate *and* the slate of electors who formally cast their votes for president a month after the November general election.

So, in two major ways the electoral college falls short. But these are just the first two counts in a long indictment. Before turning to some of these other problematic features of the electoral college, I first want to flesh out the equality issue a bit more.

Many critics of the electoral college complain about the numerical inequalities among the states or about how the institution counts some votes differently from others. Many of these related concerns flow from the disparities produced by giving each state a number of electors equal to its congressional delegation. Delaware thus receives three electoral votes, while California gets fifty-five. At first blush, Delaware and the six other states with a single House member seem to be getting away with murder. After all, their electoral votes are triple the number they would receive if population (reflected in the number of House seats) were the sole criterion. At the same time, the Senate "bonus" barely changes California's electoral total; the two extra electors pale in comparison with the state's fifty-three House members.

But Delaware's citizens understand that they do not have nearly the clout held by Californians. Under the winner-take-all rule all fifty-five of California's electors are awarded to the candidate who carries the state; Delaware's prize is tiny by comparison. Thus even with their extra electors, small states remain at a disadvantage. Moreover, anyone wanting to look at real inequality in the American political system need look no further than the U.S. Senate, which is by far the most unrepresentative major legislative body in the world. The inequalities of the electoral college pale before those of the Senate.

Ironically, the core inequity of the electoral college involves neither the largest nor the smallest states, but the handful of states (about fifteen or so in the past few elections) that are truly competitive—that is, are neither red nor blue. Not only do these states—such as Florida, Iowa, New Mexico, Ohio, Pennsylvania, and Wisconsin—receive the lion's share of the campaigns' attention, but the value of each vote in these states is magnified by the fact that the entire presidential election could well be decided by a relatively small number of votes in a single state.[4]

That said, the gravest defect of the electoral college is that the candidate who receives the most popular votes can lose the election. Before the 2000 election, the last time this situation arose was in 1888, when Republican Benjamin Harrison defeated the Democratic incumbent president, Grover Cleveland, despite the fact that Cleveland received more popular votes.[5] Prior to the 2000 election, then, defenders of the electoral college could have argued that the institution, while perhaps flawed, had generally proved a success. At the same time, skeptics could look at the narrow elections of 1916, 1948, 1960, 1968, and 1976 and express wonderment that the system did not produce more presidents who won the electoral vote while losing the popular count.

The 2000 election brought the flaws of the electoral college into full view. Republican George W. Bush received fewer popular votes than Democrat Al Gore, yet Bush won the electoral vote count by five votes. In the popular vote, Gore had a narrow but clear national plurality of more than 500,000 votes. A system of direct election would have awarded him the presidency, but the electoral college—and a razor-thin margin for Bush in Florida—created a constitutional crisis and elected the candidate who lost the popular vote count.

Unfortunately, the defects of the electoral college were obscured in the shuffle of postelection court battles and vote counting in Florida. But the simple truth remains that the popular vote count was far less ambiguous than was the result produced by the electoral college, save for the Supreme Court's late intervention on Bush's behalf.

Despite some initial calls for electoral reform after the 2000 contest, the wind soon went out of reformers' sails, and the 2004 and 2008 elections were conducted in the same manner as the 2000 election, with candidates focusing on the ten to fifteen states that were in play. A Kansan or even a Californian had no more role to play in 2004 or 2008 than in 2000. Moreover, the Bush-Kerry contest in 2004 again demonstrated the potential for an electoral college "mistake," because Bush, despite winning the national popular vote by three million votes, had only a 119,000-vote margin (of almost three million cast) in Ohio, a state essential to his victory. Democrat John Kerry could easily have become the second consecutive chief executive who lost the popular vote, in which case real concerns about presidential legitimacy would certainly have surfaced.[6]

So far, I have focused on actual problems with the electoral college. Its dysfunctional nature comes into even sharper focus when one considers what happens when no candidate receives a majority of the electoral vote and the election is thrown into the House of Representatives for resolution. This situation arose in both 1800 and 1824, but never in the modern two-party era. There have, however, been a lot of near misses, most notably in 1948, when "Dixiecrat" candidate Strom Thurmond won thirty-nine electoral votes in the South, and in 1968 when American Independent Party candidate George C. Wallace won forty-six electoral votes. In a closer election, either might have been in a position to determine the winner by negotiating a deal with one of the major-party candidates. Many states have sought to avoid such deal making by binding electors to candidates, but most constitutional scholars agree that the courts would not uphold such laws.[7]

Governments in parliamentary systems often come into existence through this kind of negotiation, but the United States does not have such a system. Americans can scarcely anticipate the possible implications of politicking for the electoral college vote, but the preparations for negotiations that third party candidate H. Ross Perot made in 1992 and the actions of both the Bush and Gore camps in 2000 are reminders of the potential for a backroom deal to decide the presidency.

And what if the deal making fails and the electoral college does not produce a majority for any candidate? As noted earlier, the House of Representatives decides who will be president; each state delegation receives one vote, with a majority (twenty-six) required for victory. Anyone who finds the electoral college unrepresentative would become apoplectic at the patent unfairness of such a decision. California would have a voice equal to that of Delaware. Indeed, California, which has more House members (fifty-three) than the smallest twenty-one states together (fifty-one), could be outvoted twenty-one to one. To be sure, small states would probably not vote as a bloc, but that does not make the process any more equitable.

The inequities of the "one state–one vote" rule pale in comparison with the political machinations it invites. Consider the following scenario: the

Democratic candidate receives 260 (of the 270 necessary) electoral votes and wins 50 million popular votes; the Republican candidate wins 230 electoral votes and 45 million popular votes; and a third party candidate receives 48 million electoral votes and 35 million popular votes. Republicans control the House delegations in twenty-seven states, Democrats in twenty, and three are equally divided. The Republican candidate won the popular vote in four Democratic states, while the Democrat prevailed in six GOP states. Would Republican House members toe the party line, elect a president who received only about 36 percent of the popular vote, and risk their seats in the next elections, especially in districts where the Democratic presidential candidate won? Would the third party candidate throw his or her support to one of the major-party nominees? And on and on. This, too, is the electoral college system at work.

DUMP THE ELECTORAL COLLEGE

A short essay cannot fully explore the many problems posed by the electoral college. But excellent alternatives are available that rely on a direct popular vote. A pure plurality vote election might be the cleanest alternative, but other systems, including runoffs between the top two candidates, would also count every vote equally and produce a clear winner more often than the electoral college, with its myriad possibilities for breaking down. And I could then cast my vote in Kansas, certain that it counted just as much as if I were in Ohio or New Mexico or any other of the so-called battleground states. We in the Land of Oz might even see a few ads and the presidential candidates in the flesh. Maybe it won't happen, but it should.

CON: Byron E. Shafer

> "Is there any other point to which you would wish to draw my attention?"
> "To the curious incident of the dog in the night-time."
> "The dog did nothing in the night-time."
> "That was the curious incident," remarked Sherlock Holmes.
>
> —Arthur Conan Doyle, *Silver Blaze*

Not one but three curious incidents characterized the presidential election of 2000. The first was manifest and dramatic: the electoral college, not the popular vote, determined the outcome. A second was latent and ironic: the electoral college kept pumping away as a device for majority formation in the usual manner despite that controversial outcome. And the third unfolded before our eyes but was frequently not tied back to its actual cause: the electoral college helped to restore "retail politics" to the presidential contest. How an observer feels about the practical balance among these three curious incidents goes a long way toward determining how that observer feels about the electoral college itself.

But first, note that neutral observers quickly came to know how the general public felt. In the face of the central fact of the 2000 outcome, whereby the winner of the popular vote and the winner of the electoral vote diverged, the general public demonstrated remarkable equanimity. Before the fact, many analysts, both supporters and opponents of the electoral college as an institution, would have predicted that the next time the institution "misfired," it would be reformed out of existence. When it did misfire, electing the "wrong" president, a few political elites attempted to raise the hue and cry. But there was no great mass response, and the matter passed quickly.

Isolating the larger systemic contribution of the electoral college to American politics, especially in that long stretch between 1888 and 2000 when it did nothing but confirm the winner of the popular vote as the next president, has never been a simple task. Worse yet, the argument on both sides has had to be about things that did not happen or were not happening—about dogs that did not bark. Yet the arguments themselves are straightforward enough. Moreover, the strategic politics surrounding these arguments has changed in our time, a fact that further justifies our returning to the debate.

The last time the electoral college received sustained scholarly attention, during the late 1960s and early 1970s, it was as part of a larger debate about institutional reform. The essence of that discussion involved participatory versus representative democracy, and reached into every institutional theater: political parties, Congress, the bureaucracy, and, by way of the electoral college, the presidency as well.

- Proponents of reform focused on procedural fairness. They argued against the "distorting" effect of the electoral college on the popular will, quite apart from the ultimate risk of electing the wrong contender, and against an institutional barrier to the direct registration of the public will, distorted or not.

- Opponents focused instead on behavioral effects. They countered that the electoral college had to be judged in the full context of the institutional structure of American government and that, when it was, the college contributed important countervailing influences to *other* distortions, lodged where they could less easily be addressed.

In pursuit of these arguments, both sides used the same basic data. Proponents of reform argued that the campaign, both the activities and the positions of the presidential contenders, was being heavily influenced—distorted—by the electoral college. What proponents saw was that candidates inevitably attended to the competitive states, where a small shift in the popular vote could swing a large bloc of electors. In the process, they did *not* go to states where the partisan outcome was obvious, and thus did not stimulate participation and turnout in these neglected areas.

Opponents agreed with the diagnosis but disagreed with the conclusion. They focused on the identity of these competitive states, which tended to be larger and more socially diverse. In practice, Republicans had to reach out to the northeastern industrial states plus California, rather than to their guaranteed base in the Midwest and Rocky Mountains. In practice, Democrats had to reach out to the same northeastern industrial states plus California, rather than to their guaranteed base in the South. Ideological liberalism, coupled with energy and innovation, were thereby fostered, compensating for other conservatizing elements in the Constitution.

Opponents won the debate in the sense that reform of the electoral college did not proceed, though it was not necessarily their arguments that carried the day. The small and less competitive states were often the most actively opposed to reform. They focused on the fact that they were over-represented within the electoral college, because every state gets two electoral votes for their two senators regardless of population, rather than on the fact that the big states gained leverage by being more competitive. And the larger and more competitive states often supported reform, because they were the home of many ideologically committed reformers.

Flash forward to 2000. Proponents of electoral college reform heard their clarion call. The "wrong candidate" won. Members of the general public were unimpressed. The winner in the electoral college was the "right candidate" by definition; that is how presidents are chosen. Yet if we refocus the argument on the two *other* things that the electoral college does, conducing toward majorities and encouraging retail politics, it should be possible to weigh the alternatives intelligently—that is, it ought to be possible to see whether these contributions are sufficient to compensate for the occasional year when the electoral college does not award the presidency to the contender with a plurality of the popular vote.[1]

CONDUCING TOWARD MAJORITIES

The surface influence of the electoral college on the way we form presidential majorities was exercised in the usual way during the 2000 campaign through its hostility toward third parties and independent candidacies. Ralph Nader, Green Party candidate for president, bore the brunt of this effect, though he bore its burden lightly. During the campaign, the electoral college produced the usual argument against supporting Nader: if a third contender cannot win, then voting for him will always benefit the major-party candidate you like least. As election day approached, the stated intention of voting for Nader did decline, and it declined most in those states where the outcome was apparently closest—states where the strategic argument was most true. Afterward, in an election in which a myriad of factors could be argued to have been sufficient to alter the outcome, the remaining Nader vote in Florida certainly qualified: had the electoral college managed to repress that vote further, Al Gore would have become president.[2]

Yet this effect still grossly understates the majority-forcing aspect of the electoral college. For in fact, the college is shaping not just the fortunes but the very field of presidential candidates. And here, the question of how American politics would handle the shaping of this field, if we imagine doing away with the electoral college, becomes critical to the argument—and critical to the functioning of American democracy. For the electoral college is not just repressing the vote for announced third candidates for president, its evident surface impact. It is powerfully reinforcing the definitiveness of the processes by which the two major-party candidates are selected. In the long run, this deeper process—another dog that does not bark—may be far more consequential.

At a minimum, the electoral college reinforces the dynamic under which, by the time a national party convention confirms a major-party candidate for president, the battle within that party is over, and the other candidates who sought its nomination withdraw from the field. Because of the electoral college, all they could alternatively do is to launch a quixotic independent bid for the presidency, thereby guaranteeing victory for the other major-party candidate—the opposition-party candidate—probably while terminating any further political career of their own.

The moment the electoral college is gone, however, this dynamic changes: aggrieved candidates for major-party nominations would no longer need to withdraw. And recurrent sources of aggravation are multiple and obvious. Some candidates always believe that their positions have been distorted by opponents or by the press. Some candidates always conclude that they have lost just because other contenders had unfair resource advantages. Some candidates always have supporters who desire—and in some sense deserve—to continue the crusade. And on and on.

Fanciful? Recent campaigns suggest not. For example, it is not difficult to imagine the 2000 contest with all four main contenders—George W. Bush,

John McCain, Al Gore, and Bill Bradley—continuing on to the general election. Indeed, it is not that difficult to imagine the nominating contests of 1992, with the senior George Bush and Bill Clinton as major-party nominees but with Pat Buchanan not dropping out, with Jesse Jackson entering—he certainly wanted to—and, of course, with H. Ross Perot staying in. We shall return to the presidential election of 2008 at the end of this essay, since it may be the clearest example of all.

Moreover, the fancy helps to underline some very real facts about the operation of the electoral college. For it emphasizes how important the new rules of presidential election would be in the absence of the college. Would the general public demand a majority of the popular vote in order to affirm a president? Possibly not—we do not demand it now—though note that this is precisely because we have an alternative majority-forcing device in the form of the electoral college. We could, of course, demand just such a majority, and we might well have to do so once the electoral college was gone, though note that this would almost certainly require runoff elections. By this standard, there would have had to be runoffs not just in 1992 and 2000 but even in 1996.

Most alternatives to the electoral college instead proceed on the theory that the plurality vote winner would become president. But this is a safe assumption only within a system that is powerfully constrained by the electoral college—that is, it assumes that the two parties will be creating the two main candidates, that this selection process will simultaneously be repressing major partisan alternatives, and that coronation of these two main alternatives will then be deterring independent candidacies. Yet these parties guarantee their two major-party nominees and deter third (fourth, etc.) alternatives *by way of the electoral college*. Both proponents and opponents agree that the existence of the electoral college shapes the field of candidates and their electoral strategies. Surely removing the college would likewise (re)shape them.

And here the alternatives become less fanciful. Surely there will often be presidential contenders who could expect to draw a substantial portion of their support from independents and loyalists of the opposite party. The current system is stacked against them, all but forcing them to run within a party. A direct plurality vote system is what they need, encouraging them to run directly for president instead. Surely there will likewise—nearly always—be presidential contenders who could expect to rally a major social group. The current system encourages them not to, since they cannot win a nominating majority with such a strategy, while they would be drawing their preferred group away from influence on the actual winner. Again, a direct plurality vote system is what they need for rallying their group and then attempting to trade off its influence.

Yet if more than two serious contenders actually ran in the general election, year in and year out, would we still be willing to elect the plurality winner? How large a plurality would you require? Would you tolerate a candidate as president who had "won" with 25 percent of the vote? Twenty-two percent? Nineteen percent? The moment you establish a system in which, say, 30 percent of the vote might win, you encourage any candidate who might hope to attain that total to run as an independent rather than seeking the Democratic or Republican nomination. The moment you address this problem by having a second round of voting—a runoff—you encourage *every* candidate to enter the first round of the "real election," the general election, rather than being content with an internal party process under which all but one would be eliminated.

In the face of these alternative rules, how fissiparous is American society, that is, how many candidates can it "naturally" support? If you believe that it is quite diverse—socially diverse, economically diverse, geographically diverse, ideologically diverse—the answer is surely, in principle, many. With the presidency, the two-party system as buttressed by the electoral college works against such a multiplication of candidacies. In its absence, at a minimum, the strategic calculations of many potential candidates would be altered. Yet the chain of impacts would likely go on and on. A presidency that is either balkanized by major ongoing social divisions, each with their own designated candidate, or "unified" by standing apart from those divisions and thus obscuring candidate attachments, will be a weakened institution: either devoid of mandate or devoid of program.

ENCOURAGING RETAIL POLITICS

We are not, however, reduced to imagining that the interaction of social change with institutional rules might alter the character of politics. For in our time, the combination of the electoral college as the central institution for presidential elections with the changing nature of American society has already transformed the character of presidential politicking. This impact is widely recognized, though the role of the electoral college in creating it is less so. Nevertheless, this impact is yet another reason one might—or here, might not—desire to see the electoral college continue to perform its major roles. For what the electoral college has done, when imposed upon partisan shifts in the states and localities, is to restore what is known as "retail politics" to the presidential campaign.

This is a terminology more commonly recognized at the nomination stage. We say that the opening contests—Iowa, New Hampshire, maybe South Carolina, sometimes one or two others—feature a retail politics in which candidates meet voters face-to-face in their localities. After this opening phase, we switch to "wholesale politics," the politics of the tarmac, in which candidates are flown from airport to airport delivering set speeches while the bulk of the campaign switches to televised advertising. There are proponents and opponents of this system as well, and it is true that we emphasize these early contests in small places at the cost of later and usually larger ones. But both proponents and opponents recognize that the country has designed a process privileging retail over whole-sale politics, at least at the start.

This was long thought to be part of the impact of the electoral college too, forcing candidates to address individual states on the way to the general elec-tion. In recent decades, much of this effect appeared to go away, replaced by fully national campaigns—retail campaigns, tarmac campaigns, media cam-paigns. Now, as evidenced by 2000 and again by 2004 and 2008, the old effect is back with a vengeance. The two major contenders focus on a small set of what are widely recognized as "battleground states," and they do so with events which are radically scaled down from those of only a few years ago. No one can deny that many states are thereby ignored. But nor can one deny that both the focus and the character of campaigns have changed.

How did this come about? Apparently through the impact of partisan shifts *as funneled through the electoral college.* In truth, what was previously viewed as a national campaign was in part illusory, resulting from the fact that the elec-toral college focused the campaign on the bigger (and more socially diverse) states. If you have to worry about California, New York, Pennsylvania, and Illinois, the result will *seem* like a national campaign. More to the practical point, it will inevitably be wholesale politics. You cannot campaign in California as you would campaign in Wisconsin; scale alone forbids it. But if, as in 2004, you have to worry instead about Wisconsin, Iowa, Minnesota, New Hampshire, and New Mexico—even throwing in Florida and Ohio—the story is different. The fact that you are campaigning within states is no longer hidden. The retail character of that campaign is likewise evident.

The result is not as self-evidently virtuous as the majority-forcing impact of the electoral college, and the effect of removing the college is thereby not as self-evidently disastrous. But the point here is a different one. What needs emphasis is that the choice between electoral college or not is inherently a choice between one vision of politics and another. It is not between one set of rules and "no rules." It is not between one impact and "no impact." The choice is instead between majority-forcing and minority-inducing strictures. It is between incentives toward retail and wholesale politicking. It is between one set of institutionalized "distortions" and another. In such a world, anyone who opposes the electoral college without specifying an alternative and then elaborating the consequences cold-bloodedly is irresponsible at best, pernicious at worst.

A BITE WITH NO BARK?

The charm of 2008, by these lights, was that the electoral college was functioning in the same fashion as it had in 2000—and every bit as forcefully—yet no one appeared to notice, much less complain. It was Barack Obama rather than George W. Bush who was the beneficiary this time, because 2008 was the kind of election that would most plausibly have spawned multiple candidates under reformed arrangements, that is, in a process of presidential selection that encouraged some contenders to undertake an independent candidacy while it encouraged others to fight for a major-party nomination but then continue on to the general election.

To help make this implicit impact explicit, consider the candidate array of 2008 as it began to emerge. Begin with those who obviously did feel encouraged to seek major-party nominations, including John McCain, Mike Huckabee, and Mitt Romney among Republicans, along with Barack Obama and Hillary Rodham Clinton among Democrats. Then consider their strategic alternatives in the absence of the electoral college, once the process of delegate selection had concluded:

- For the Republicans, their party was left with a maverick nominee, John McCain, who had been an intermittent thorn in the side of the regular party for many years. Said the other way around, the active base of the Republican Party was left without a candidate. The electoral college nevertheless made this the end of the line, but in its absence, this active base would have been free to continue to search for a champion. Indeed, under reformed arrangements, major losing contenders like Fred Thompson might have been better advised to delay entry and wait for just such an appeal from the regular party, making them into heroes rather than spoilers in the process.

- For the Democrats, the situation was opposite but the result was the same. For them, the candidate who had arguably received the most votes toward a nomination—counting only the primaries, but counting them all—was actually defeated. In the absence of the electoral college, and even more so if it had been replaced by a two-stage runoff process, Hillary Clinton would have had to think seriously about continuing on. Indeed, even if she had been privately disinclined, she would have had to deal with an outraged campaign whose active members believed that she, not Barack

Obama, John McCain, or Fred Thompson, would ultimately emerge from a multicandidate opener and a two-candidate runoff.

And at that point, the floodgates would open: other candidates who had not seriously considered the run for a major-party nomination would have been encouraged to consider running for president as independents. The two most obvious examples stayed out in 2008, despite evident indications of interest. In the absence of the electoral college but in the presence of *four* presidential candidates for the general election, the strategic environment would have been aligned with—not against—their inclinations:

- Michael Bloomberg, mayor of New York City, had thought seriously about just such a run, to the point of establishing a shadow campaign staff charged with developing themes, issues, and strategies. Like Ross Perot before him, Bloomberg was sufficiently wealthy that he could have funded such an effort out of his own pocket if need be.

- Jesse Jackson, who had run for the Democratic nomination twice before, was volcanically—even scatologically—angry at the prospect that Barack Obama would come to be seen as the premier champion of black America. If he never looked like the ultimate winner, Jackson had the name recognition and activist connections necessary to enter as an explicit spoiler, in hopes that his first-round support—even 2 or 3 percent would do—could be traded at the second round of the general election.

Would these candidates ever actually have responded to their personal siren songs? If they had, what would the ultimate vote actually have looked like, in round one and then in round two? No one knows the answers, but it hardly matters: these are the wrong questions. Instead, ask yourself how sure you are that none of this would have come to pass. Then ask yourself how many times it would have to hap-pen before it was a common—even expected—occurrence. And once you have done all that, ask yourself whether American politics would work better by your lights with fragmented candidacies or nonmajoritarian presidents.

Let me say the same thing differently. The fact that the existing dogs do not normally bark does not mean that they are not standing by the gate, protecting the commonwealth. If they are slain by accident, no less than if they are slain deliberately, the majoritarian process in American politics—a politics riddled with nonmajoritarian elements in its institutions and in its society—can hardly be said to have been reinforced. If that process is weakened, it is hard to see how government would become either more effective or more responsive. Holmes would have known how to make the proper deduction.

RESOLVED, the Twenty-second Amendment should be repealed

PRO: David Karol

CON: Thomas E. Cronin

How many four-year terms should a president be allowed to serve? From 1789 to 1951, the Constitution's answer to that question was: as many as the president chooses to seek and the voters choose to grant—in other words, an unrestricted number of terms. With the addition of the Twenty-second Amendment to the Constitution in 1951, the answer changed: no more than two.

The belief that the president should always be eligible for reelection was important to the delegates at the Constitutional Convention. Throughout most of their deliberations, they maintained that the president should be elected by Congress to a seven-year term. A necessary corollary to this provision, they believed, was that the president could only serve one term. Otherwise presidents would spend all their time conniving to get reelected by, in effect, bribing members of Congress with political patronage and illegitimate favors.

As they deliberated further, however, confining the president to one term eventually struck most of the delegates as a bad idea, so much so that they jettisoned the provision for election by Congress and created the electoral college. Reeligibility would allow the country to keep good presidents in office and give every president what Pennsylvania delegate Gouverneur Morris called "the great motive to good behavior, the hope of being rewarded by a reappointment." More ominously, Morris warned, "Shut the Civil road to Glory & and he may be compelled to seek it by the sword."

Once the Constitution was ratified and took effect, the absence of term limits became in practice a two-term limit. George Washington, who retired at the end of his second term, is often credited with inventing this tradition. In truth, Washington meant to do no such thing: he stepped down because he longed for the "shade of retirement" and also because he thought it was important for the country to learn that the new Constitution would work just as well without him as with him. The real inventor of the two-term tradition was the third president, Thomas Jefferson, who served in France during the Constitutional Convention and thought that the lack of a term limit on the president would lead to a kind of elective monarchy.

The two-term tradition endured until Franklin D. Roosevelt broke it by being elected to a third term in 1940 and a fourth term in 1944. Indeed, twenty of FDR's thirty predecessors actually served one term or less. Some presidents, including Andrew Jackson, even argued for a constitutional amendment that would confine the president to one term but lengthen it to six years. The best argument for this proposal was that it would free presidents from all concerns about getting reelected while giving them time to see their initiatives through to completion. The best argument against it was that with the single six-year term the country would have a president it liked for two years less than it does now and a president it disliked for two years more.

The single six-year term still has adherents, but the change in the original constitutional arrangement that actually was made was for a maximum of two four-year terms. The Twenty-second Amendment stipulates that "No person shall be elected to the office of the President more than twice." An exception applies to presidents who succeed to the office less than halfway through their predecessor's term, as Gerald R. Ford did when Richard Nixon resigned nineteen months into his term. These presidents may be elected only once.

Politically, the enactment of the Twenty-second Amendment expressed the conservative backlash against FDR that followed his death in 1945. Every Republican in Congress voted for the amendment in 1947, along with many southern Democrats. Liberal Democrats from the North opposed it. The amendment remained controversial when it was sent to the states for ratification. It required an unusually long period (nearly four years—a record at the time) to be approved by the same coalition of Republican and southern Democratic state legislatures.

Controversial at its birth, the two-term limit has remained controversial ever since. Three of the four presidents who have bumped up against the limit by serving two terms—Dwight D. Eisenhower, Ronald Reagan, and Bill Clinton—favored repealing it. So does David Karol, who argues for the resolution that "The Twenty-second Amendment should be repealed" in the face of Thomas E. Cronin's defense of the amendment.

PRO: David Karol

The simplest case against the Twenty-second Amendment is that it is undemocratic. If voters think that an individual who has already served two terms in the White House is the best candidate for the next four years, then their wishes should be respected. Although the undemocratic aspect of the amendment is its most offensive feature, there is also reason to believe that it makes presidents less effective without curbing their abuses of power.

The Twenty-second Amendment is based on a fundamental mistrust of the democratic process. Admittedly, the presidential term limit is far from the only antimajoritarian provision of the Constitution.[1] Because majority rule is not the only value dear to Americans, some of the Constitution's deviations from it can still be justified. The Bill of Rights and the post–Civil War civil rights amendments protect fundamental liberties of individuals whose religious practices or political speech may be abhorrent to the majority, and they ensure minorities equal protection. Other Constitutional provisions, including the separation of powers and bicameralism, encourage deliberation and promote stability by impeding policy changes that lack broad support. Still other aspects of the Constitution protect federalism, a value important to the founders if not always to later generations.

Yet, although all of these values have some weight against the claims of majority rule, the Twenty-second Amendment promotes none of them. It does not protect individual liberties or minority rights. Nor does it encourage deliberation, stabilize policy making, or preserve federalism.

Moreover, American values have long been more democratic than those of the founders, to whom "the people" meant white, propertied males. As a result, with the glaring exception of the Twenty-second Amendment, constitutional reforms affecting the electoral process have consistently moved toward greater democracy. Constitutional amendments mandated the direct election of senators; granted electoral votes to the District of Columbia; guaranteed voting rights to African Americans, women, and young adults; outlawed the poll tax; and shortened the lame-duck period in which officials no longer accountable to voters can govern.[2] In considering these reforms, Americans had to choose between the founders' careful design and their own growing preference for democratic values.

By contrast, the question of the Twenty-second Amendment's repeal does *not* force us to choose between the founders' design and democratic values, since that amendment uniquely overturned the considered judgment of the founders at the same time that it restricted voters' rights.

We know from James Madison's notes that the delegates to the Constitutional Convention considered and ultimately rejected a term limit for the chief executive. Early in the convention a majority did support a single seven-year term for the president. Yet delegates favored a single term at a time when they were planning to have Congress elect the president and feared that a chief executive who knew his reelection was in the hands of the legislature would not be sufficiently independent of it. Later the delegates accepted a committee proposal that created an electoral college to choose the president. Having removed presidential election from Congress, the committee decided to make presidents eligible for reelection. Several delegates saw preserving the president's "re-eligibility" as an important advantage of the electoral college.[3]

Why did many of the founders think it was useful for a president to be reeligible? It is notable that the opponents of term limits did not ground their arguments on a naive or optimistic view of human nature and took seriously concerns about tyranny. For Gouverneur Morris, the most vociferous opponent of term limits at the convention, barring the president from seeking reelection "tended to destroy the great motive to good behavior, the hope of being rewarded by a re-appointment. It was saying to him, make hay while the sun shines."[4] Morris worried that a term-limited president might be corrupt or tempted to create a crisis or stage a coup to remain in office.

In *Federalist* No. 72 Alexander Hamilton defended the Constitution's lack of a presidential term limit. Hamilton built on Morris's arguments, noting that such a limit would reduce the president's incentive to perform well, especially to undertake projects that would have no immediate reputational payoff and whose success would depend on his successors' actions. Hamilton also noted that the country would be depriving itself of experienced leadership and might be unable to select the person best suited to deal with a pressing problem. Term limits might also require turnover in the presidency during a war or other crisis and in general would lead to unhelpful policy instability.

Supporters of the Twenty-second Amendment make several claims. They allege that George Washington believed two terms were sufficient for a president and that Jefferson agreed, and that their examples convinced Americans of the wisdom of this view. Therefore, some have contended, the amendment merely codifies what had been an entrenched norm dating from the days of the first president until it was recklessly cast aside in 1940. Yet scholars have shown that the two-term tradition prior to the second reelection of Franklin Roosevelt was both less venerable and more tenuous than advocates of the Twenty-second Amendment claim. Washington did indeed retire when he could have won a third term. Yet Washington's own explanation for this decision was *not* that he believed that presidents should serve no more than eight years.

In correspondence with Lafayette, Washington disputed the value of term limits.[5] Rather the first president claimed to want to show that the new political system did not depend on any individual. He also said he was exhausted and eager to return to private life.

It was only starting with Thomas Jefferson's renunciation of a third term and his dubious interpretation of the motives underlying Washington's decision that the two-term norm began to gain currency.[6] Until 1940 no president had served more than two terms, and many thought this was proper. Some presidents even tried to establish a norm that a president should only serve one term.[7]

Yet in practice many Americans were not wedded to the notion that presidents could serve only two terms. In 1880 former president Ulysses S. Grant sought a third term and won much support despite having already served two terms. Grant led on the first 34 ballots at the Republican National Convention that year, before a compromise dark-horse candidate was selected.[8] Similarly in 1912 former president Theodore Roosevelt, who had served more than seven years after succeeding the assassinated William McKinley, won almost all the Republican primaries only to be denied the nomination by the party machine that preferred President William Howard Taft. A defiant Roosevelt went on to run the most successful third party campaign in history as the candidate of the Progressive Party. Running as the "Bull Moose" candidate, Roosevelt outpolled Taft and carried several states. Clearly in the late nineteenth and early twentieth centuries many Americans had no strong objection to a president serving more than two terms. And in 1940 and 1944 Franklin D. Roosevelt won his third and fourth terms by solid margins.

If the founders rejected term limits for the chief executive and many voters in both parties favored presidential candidates who sought more than two terms, why was the Twenty-second Amendment adopted? As historian Henry Steele Commager argued and President Ronald Reagan later agreed, "There is simply no denying that in many ways the two term limit 'was imposed as posthumous vengeance on Franklin D. Roosevelt.'"[9] In the 80th Congress, the first one with a GOP majority since the beginning of the Great Depression, the Twenty-second Amendment won unanimous support from Republicans as well as the backing of some Southern Democrats who had fallen out of sympathy with Roosevelt's New Deal policies. FDR's political opponents, temporarily in the majority, made sure that no one else would repeat his feat.

Yet if partisanship indisputably motivated the adoption of the amendment, it should play no role in consideration about repealing it. It is not merely that a constitution ought to transcend partisan concerns, but from a more practical standpoint, we simply cannot know which party will be advantaged by repeal in coming decades. The Twenty-second Amendment was a Republican initiative.

Yet it did not affect a Democratic president who was in good enough physical and political shape to aspire to a third term until Bill Clinton left office almost fifty years after the amendment came into force. By contrast, there is reason to believe that Dwight D. Eisenhower, a Republican, might have secured a third term in 1960 had he sought one. And despite his advanced age Republican Ronald Reagan might have won a third term had he desired it in 1988.

A more valid concern raised by advocates of the Twenty-second Amendment is excessive presidential power. Charges that FDR had been or verged on becoming "a dictator" were partisan hyperbole, but the power of the presidency vis-à-vis Congress and the broader society definitely increased greatly during Roosevelt's time in office and subsequently. Given this unmistakable trend, concerns about presidential abuse of power are reasonable, but term limits are not the answer.

Generally, presidential power is greatest and the risk of abuse most serious in the fields of national security, foreign policy, and law enforcement. Yet the growth of the so-called imperial presidency largely postdates the Twenty-second Amendment. The actions that led Congress to enact the War Powers Resolution in 1973 were taken mostly by term-limited presidents.[10] The only president forced to resign over abuse of power, Richard Nixon, was term limited, as was George W. Bush, who made many assertions of presidential power that remain controversial.

It still might be argued that presidential abuses of power would be even worse were it not for the Twenty-second Amendment, since "power corrupts" over time. Yet this contention is undermined by a review of the record. Many of the most widely criticized presidential actions in recent decades were undertaken in presidents' first terms. Lyndon B. Johnson's misleading of the public over the Gulf of Tonkin incident, which led to an escalation of U.S. involvement in Vietnam, occurred in his first term. The secret bombing of Cambodia as well as the Watergate break-in and ensuing cover-up took place during Richard Nixon's first term. Similarly, many of George W. Bush's most controversial actions in the realms of national security and civil liberties occurred during his first term. We do not want presidents to conduct unaccountable foreign policies, to undermine civil liberties, or to turn law enforcement agencies into tools for partisan or personal vendettas. Yet there is little evidence that term limits address these problems.

Although the consequences of repealing the Twenty-second Amendment are inevitably somewhat uncertain, it is useful to examine evidence from other political systems both in the United States and around the world in order to come to a more informed judgment of the merits of presidential term limits. Presidential term limits exist in many countries that lack long traditions of stable democracy, including much of Latin America and Africa. In Russia, where democratic traditions and values are weak, a two-term limit achieves little; although he stepped down from the presidency, Vladimir Putin has continued to dominate politics via a hand-picked successor. Similarly, the example of Hugo Chavez in Venezuela shows that, faced with a popular leader with authoritarian tendencies, term limits might be eliminated. It is the least dangerous leaders in the most stable democracies who are most affected by term limits.

In long-standing democracies more comparable with the United States many chief executives have served for more than eight years in the modern era without those countries devolving into tyrannies. In Canada Pierre Trudeau was prime minister from 1968 to 1979 and again from 1980 to 1984 and Jean Chretien held that office from 1993 to 2003. In Australia Robert Menzies was prime minister from 1949 to 1967 as was Michael Howard from 1996 to 2007. In the United Kingdom Margaret Thatcher was prime minister from 1979 to 1990 and Tony Blair from 1997 to 2007. In the Netherlands Ruud Lubbers was prime minister from 1982 to 1994. In Germany Konrad Adenauer was chancellor from 1949 to 1963 and Helmut Kohl served from 1982 to 1998. All these examples are drawn from parliamentary systems, but in France Charles de Gaulle was president from 1958 to 1969, Francois Mitterrand served from 1981 to 1995, and Jacques Chirac from 1995 to 2007.[11]

We can also find examples of polities that function well absent term limits without venturing abroad. The American office most analogous to the presidency is the governorship. So it is notable that the lifetime two-term limit that the Twenty-second Amendment imposes is more restrictive than the rules that exist in a majority of states. Lifetime bans after two terms are in force in only twenty states. Nineteen states limit the number of consecutive terms a governor can serve, generally to two, but permit a subsequent return to office after a designated period of time. Finally, a diverse group of eleven states still do not limit governors' terms at all.

The states have been called the "laboratories of democracy," and the diversity of arrangements concerning governors' terms allows us to draw some inferences about the effect of term limits on chief executives. Given concerns about power corrupting over time, it is notable that little correlation is evident between corruption and gubernatorial term limits. Louisiana, a state with a tradition of corrupt governors, has long had term limits, while good-government Minnesota does not. Illinois governors are notorious and the state lacks term limits, but the record of governors in neighboring Wisconsin and Iowa is far better and neither state has term limits.[12] A systematic study finds no significant relationship between states' term limits for governors and rates of corruption in state government.[13]

Yet if there is no evidence suggesting the Twenty-second Amendment limits abuse of power and corruption, there is reason to believe it does reduce the political and administrative effectiveness of chief executives. Despite a persistent notion that presidents could somehow do a better job if they did not have to worry about reelection, there is little evidence supporting this view. Lame-duck presidents are less successful than first-term ones in getting Congress to enact legislation they support.[14] Presidents also have difficulty retaining staff as turnover increases in their lame-duck terms.[15] Staff members believe that a lame-duck administration, especially in its last two years, is unlikely to achieve much and are tempted to leave office and cash in on their experience. Similarly, it is harder for presidents to attract replacements of the same high caliber, because individuals are less attracted to serving in an administration that is clearly on its way out. These are costs of term limits. Even a president who ultimately declined to seek a third term might be more effective during his second administration were his lame-duck status not certain from the outset. Americans want a president who does not abuse the office, not one who cannot exercise the powers of the office effectively.

Repeal of the Twenty-second Amendment may have one downside. Sidney Milkis and Michael Nelson argue that the "Twenty-second Amendment has strengthened the vice presidency by allowing vice presidents to campaign for the presidency during the second term of an administration without competing with the sitting president." These scholars contend that "the Twenty-second Amendment gives second-term presidents a stake in the success of their vice presidents, which is the closest to vindication and continuity they will achieve."[16] As the vice presidency has come to be seen as a stepping-stone to the presidency, it has attracted more able politicians who have been given more responsibilities that prepare them for a possible ascension to the Oval Office.

The strengthening of the vice presidency is a positive trend that repeal of the Twenty-second Amendment could counteract. Yet it is doubtful that repeal of the Twenty-second Amendment would lead to the wholesale deinstitutionalization of the vice presidency, which now includes a large staff, a residence, Secret Service protection, and a seat on the National Security Council. In any case, this modest benefit is far outweighed by the costs the Twenty-second Amendment imposes on voters and the reduction in presidential effectiveness it produces.

None of this is to suggest that we need presidents in perpetuity. For most chief executives, Thomas Cronin is surely right that "eight years is enough."[17] Starting with John Adams in 1800 voters have often decided that one term was enough and evicted presidents from the White House. History suggests that even absent the Twenty-second Amendment, many reelected presidents would still not be in physical or emotional shape or retain sufficient political support to secure a third term.

Yet there was an exceptional case earlier in our history when in the midst of a crisis voters decided a chief executive should serve more than two terms. Many decades later he is widely considered one of our greatest presidents. Who is to say another such crisis and another such leader may not one day emerge? There is no reason to tie voters' hands. The historical record does not justify the extreme distrust of the electorate that the Twenty-second Amendment embodies. While voters' knowledge and attention spans are quite limited, they do react predictably, rewarding leaders who preside over "peace, prosperity, and probity" and punishing those who do not.[18]

The Twenty-second Amendment is the only revision to the U.S. Constitution that reduces the ability of voters to influence their government. It restricts voters' choice of presidential candidates by ruling out those individuals about whom voters know the most. It is the residue of a spasm of vindictive partisanship. It reduces presidents' effectiveness as leaders and administrators without curbing their abuses of power. Alexander Hamilton said it best in 1787: "There is an excess of refinement in the idea of disabling the people to continue in office men who had entitled themselves, in their opinion, to approbation and confidence; the advantages of which are at best speculative and equivocal, and are overbalanced by disadvantages far more certain and decisive."[19] The Twenty-second Amendment should be repealed.

CON: Thomas E. Cronin

The Twenty-second Amendment to the U.S. Constitution should be retained. It was added to the Constitution in 1951 after 70 percent of those voting on it in the U.S. Congress approved it and the requisite thirty-six state legislatures ratified it. Nearly 70 percent of the American people, when polled over the years, have indicated support for retaining the Twenty-second Amendment.

This idea was hardly new in 1947 when it passed Congress by two-thirds majorities. It had been in both Republican and Democratic party platforms at various times. It was proposed and approved in a few of the state ratification conventions, including in New York, back in 1788. Thomas Jefferson and other founders as well as the Anti-Federalists favored term limits for the proposed new presidency.

Democratic icon Andrew Jackson embraced it. It was in the populist-leaning Democratic Party platform of 1896. And the legendary progressive U.S. senator, Robert M. La Follette, R-Wis., introduced a two-term limitation measure back in 1927, and his Senate colleagues voted for it with a bipartisan 56-26 vote. His resolution was similar to many that had been previously introduced in Congress. The wording of his resolution is noteworthy:

> *Resolved:* That it is the sense of the Senate that the precedent established by Washington and other Presidents of the United States in retiring from the Presidential office after their second term has become by universal concurrence, a part of our republican system of government, and that any departure from this time-honored custom would be unwise, unpatriotic and fraught with peril to our free institutions.[1]

John F. Kennedy voted for it in 1947 as a young member of the U.S. House of Representatives. Asked about it again when he was in the White House in 1962, he reaffirmed his belief that two terms were enough for any president.

Here are the four most important reasons for retaining the Twenty-second Amendment.[2]

First, national security, social, economic, and globalization developments have conspired to centralize and strengthen our national government, and especially the presidency and the executive branch of our government.

The powers of the American presidency have grown enormously, especially in recent generations, and this will surely be the case in the coming generations. This does not mean presidents regularly get their way. Rather it means that their responsibilities have grown so large that the American people and the Congress increasingly turn to presidents for leadership and often delegate great discretion to presidents.

Presidents, to be sure, have always had considerable formal authority. But the cold war and the post–September 11, 2001, age of terrorism have irreversibly led to a presidency-centric system. Nuclear weapons, covert operations, satellite intelligence systems, wiretapping technologies, extraordinary prisoner rendition policies, huge government interventions in the financial and automotive industries, and U.S. military bases or installations in nearly sixty nations around the world are but a few of the enlargements that have reshaped the modern presidency.

Second, the Twenty-second Amendment allows a citizen to serve four or eight years in one of the world's most demanding and influential political positions while protecting the country from the potential excesses of power that could come with extended tenure.

There has been, over the years, a general decline of Congress as a checking and balancing branch. Congress may not be a broken branch, yet it sometimes fails to exercise fully its prerogatives, especially in relations with the White House and the executive branch. We cannot, therefore, expect Congress to safeguard against all executive abuses.

We have had a series of presidents (and White House staffs) that remind us that power has a tendency to corrupt. The presidency is now a place of considerably more powers, more responsibilities, *and* more temptations.

Thomas Jefferson, Andrew Jackson, and John F. Kennedy all supported the rotation-in-office principle—the notion that a vigorous constitutional democracy needs continually to generate new and capable leaders. Rotation in office is part of our tradition of citizen leaders, our notion of fair play, the idea that our leaders can come from any part of the country, from an underrepresented minority group as well as from the establishment, and that talented men and women should be given the chance for this high honor. Note, too, that our population is more than one hundred times the size it was in the 1780s. Our eligible candidate pool may be at least three hundred times that of the 1780s.

The Twenty-second Amendment may not have been needed in 1947 yet it will likely prove to be an invaluable additional check and balance in the future. It is a check against the ultimate type of corruption—the arrogance that a leader is indispensable. It was precisely this assumption of indispensability that led Venezuela's Hugo Chavez to campaign for the end of term limits in his country, Robert Mugabe in Zimbabwe to rig his staying in office, to the antics of Ferdinand Marcos in the Philippines, and to the schemes of countless similar would-be saviors.

Calvin Coolidge put it well in his autobiography when he warned: "It is difficult for men in high office to avoid the malady of self-delusion. They are always surrounded by worshipers. They are consistently … assured of their greatness." Coolidge understood that presidents live in an "artificial atmosphere of adulation and exaltation which sooner or later impairs their judgment. They are in grave danger of becoming careless and arrogant."[3]

The Twenty-second Amendment, like impeachment, might come into play only once a century or even less often, yet it would be there—as the reality of impeachment was in the case of Richard Nixon—to ensure constitutionalism, respect for law, and the survival of republican practices, processes, and principles.

A look at many of the big-city mayors who have stayed for third, fourth, and fifth terms provides additional grounds for skepticism about repealing the Twenty-second Amendment. Of course there are exceptions. Yet in Boston, Chicago, Detroit, Newark, Kansas City, Providence, Syracuse, and Washington, D.C., to suggest a few, multiterm mayors and their associates, especially during their later terms, have often been less responsive, less accountable, and more tempted to become arrogant and corrupt than in their first or even second terms.

Third, the two-term limit is healthy for our two-party system and for our democracy. It helps prevent political stagnation. The two parties benefit and are rejuvenated by the challenge, at least every eight years, of nurturing, recruiting, and nominating a new team of national leaders. In this sense, the very existence of this amendment prevents the hardening of political arteries. Change every eight years adds a degree of freshness and new energy—elements our Madisonian system can usually use.

One of the strengths of our evolving constitutional democracy is its ability to renew and revitalize itself. It requires new ideas, new energy, and a periodic changing of the guard. The Twenty-second Amendment is just one of many aspects of our system that helps guarantee the infusion of new ideas, new blood, and the fructifying vitality needed to counteract calcification and policy stagnation.

More than a few scholars have rightly worried that the presidential appoint-ive power coupled with presidential influence over appropriations, tax benefits, and bailouts may be used to influence renomination and reelection.[4] One of the stronger arguments for the two-term tradition involves the vast appointive power presidents have. A president who stays in office for twelve or sixteen years would likely be able to stack, if not pack, the Supreme Court and fundamentally alter the partisan and ideological leaning of the entire federal judiciary. Franklin D. Roosevelt, for example, appointed nine justices in his twelve years. Nixon appointed four in just five years. George W. Bush appointed only two Supreme Court justices yet appointed nearly half of the judges in the federal district courts around the country.

Most of us do not want a president who could dominate and in effect pack the judiciary and thus influence two of our three "separate" branches. We have enough to worry about with the evolution of the so-called unitary executive, the idea that on any number of administrative and national security matters a president should exercise the primary if not sole decision-making authority.[5]

Fourth, eight years in the job is long enough and longer than many presidents should be given. We need to remember that nearly half of our presidents have been disappointments. Americans may have enormously high expectations for their presidents; yet they do not view the presidency as a career job with tenure, but rather as a temporary honor to be exercised with Lincolnian humility. Americans rather like the idea of a rotation in office and, along with Jefferson, Jackson, and Kennedy, think of this as healthy and desirable.

Eight years should be ample time for a president and an administration to introduce and bring about major policy changes. If such changes are valued, needed, and acceptable to majorities of Americans, they will doubtless be continued and honored by the succeeding presidents.

There is little evidence that the two-term limitation hastens the onset of lame-duckness. Second terms were almost always harder than first terms well before the ratification of the Twenty-second Amendment. Madison, Grant, Cleveland, Wilson, and Truman are classic examples of "second-termitis." Eisenhower, Reagan, Clinton, and George W. Bush, to be sure, all had less-successful second terms than first terms. Some of that was due to the failing health and vitality of the older presidents, although some of the problems can be attributed to the hubris and power-corrupting inclinations associated with longer tenure. Some of it was also due to the reality that eight years in the presidency is inevitably and increasingly a bruising experience. Said Jefferson as he was about to retire: "Never did a prisoner, released from his chains, feel such relief as I shall on shaking off the shackles of power."

Second terms, it seems, are usually marked by more trials than triumphs. James Madison had to flee Washington, D.C., as the British burned down both the White House and the U.S. Capitol. Things got so bad economically and politically for Grover Cleveland that he wished he could flee town. Nixon was kicked out of town. Bill Clinton was impeached in his second term. Wilson had a stroke and became an invalid. George W. Bush had an average approval rating that was 26 percentage points lower in his second term than in his first. With few exceptions—regardless of whether they were presidents before the Twenty-second Amendment or after it was adopted—the perils of second terms, or the second-term blues, are the norm, in part because Congress and the media are almost always tougher on presidents in their second terms.

This is not to say presidents cannot do some important things in their second terms. Woodrow Wilson in his second term helped win the First World War and provided the vision for enduring transnational collaboration. Ronald Reagan in his second term helped enact needed tax reform and conducted important diplomacy that helped lead to the end of the cold war.

In sum, eight years are enough. George Washington retired in part because he was exhausted, and he died three years later. Lincoln, according to his friends, aged enormously in his four years. Eisenhower nearly died in his second term. If Reagan had been elected to a third term, he would have struggled with Alzheimer's disease during his final years in office. Kennedy was right: two terms are plenty for any human being.

Those who favor the repeal of the Twenty-second Amendment share some reasonable concerns. Let me offer a few counterarguments to some of these concerns.

First, repeal proponents contend that this third-term ban diminishes a voter's right to select a preferred candidate for president. Further, it is observed, this straitjacketing of future voters was done by Republicans and anti–Franklin Roosevelt partisans largely motivated by ideological revenge. They disliked Roosevelt and wanted to ensure that another popular progressive Democratic president (or Roosevelt clone) could serve in the office for at most two terms. (A few wags joked that this amendment would also be especially convenient should FDR himself somehow come back to life.)

True enough, there was at least some paternalism or "neo-nannyism" among the backers of this amendment in the 80th Congress. They, in effect, prevented future voters, for their own good, presumably, from selecting as their president someone whom they might deem to be the best candidate. These backers had seen firsthand how FDR had mastered the patronage system, had shaped the judiciary by his partisan appointments, and had become a veritable "spinner in chief" via radio. They worried about this, not without some justification—especially as it affected the Republican Party.

Those who favor retaining this amendment concede that on some future occasion a voter's right might indeed be diminished by this ban on third terms. That limitation has to be viewed as a trade-off for the protection of our liberty and as a price we pay for enforcing the democratic principle of rotation in office.

The American people would not support the Twenty-second Amendment if they believed it measurably diminished their democratic voting rights. Public opinion supportive of the Twenty-second reflects both a fondness for the idea of rotation in office as well as an ingrained fear that power held and wielded for long periods can breed abuse.

Second, repeal proponents, echoing Alexander Hamilton's argument in *Federalist* No. 72, contend that curbing reeligibility would help make a president unaccountable to the American public. "One ill effect of the exclusion would be a diminution of the inducements to good behavior," wrote Hamilton. "There are few men who would not feel much less zeal in the discharge of a duty, when they were conscious that the advantages of the station with which it was connected must be relinquished at a determinate period, than when they were permitted to entertain a hope of obtaining, by meriting, a continuance of them."[6]

The quasi-monarchical Hamilton was prescient on many things, but on this point he exaggerated. There are, in fact, plenty of inducements to good behavior or excellence in a second term. Presidents naturally will want to earn the honor of being a great or near-great president. They'd all like to be the next president to be added to Mount Rushmore.

Presidents want to excel so they can enact and implement their priorities. They want to be liked and respected. They want a positive legacy. Moreover, most of them want to have their party and their chosen successor succeed them in office. If these incentives are not enough, they also have to worry about being impeached, shamed in the polls, and condemned as ineffective or failures by opinion makers and Internet bloggers.

Third, proponents of repeal contend that someday we will need that tried, tested, and indispensable leader on the proverbial white horse to continue in our White House. This "pernicious ban" on third terms, they argue, would deny us this potential savior.

Writes political scientist Larry Sabato: "America benefited from Roosevelt's strong hand as we semi-secretly prepared to enter war, but it is very possible that the impressive, internationalist Republican nominee Wendell Willkie or an able Democrat of Roosevelt's stripe could have led the country well, had either been elected in 1940." And, adds Sabato, "if we can credibly suggest that a presidential giant like FDR was replaceable, then any president is."[7] On this point France's Charles de Gaulle is said to have once commented that "the cemeteries of the world are filled with people once deemed irreplaceable."

If a president of the ability, agility, and savvy of a Washington, a Lincoln, or an FDR were available at the end of a second term, and if the nation were facing dire emergencies such as Pearl Harbor, 9/11, or the Cuban missile crisis, the services and leadership of such a person need not be thrown out and ignored merely because a successor president had been elected. Common sense would suggest that these exceptional public servants be retained as senior counselors, roving ambassadors, or cabinet members without portfolios—precisely in order to take advantage of their experience and expertise. After John Quincy Adams finished his presidency, for example, he served admirably in the U.S. House of Representatives for seventeen years. Former president Jimmy Carter even won a Nobel Peace Prize for his post–White House leadership.

Thus, we want a strong, energetic and effective American presidency, yet we rightly fear the potential abuse of power by presidents who may someday delude themselves into believing they are indispensable. Without a Twenty-second Amendment we might someday be subject to the judgment, temperament, and unilateral biases of a single person, perhaps hardened, isolated, and increasingly insulated from public pressures by virtue of additional years in office.

George Washington was a terrific role model in so many ways, including his refusal to succumb to a "cult of indispensability." Other leaders of national liberation movements, such as Mao Zedong, Fidel Castro, and Robert Mugabe, seem to have believed themselves indispensable and therefore thought that they should serve for life.

Royal governors and an out-of-touch monarch helped foment our fighting of the American Revolution. Today's twenty-first-century presidency has become, for understandable and generally valid reasons, a more powerful institution than was ever imagined in 1787. Most of this cannot be reversed. Consequently, the Twenty-second Amendment is a modern "auxiliary precaution" in the finest sense of Madison's usage in the *Federalist*. The Twenty-second Amendment is an imperfect yet increasingly acceptable solution. It is a practical compromise between the need for Hamiltonian energy and continuity on the one hand and republican and democratic principles on the other.[8]

RESOLVED, the media are too hard on presidents

PRO: Matthew R. Kerbel

CON: Bartholomew H. Sparrow

One of the qualities that distinguishes the modern presidency from the traditional office of the eighteenth and nineteenth centuries is that modern presidents—that is, every president since Theodore Roosevelt—have been the figures most in the spotlight on the political stage. And who shines that spotlight on presidents? The mass media.

In the era of the traditional presidency, *mass media* meant local newspapers with a local focus. As a result, mayors, governors, and local representatives in Congress usually loomed larger in media coverage than presidents. But in the early twentieth century, the media expanded to include national magazines with a national focus. The editor of a popular magazine such as *Collier's* or *McClure's* knew that, even though subscribers in Virginia probably would not care to read about the governor of Nebraska or the mayor of Buffalo, readers everywhere were interested in the president. Indeed, it was at this time that enough reporters began covering the president to form the White House press corps and presidents began to hold regular news conferences.

The next major innovation in mass media—and arguably the most important one politically—was radio. For the first time, radio brought the president into people's homes, making him not just a familiar figure but also an intimate one, the personification of the entire federal government. Although radios became a standard fixture in American homes during the 1920s, Franklin D. Roosevelt was the first president to figure out how to use the new medium effectively. In place of loud oratory—suitable for addressing large crowds but not for visiting families in their living rooms—FDR offered "fireside chats."

Television, the new technology that swept the country during the 1950s, added pictures to the words that radio conveyed. As with radio, however, it took a while before a president was able to figure out how best to use this new medium. In 1961 John F. Kennedy began holding news conferences on live television—mini-dramas in which viewers saw their president coolly fending off seemingly difficult questions from an army of reporters.

The most recent major addition to the nation's mass media is the Internet. Like radio and television, this technology spread widely over the course of a decade—roughly the mid-1990s to the mid-2000s—from being a medium that a few people used to one that is used widely. But so far, no president has figured out how best to use this new medium for maximum political effect, although Barack Obama used it masterfully to raise money and mobilize volunteers for his 2008 campaign.

New media have offered presidents new tools to communicate with the American people and, in doing so, have elevated the prominence of the presidency in the political system. But with this increased prominence has come increased scrutiny. The media are not mere conveyor belts bringing presidential words and images to the American people. They are journalistic organizations whose reporters can ask challenging questions, report news that undermines the president's message, give voice to the president's political opponents, and interpret critically what the president says and does. Bloggers and other Web users further amp up the scrutiny. The media spotlight shines brightly on the modern presidency, but, while doing so, it brings both the good and the bad into sharp prominence.

Are the media—newspapers, magazines, radio, television, and political Web sites—too hard on presidents? Yes, argues Matthew R. Kerbel, and, still worse, their harshness has provoked presidents to act in ways that do not serve the national interest. Bartholomew H. Sparrow dissents from this view. To be sure, Sparrow argues, presidents may not be able to prevail in an open contest with the news media, but they have more subtle and more profound means of exercising their domination.

PRO: Matthew R. Kerbel

By going on the offensive on Afghanistan and by arranging a schedule that provides lots of colorful pictures, the President has sought to override criticism that he's a weak leader of the Western alliance while at the same time dominating the nightly television news. It may not have worked but as this trip demonstrates once again Mr. Carter's image makers know how to give this sort of thing an awfully good try.

—Sam Donaldson, *ABC World News Tonight*, June 26, 1980

Out for his morning jog, President [George] Bush dished out his own spin on how reporters should write about new figures showing surprising growth in the overall economy the last three months.... The president is seizing on a quarterly bump of 2.7 percent in the gross domestic product, which is the best measure of the economy's growth. Economists say that's a notoriously volatile number that does not necessarily mean a trend.... Voters tend to make up their minds not by statistics but by assessing their own economic situation. And for many voters who have seen plants close and safe jobs disappear, the highest of the measurable economic indicators is anxiety.

—Eric Enberg, *CBS Evening News with Dan Rather*, October 28, 1992

I think, Mary, the best thing you can say about this process right now is that it's chaotic and also that [President Bill Clinton] is having a terrible time in part because a lot of the people out in the public are more concerned about things like crime and certainly things like O. J. [Simpson] and the economy than they are about changing the healthcare program and that—here we are at the last minute. There are only a couple of weeks to go. They have to throw together something for which neither party has a majority, ... which the public has not agreed on, and I think that this is a very, very hard row for the President.

—Julia Malone, *CNN and Company*, July 18, 1994

Back in this country, the debate over Social Security. Today another leading Republican raised doubts about [President George W. Bush's] plan to revamp the program, a sign that it may be in serious trouble.

—John Seigenthaler, *NBC Nightly News*, February 13, 2005

A sign for the president, indeed. Anyone who has paid casual attention to television news over the last three decades should find these comments so familiar as to be unremarkable, which is precisely why the media have caused vexing problems for presidents unlucky enough to serve during the heyday of network and cable television news. There is nothing special about reporters pointing out the failed but determined media manipulation efforts of Presidents Jimmy Carter and George Bush, or the hopeless policy predicaments of Presidents Bill Clinton and George W. Bush. A Google search on news coverage of any contemporary president would generate a bonanza of negative stories about his failed or long-shot attempts at political, policy, and media control. Such negative themes bring drama to coverage in the television age.

Presidents throughout history have felt the burden of a constitutional separation of powers that requires them to cajole, threaten, charm, and otherwise manipulate those in Washington who stand in the way of their agendas. But only presidents of the television era have been subjected to having these efforts laid bare for a national audience, as well as having the results of presidential politicking evaluated against the unrealistic expectation that these presidents' efforts will end successfully. Constitutional design sets up presidents to fail by making them simply one actor in a system of competing actors with different political interests. Media scrutiny compounds this disadvantage by portraying presidents in a negative light that does little to enhance either their positions with the public or their strategic positions in Washington. This is not to suggest that the media should give presidents the benefit of every doubt, or that journalists should not be critical of presidential initiatives. But when reporters dwell on the manipulative underbelly of the political system and harp on political or policy failures, they do a disservice to everyone with a stake in the governing process, presidents included.

Television requires that presidential politics be portrayed as problematic. In a fashion that suits television's need to tell a story, media narratives since the 1960s have increasingly emphasized all manner of competition, from odds making on presidential policy efforts to dissecting the president's public standing.[1] Could President George W. Bush convince a reluctant Congress of his own party to change the popular Social Security system? Could President Clinton win ratification of the North American Free Trade Agreement (NAFTA) treaty? Could the first president Bush convince fellow Republicans to raise taxes? Could President Carter win the release of American hostages in Iran? How would President Gerald R. Ford convince the public that he could rein in inflation? If any of these presidents failed at any of these initiatives, how badly would it hurt his public standing or his chances for reelection? Suggesting the possibility of presidential failure was an integral part of each storyline. Discussing the race to replace the incumbent was an ever-present accompanying theme, along with periodic accounts of presidential missteps and scandals.[2]

Negative media frames prime the public to assess the president in the context of failed policy initiatives, unattractive strategic maneuvering, or both.[3]

Such negativity adversely affects how the president is evaluated by the public, which, in turn, constricts the president's ability to influence official Washington by virtue of diminished public support.[4] The interplay between media frames and the public's response is self-fulfilling: the president is portrayed as trying desperately but unsuccessfully to control the news and policy agenda, which primes the public to experience the president negatively, thus validating reporters' expectations about presidential failure. Media coverage then shifts from negative reporting of presidential actions and outcomes to negative coverage of declining public support for the president, guaranteeing that public support will remain low.[5]

This dynamic has touched every president of the television age to some degree. For Presidents Ford, Carter, and Bush senior, it contributed to a tailspin in public support from which the incumbent was unable to recover. A content analysis of network evening news coverage conducted by the Center for Media and Public Affairs divided the first three years of the Bush (senior) and Clinton administrations into twenty-four quarters and found that the incumbent averaged positive coverage in only three of them. Even when Bush had an 88 percent approval rating after the Persian Gulf War, his coverage barely averaged in the positive range.[6] More recently, the Center for Media and Public Affairs found that in the critical last months of the 2004 presidential campaign almost two in three mainstream media references to George W. Bush were negative.[7]

The phenomenon of the media combating the president became more pronounced as the influence of television expanded. Although television has been around since the late 1940s and had national reach by the 1950s, it did not emerge as a dominant political force until the 1960s. At the beginning of the television era, a series of dramatic national events satisfied television's demand for gripping plot lines. They included political assassinations, the civil rights and women's rights movements, the Vietnam War, the Watergate scandal, and President Ford's pardon of Richard Nixon. But social activism dissipated as twenty-four-hour cable news emerged, leaving news producers with fewer inherently compelling news items at a time when increased media competition had upped the demand for gripping content. As captivating plot lines became harder to find in daily political events, reporters turned to the competition inherent in the political process to keep viewers engaged.

By emphasizing the political process over political events, television bolstered the personal presidency. It turned the president into "communicator in chief" in an era characterized by the struggle between reporters and presidents over message control. Incumbents had to operate in a political-media environment in which reporters cast presidents as political losers in an ongoing game of "gotcha." Presidents, not surprisingly, found governing difficult under these conditions.

One measure of the intensity of the struggle between reporters and presidents since the 1950s is the steadily increasing number of "feeding frenzies"—that is, exercises in pack journalism in which candidates or office-holders face the full wrath of a media hoard fixated on saturating the airwaves and dailies with juicy details about scandalous behavior. Sorting through major stories about presidential politics and governance, political scientist Larry J. Sabato identified one such frenzy in the 1950s, three in the 1960s, six in the 1970s, and fifteen in the 1980s.[8] And all this was before Bill Clinton, the walking feeding frenzy, came to power in the 1990s.

Presidents predictably pushed back. White House communications offices evolved into war rooms devoted to crafting, controlling, and disseminating administration-friendly messages.[9] Governance morphed into marketing. Administration officials spent most of their tenure competing with reporters over the content of the news agenda.[10]

A clear line of demarcation separates practices such as these—hallmarks of the television era—and earlier presidential efforts to shape news coverage. The differences are of type and degree. In 1960 presidential scholar Richard E. Neustadt commented that presidents could sometimes manufacture events to move opinion in their direction, but that the conditions for doing so were not readily available to them and that, in any event, the press would rarely cooperate for long in such initiatives.[11] In the political environment that developed over the following decades, however, White House–manufactured events became presidential job one. Similarly, when Neustadt wrote that "an image of the office, not an image of the man, is the dynamic factor in a president's prestige," Washingtonians were still talking to taxi drivers to sample public opinion.[12] Since then, ad hoc soundings have given way to wall-to-wall polls and media analysis of wall-to-wall polls, which presidential advisers attempt to shape by carefully crafting a positive image of their boss.

Although presidents since Franklin D. Roosevelt have paid attention to public opinion polling,[13] not until Lyndon B. Johnson did presidents actively attempt to influence opinion poll results.[14] In the 1940s, FDR used polling, then in its infancy, as a way of guiding his leadership decisions, but not as a device for image manipulation. According to his pollster, Hadley Cantril, Roosevelt did not alter or even shade his policy objectives to bring them in line with public opinion, choosing instead to use polls to find ways "to try to bring the public around more quickly or more effectively to the course of action he felt was best for the country."[15] His successor in office, Harry S. Truman, was notoriously hostile to opinion polls, and Dwight D. Eisenhower, who succeeded Truman, preferred to ignore them altogether.[16] These presidents had the luxury of operating without television reporting every strategic turn of events.

All this changed in the 1960s with Johnson, who tried to shape poll results by attacking negative public polls and attempting to influence them; he planted favorable information from in-house polls with sympathetic columnists and courted the favor of pollsters.[17] Nixon and Carter viewed negative poll results as an invitation to engage in public relations efforts to improve their public standing rather than to identify possible problems with where they were leading the nation.[18] Soon, political scientist Theodore J. Lowi contends, presidents essentially became spin machines, devoting the latter portions of their tenures to convincing the public that the early portions of their tenures were more successful than they appeared.[19]

For all his work, Johnson's effort to manipulate pollsters and their numbers was ineffectual.[20] Most of his successors fared no better. The clear direction of public support for presidents of the television age has been downward.

Yet, it was not always like this. In the 1950s, Eisenhower's support was steady and strong, resting in the 70 percent range for much of his two terms in office and falling only slightly at the end. His successor, John F. Kennedy, claimed comparable approval ratings for his first two years in office, and this rating hovered at about 60 percent support at the time of his death.[21] After that, things changed. Most presidents of the television era came to office with strong support, only to see it drop—sometimes sharply—during their first three years in office, never to see it return.[22] George W. Bush failed to receive even this initial burst of goodwill, coming to office in 2001 with middling approval scores, which, after skyrocketing to record levels in the wake of the 2001 terrorist attacks on the United States, followed a steady downward trajectory over the next seven years to some of the lowest depths recorded in modern times.

Notably, in the 1980s, Ronald Reagan bucked the trend, turning an initial two-year decline into sustained support that lasted well into his second term.[23] The Reagan White House figured out how to wage a successful public relations and media relations battle, blending the former actor's communications skills with a disciplined message development and management apparatus to form the perfect combination for governing in the television age. But his efforts did not put an end to negative press coverage; the Center for Media and Public Affairs found that Reagan received a record 91 percent negative coverage while he was running for reelection.[24] Reagan's team responded by devoting a lot of energy to figuring out how to work around the critical media.

The positive trajectory of Reagan's public standing and his ability to win reelection and complete his second term unscathed were the calm exceptions in an otherwise turbulent era of television-centered administrations. Table 5-1 compares the fate of twentieth-century chief executives pre- and post-television. Before 1960,

Table 5-1

Stability and Change among Incumbent Presidents, 1900–2008

Stability		Change	
1900–1956			
Elected/reelected		Defeated	
1900	McKinley	1912	Taft
1904	T. Roosevelt	1932	Hoover
1916	Wilson		
1924	Coolidge	Open seat, vacated by incumbent	
1936	F. Roosevelt	1908	T. Roosevelt
1940	F. Roosevelt	1920	Wilson
1944	F. Roosevelt	1928	Coolidge
1948	Truman	1952	Truman
1956	Eisenhower		

Stability		Change	
1960–2008			
Elected/reelected		Defeated	
1964	Johnson	1976	Ford
1984	Reagan	1980	Carter
1996	Clinton[a]	1992	G. Bush
2004	G. W. Bush		
		Involuntarily retired	
		1968	Johnson
		Reelected, forced to resign	
		1972	Nixon
		Open seat, vacated by incumbent	
		1960	Eisenhower
		1988	Reagan
		2000	Clinton
		2008	G. W. Bush

Source: Matthew R. Kerbel.
[a] Impeached, not convicted.

incumbents were returned to office nine times. A change in administrations was more likely to be caused by an incumbent voluntarily stepping aside (four times) or dying (three times) than by an incumbent being voted out of office (twice). From 1960 to 2004, during the emergence of television-centered politics, three incumbents were turned out by voters, one (Johnson) was forced by political circumstances to abandon a reelection bid, and one (Nixon) was forced to resign in the face of certain impeachment and removal. One more had to confront the possibility of involuntary removal from office: Bill Clinton was impeached but survived the Senate trial.

Although George W. Bush survived a close reelection contest in 2004, he began his second term without a honeymoon and with the lowest approval ratings of any modern reelected president. His response, famously, was to claim a mandate despite receiving the narrowest reelection victory since 1916. It was a public relations effort that typifies presidential governance in this era: if a mandate was not forthcoming, Bush would try to create one via television. If enough people then believed he had a mandate, his public relations effort would render the same political benefits as if he had been reelected in a land-slide. In keeping with the fates of contemporary presidents, the maneuver failed. Within one year of his reelection victory, Bush faced slipping job approval ratings that rendered him a lame duck long before his term ended.

It would be stretching things to say that the ascendancy of television is the cause of the turbulence experienced by modern presidents, but the two are strongly correlated. One might expect an era of enormous political, economic, and social change to lend instability to politics, and the period since 1960 has certainly been such a time. But then so was the rest of the century. Social and economic dislocation was a constant in the twentieth century, but the existence of a saturated media environment characterizes only the last several decades.

The election of Barack Obama following a campaign that relied heavily on the Internet may herald the end of television's exclusive hold on politics. The level of engagement reported by people who participated in the Obama cam-paign online may be a positive development for the public and politicians alike. A decentralized medium that does not need to capture a mass audience to be commercially viable, the Internet hosts a lively, colorful discourse that does not always dwell on the negative, process-oriented, horserace-centered, scandal-heavy coverage that is the staple of television news.[25] It is discourse produced by the collective contributions of numerous voices with broad, cross-cutting agendas—ordinary individuals writing on multiple Web sites who provide alternative perspectives on political matters to the rather small cadre of elite political reporters who previously defined the agenda by themselves.

Should the Internet return politics to its rightful place as a participant sport, rather than the distant spectator sport it had become in the television age, every-one would stand to benefit, because a political process built to gratify television's competitive needs is destined to undermine debate and decision making. It is bad for the polity, because it detaches people from their government. It is bad for governance, because the relentless focus on Washington's "winners and losers" detracts from examining the merits of policy. It is certainly bad for presidents, who find themselves caught up in a battle with reporters over message control that most have found they cannot win.

CON: Bartholomew H. Sparrow

Scholars have traditionally portrayed president-media relations as being balanced and two-sided. As Doris Graber writes, presidents "desperately" need the media, and the media need them just as much, if not more. Presidents and the media may have a love-hate relationship, but they do not dare go their separate ways.[1] In the battle between the White House and the media, another media observer agrees, both are fully aware of their mutual dependence and the fact that neither can dominate the other.[2]

There is validity to these views. Neither presidents nor the media *can* wholly dominate the other; presidents and journalists *have* conflicting motivations and interests; and the two parties *are* unavoidably interdependent. But surely it is possible to be more specific, since whether the media are too hard on U.S. presidents or vice versa is an empirical matter that ultimately comes down to a question of power, specifically the question of which actors are better at determining the political news Americans receive—presidents or the media?

Answering this question, though, demands considering two things: what we mean by *power* and what we mean by *media*. Power, as Stephen Lukes points out, has multiple dimensions: it is revealed in open contests taking place between persons or parties; it is manifest by who is able to set the political agenda and thereby determine what is, and what is not, subject to open contestation; and it is implicit in how meaning gets attributed—and thus how political culture gets defined.[3] Lukes's threefold typology may accordingly be applied to president-media relations in the study of which actor (1) dominates those issues being openly fought over in the media; (2) sets the news agenda; and (3) is able to frame the news—that is, to determine how political information gets categorized, is connected to the preexisting news, and becomes linked to particular problems and solutions.[4]

An investigation of president-media relations also requires a reexamination of the media, since it is obvious that the "golden age of presidential communication"[5] has passed. Not only have the elite print and video media—the mainstream media (MSM)—lost influence relative to niche political cable channels, comedy shows, and talk television, but political discourse is increasingly taking place on the Internet. The new media offer a vast realm of politically relevant communication, from the political tabloids of the Huffington Post and Drudge Report (the top two Internet political sites) to more neutral political Web sites such as Politico, NewsMax, and Salon, the next three most highly trafficked political Web sites.[6] Then there are the almost countless videos, photographs, alternative and foreign news stories, and blogs that daily swirl around the Internet—sometimes with significant political consequences.

The Internet has put the brick-and-mortar MSM under tremendous pressure, not only in small and midsized cities but also in the country's largest cities. Witness the fate of the *Wall Street Journal* (sold to Rupert Murdoch's News Corporation); the indebtedness of the *New York Times* (selling and leasing back its brand-new office building, laying off reporters); and the demise of Denver's *Rocky Mountain News* (out of business), the *Christian Science Monitor,* and the *Seattle Post-Intelligencer* (the latter two now online only). Meanwhile, the MSM's own Web sites exacerbate the difficult position of the MSM: they offer both a larger news hole—additional letters, guest editorials, reporters' blogs, video clips, and links to still more sources and sites—and more timely, updated content.

The emergence of the new media, with the tremendous range of politically relevant news on the Internet, has complicated the relationship between presidents and the media. Yet Lukes's threefold typology still provides insight into the relationship, one in which the president retains an advantage over the media.

CONTESTED ISSUES

During its first term the George W. Bush administration received the coverage it wanted on the major issues of the day. The media gave short shrift to the political opponents of the president's programs, and what opposition there was found expression in newspapers' op-ed pages rather than in the news itself. Coverage was even more one-sided in television broadcast or cable news. This was true of media coverage of the USA PATRIOT Act, the wars in Afghanistan and Iraq, the creation of the Department of Homeland Security, the passage of the tax cuts, and the booming federal budget deficits. The Bush administration further benefited from the Republican Party's control of both houses of Congress between 2001 and 2006, from strong GOP leadership in Congress, and from the discipline with which it ran the White House. The Bush presidency profited, too, from the rise of Fox News, the growth of Christian television and radio broadcasting, the popularity of conservative talk radio, and the influence of the *Wall Street Journal, New York Post, Washington Times,* and other conservative papers. These developments pushed the centrist MSM, such as the *New York Times, Washington Post,* and *Time* magazine, more to the right. The first-term Bush administration was able to create its own political reality, to paraphrase one anonymous official, a reality that after September 11, 2001, the president and his staff parlayed into fundamental changes in U.S. domestic and foreign policies.[7]

But the external political reality interfered with the Bush administration's own political reality. Not long after Bush's reelection in 2004, the media turned against him. With the news of the Abu Ghraib prison abuses, the mounting numbers of American deaths in Iraq, and the rising cost of the U.S. occupation of Iraq, Bush's popularity began to fall even before the election. Afterward, with the Hurricane Katrina catastrophe, indictment of I. Lewis "Scooter" Libby, and continued gloomy news from Iraq and Afghanistan, the press got worse. As a result, President Bush was unable to privatize the Social Security system, pass his faith-based initiative, or stop the slide of the American and global economies.[8] The Democrats regained control of both houses of Congress in 2006, and in January 2009 President Bush left office with a 22 percent job approval rating, the lowest of any president since Gallup began polling in the late 1930s.[9]

The dismal economic news of 2007 and 2008, together with the revelations that there was no basis for the administration's main rationale for attacking Iraq, sapped the enthusiasm that the nation's leading reporters, columnists, and talking heads as well as their publishers, editors, producers, and news executives had had for the Bush administration, so much so that both the *New York Times* and *Washington Post* apologized for their earlier news coverage of the Bush presidency. And yet President Bush arguably did better than expected in view of Bush's troubled foreign policy and, later, the cratering economy. The MSM did little to undermine the Bush administration's most important legacies: support for U.S. forces in Iraq and Afghanistan, support for lower taxes and the repeal of the estate tax, appointments of John Roberts and Samuel Alito to the Supreme Court, and passage of the Troubled Asset Relief Program (TARP) in November 2008. Such a result may reflect what W. Lance Bennett identifies as the media's indexing: typically, the media report critically on U.S. presidents and major public policies only when there is significant political division within an administration or between branches of government.[10] That is to say that the Democratic Party leaders were complicit in the Bush administration's successes, partly because of their fear of retribution from the Bush White House (which would then be repeated and amplified in the media).

It is perhaps too early—with President Barack Obama's only a few more than one hundred days in office, as of this writing—to reach any conclusions about what the new president's success with the media will be with respect to openly contested issues. But Obama did get a major stimulus bill through Congress, order the timely closing of the Guantanamo Bay detention center, and succeed in getting his budget extension bill through Congress, among other initiatives. In fairness, the president had to compromise with congressional Republicans on the specifics of the stimulus bill, the amendments to TARP, and the proposed budget. And he was roundly criticized for the bailouts of AIG and the banks. Perhaps of equal significance, however, is that despite the dire economy of the first quarter of 2009 and despite the continued bad news coming out of Iraq and the president's commitment of a further ten thousand troops to Afghanistan, Obama's job approval rating remained at about 60 percent.[11] Despite the grim news on housing foreclosures, job losses, and stock market levels; the ambition and scope of the president's programs; and the challenges that the administration's programs pose to the status quo, Obama got off to a strong start. Certainly he did not experience the media (and policy) setbacks of President Bill Clinton when he first came into office (health care and gays in the military) and President George W. Bush at the start of his second term (Social Security reform and other major legislation).

One reason for Obama's early good fortune was his use of the new media. The practices of the Obama administration, like those of his campaign and his transition team (he was the first president-elect to have a Web site—change. gov—dedicated to the transition to office), mark the dawn of a new era. The administration as well as the Democratic Party and allied persons and groups use the new media to attract and inform their supporters and independent voters, and the use of this new media, such as the electronic town hall held by the president in mid-March 2009, has helped undergird the favorable coverage in the new media and much of the MSM. Such measures have also served to suppress Republican opposition and perhaps helped to dampen the MSM's opposition to the administration's programs.

Another reason for the Obama presidency's relative success has been its ability to communicate by going around the MSM and the Washington press corps. The president held in-person town hall meetings in Elkhart, Indiana, and in Los Angeles. He also reached out through prime-time press conferences and national addresses, including in a State of the Union–style speech in late February 2009, only weeks after taking office, as well as in soft news shows.

AGENDA SETTING

As the head of state, the president personifies the federal government. Presidents, not the media, are able to dictate what is, and what is not, news. They can thereby set the national political agenda.[12]

George W. Bush was an expert at using the MSM to set the agenda. In one case he did so through omission, by avoiding occasions when he would have had to field questions on topics on which the administration might be vulnerable to criticism. Bush held fewer solo press conferences per month in his first term than any president since Woodrow Wilson. Bill Clinton held the third-fewest press conferences during his second term, and Richard M. Nixon held the second-fewest press conferences during his Watergate-shortened second term.[13]

The Bush administration also made news inconvenient by releasing statements to the press right before the weekend or during holidays. On August 30, 2002, for instance—the Friday before Labor Day—it announced the appointment of Allan Fitzsimmons, a supporter of more logging, to oversee the Healthy Forests Initiative. On Christmas Eve 2002, it announced that state and local governments would have more control over the Bureau of Land Management's roads, trails, and paths. And on December 31, 2002—New Year's Eve—the White House announced new regulations that made it easier for manufacturing and refining companies to avoid installing expensive pollution controls.

Presidents also use secrecy to avoid media scrutiny. After September 11, 2001, the Bush administration persuaded Congress to pass the Intelligence Authorization Act, which criminalized the disclosure of information that the executive branch determined should be classified. The administration also removed the presumption of disclosure in response to Freedom of Information Act (FOIA) requests, allowed former presidents and their heirs to veto access to their presidential papers, and delayed the opening of federal records to journalists and the American public. The media cannot report what they do not know.

Obama took steps consistent with his promise to make the federal government more transparent. He issued an executive order overturning the veto that presidents and their heirs had over FOIA requests, and although he preserved the executive's power of rendition, he added two important caveats: that there be no torture and that the International Committee of the Red Cross be notified. Time will tell the degree to which the Obama administration actually increases transparency and removes much of the secrecy that cloaks the executive branch.

Presidents also set the news agenda in more prosaic ways. They limit the length and number of their messages. They make speeches and release statements on targeted themes only. They stage attention-getting events, such as Bush's "mission accomplished" appearance on the deck of an aircraft carrier at sunset on May 1, 2003, and his Thanksgiving Day dinner with U.S. troops in Iraq on November 27, 2003. The Bush administration also introduced the use of political slogans as visual backdrops at presidential public appearances—slogans that are seen in television footage or still photographs but are less visible to the audience in attendance. The Bush presidency was probably most successful at setting the media agenda when it embedded reporters with American troops in Iraq. The media produced stories favorable to U.S. and coalition soldiers but neglected stories on civilian casualties, the dead and injured U.S. and coalition soldiers, and the damage to and reconstruction of Iraq.[14] The media gave Americans a "sanitized" view of the war, "free of bloodshed, dissent, and diplomacy but full of exciting weaponry, splashy graphics, and heroic soldiers."[15]

In short, the Bush administration was able to set the news agenda by scheduling few press conferences, by releasing controversial news quietly, by increasing government secrecy, and by employing masterful public relations strategies. During Bush's first six years in office, the media covered little in national politics other than those topics promoted by the president and his staff. Even in the final two years of the Bush presidency, when the White House received its worst publicity, the media turned away from directly examining the president's record and focused, instead, on the extended Democratic primaries and the general elections.

Obama also successfully set the news agenda at the start of his administration. He used press conferences, speeches, and presidential travel to communicate his domestic and foreign policy objectives to the public. In the news conferences, he called on reporters from the Huffington Post, the Spanish-language Univision, and Agence France-Presse (the French news service) before (or instead of) calling on prominent reporters from the MSM. President Obama also went around the White House press corps and MSM by turning to less-traditional venues: appearing on CBS's *60 Minutes* and Jay Leno's *Tonight Show*, writing an op-ed piece that simultaneously appeared in dozens of newspapers in the United States and around the world, and filling in his March Madness basketball bracket on ESPN.

In fact, the Obama administration's use of such popular, less traditional media dovetailed perfectly with the themes of President Obama's 2008 campaign and the message of his inaugural address: that Americans need to engage and participate in politics, and that government cannot be left to lobbyists, Congress, and—implicitly—the MSM. Indeed, the fact that Obama did not appear at the 2009 Gridiron Dinner—the first president since Grover Cleveland to skip this staple of Washington politics—is suggestive of the Obama administration's confidence in its ability to reach Americans through the new media and other nontraditional channels. And it bespeaks the administration's commitment to ending business as usual in Washington.

By using press conferences, public speeches and town halls, and appearances in nonconventional media venues and in the new media, the Obama presidency was able to set the country's agenda, laying out an ambitious program of domestic spending, foreign policy, health care, and other issues.

NEWS FRAMING

The media framed the politics of the first years of the Bush administration much as the White House wanted. News organizations covered the September

11, 2001, attacks as "national identity–affirming" events, and the media followed the administration's lead on the placement of blame, the reaffirmation of American values, and the assertion of U.S. strength. Similarly, the Iraq War was overwhelmingly framed in terms of military conflict, human interest, and moral righteousness, the frames promoted by the Bush administration.[16] The first several years of the Bush presidency were marked by the presence of an unquestioning MSM with little appetite for genuine controversy or dissent. Much of the American public consequently saw the Iraq War in the same way: as a patriotic mission against an evil Iraqi regime, and, after the invasion, as a battle pitting nice, well-intentioned young men and women against irrational, zealous insurgents.

Not only did the media frame the terrorist attacks of September 11 as a "war," as the White House intended, but they cooperated with the administration on other frames: calling the estate tax a "death tax"; labeling intact dilation and fetus extraction as "partial birth abortion"; and identifying the proposed privatization of the Social Security program as "Social Security reform." The media by and large reported the administration's frames uncritically, and much of the American public consequently understood these issues precisely in these terms. If presidential rhetoric "defines political reality," the media reinforced the Bush administration's framing of the news.[17]

President Obama has also been successful in framing the news. Guantanamo Bay was an unseemly site for torture and illegality, not a necessary location in the greater cause of U.S. national security; so it could be closed. Stem cell research was needed for the public health of Americans; hence the lift of the ban on stem cell research. And the "stimulus bill" of early 2009 was received as a stimulus measure rather than a spending bill, which of course it was, consistent with Keynesian economics. Finally, pending further terrorist incidents on U.S. soil and worldwide, the Obama administration dropped the phrase "war on terror." Yet the administration continues to conduct counterterrorist activities and work with the security forces of other countries to fight terrorism, just as the Bush administration did.

In sum, a look at president-media relations in the first decade of the twenty-first century shows that U.S. presidents have prevailed over the media on at least two of Lukes's three dimensions of power. The first—open contestation of power—has been where presidents have been least successful, as suggested by the examples from Bush's second term and some of the evidence of the Obama administration's first hundred days in office. The media may have minimized the conflicts and disagreements over the president's initiatives in Bush's first term, but that was less the case in his second term. And if the media trumpeted President Obama's ambitious programs during his first few days in office, they have also been more critical of his financial plans, especially the bank bailout and rescue of AIG, notwithstanding the Democrats' control of both houses of Congress.

With respect to the second dimension of power, both the Bush and the Obama administrations succeeded at setting the political agenda, albeit in different ways. The dominant media topics were the White House's topics of emphasis. As for Lukes's third form of power, the Bush administration was able to define the political culture being communicated in the media, just as the Obama administration has so far succeeded in communicating centrist and left-of-center meanings to political news in the MSM and new media alike.

CONCLUSION

President-media relations in the twenty-first century occupy barely charted waters. First, there was the remarkable convergence of a conservative president, an increasingly conservative media, and the Republican Party in control of the legislative and executive branches of government. George W. Bush further bolstered his presidency through a disciplined leadership style that demanded personal loyalty and tight control of information and decision making. The Bush administration succeeded at managing the media by fusing national security with control of political communications, by relying on secrecy and slogans, by carefully staging appearances, and by using an assertive rhetorical style. This lasted for six years, until the Democrats took control of the Congress and then, in 2008, also the presidency.

The success of the Bush administration does not mean, though, that the Obama administration will use the same tools; its commitment to transparency and its opposition to many of the policies and practices of the Bush administration indicate a different style of communication. But smart presidents use what they have to their advantage, and Obama is more comfortable with press conferences and public addresses than was his predecessor. As a populist and a Gen Xer—not a baby boomer—Obama also happens to be more at ease with the new media and with the words, gestures, music, and culture of the younger generations.

Not all presidents are equally skilled in using the tools at their disposal to manage the media. George W. Bush was clearly better at this than was his father; Bill Clinton was better than Jimmy Carter; and Barack Obama seems to be at least as skilled as President Clinton. Thus far, President Obama has shown an ability to reach out to an easily distracted, only occasionally attentive audience. Indeed, the presidency in general has been helped by the rise of the new media and loss of dominance by the MSM. A world in which fewer people are reading newspapers, watching the nightly news, and seriously attending to politics—the "short attention span presidency"[18]—strongly favors organized and disciplined presidencies versed in the new media. This has been true of the Obama campaign and new administration, and it will almost certainly obtain for subsequent U.S. presidents. Future presidencies, like the current Obama administration, should continue to be able to win most of the issues coming under political debate, control the political agenda, and frame political reality as they see it.

With the proliferation of news channels and with the increase in the kinds of political communication now possible, political communication arguably now better matches John Stuart Mill's "marketplace of ideas." The rise of the new media and parallel fall of the MSM have their costs, however: the decline of a shared American political culture and, with the deterioration of traditional print journalism, the diminished role for investigative journalism and the lesser and more diffuse impact that investigative journalism is likely to have. In fact, the proliferation of the numbers of channels and forms of political communication in conjunction with the overall explosion of information and entertainment now available in the public sphere make the American public that much more susceptible to the charms of human interest stories, the happy lessons of political theater, the attractions and simplifications of political advertising, and the manipulations of public relations.

RESOLVED, the president is a more authentic representative of the American people than is Congress

PRO: Marc J. Hetherington

CON: Richard J. Ellis

Imagine the scene on inauguration day, the start of the new presidential term. Incoming president McClain Alexander strides to the front of the stage on the west front of the Capitol, faces the chief justice, places one hand on the Bible and raises the other heavenward, and takes the constitutional oath: "I do solemnly swear that I will execute the Office of President of the United States, and will to the best of my Ability, preserve, protect and defend the Constitution of the United States." Then, instead of turning to the audience to deliver his inaugural address, President Alexander steps back and waits as incoming presidents Kyle Ference and Michael Lamb, each in turn, come forward to take the identical oath.

Three presidents at the same time? The idea seems far-fetched, almost inconceivable. But to Edmund Randolph, the governor of Virginia and a delegate to the 1787 Constitutional Convention, a plural executive made perfect sense. Entrusting the executive power of the new national government to a single person struck Randolph (and some other delegates, including Benjamin Franklin) as a dangerous folly. A unitary executive would be the "foetus of monarchy," Randolph warned. To represent the thirteen states in all their variety, he proposed a three-person executive: one from New England, one from the South, and one from the Middle Atlantic states.

Randolph's fellow delegates voted down his proposal. Some, perhaps most of them, were persuaded that entrusting the executive power to more than one person would make it impossible to assign responsibility when something went wrong. Each of the three co-presidents would point the finger of blame at the other two, and there would be no way to tell who was right. Besides, these delegates reasoned, the president would not be the people's chief representative anyway. That would be the responsibility of Congress, whose members would live in and be chosen by every part of the country.

A few delegates, however, saw the issue differently. Two Pennsylvanians in particular, James Wilson and Gouverneur Morris, worked throughout the convention to make the presidency a stronger office than most of their colleagues initially wanted. For Wilson and Morris, only a unitary executive could act with the "energy" and "dispatch" that are essential for strong leadership. Strong presidential leadership was important to them, because they believed the president was the true representative of the people. Wilson envisioned the president as "the man of the people," and Morris described the president as "the great protector of the mass of the people."

In practice, few eighteenth- and nineteenth-century presidents (Andrew Jackson was a notable exception) spoke of themselves as being more authentic representatives of the American people than Congress. President William Henry Harrison, for example, deemed "preposterous" the idea that a president could "better understand the wants and needs of the people than their representatives" in Congress. The rise of the modern presidency during the twentieth century, however, was propelled by a different theory of representation—one that regards members of Congress as servants of the special interests in their states and districts and sees the president, who alone is elected by the entire country, as representing the national interest. Congress's arcane and antimajoritarian procedural rules, as well as the Senate's overrepresentation of people who live in small states, were also thought by some observers to warp the legislature's representative character. Of course, at any given moment those whose political party controlled the presidency were more likely to make this argument than those whose party was stronger in Congress.

As Marc J. Hetherington, who regards the president as the people's more authentic representative, and Richard J. Ellis, who defends the representative primacy of Congress, reveal in their essays, the debate that began in Philadelphia in 1787 continues. Each author adds a new element—the contemporary era of ideologically polarized political parties—to the two-centuries-old controversy, but each finds in this development further grist for his mill.

PRO: Marc J. Hetherington

When the founders devised the new nation's constitutional structure, they wanted the presidency, House of Representatives, and Senate to differ in their responsiveness to the public. Thus they varied both the lengths of the terms assigned to the offices and the constituencies that would elect them. With its two-year terms and direct election by the public, the House was intended to be the most responsive. House members would serve and also reflect their relatively homogeneous constituencies. The Senate, with its six-year terms and indirect election, would be insulated from the public. Even so, because each state is smaller and more homogeneous than the nation as a whole, the Senate would be relatively consonant with the wishes of the public. Finally, the founders provided for the indirect election of the president through the electoral college. They wanted the president to be accountable to the public—the provision for reelection in the Constitution is proof. Yet the relatively long four-year term meant that the president would not need to reflect the public's wishes at all times.

If the founders could observe their handiwork today, they would be surprised. Most Americans are politically moderate; ideology does not structure the thinking of many voters. In Congress, however, few voices sound like those of the American people's. In the last twenty years, the House has evolved, at least ideologically, into the least representative branch of the federal government. In a political environment driven by ideological activists in districts with hardly a trace of interparty competition, House members have grown increasingly extreme in their views and voting patterns. The Senate is not far behind, because specific states are becoming increasingly "red" or "blue," with little room for ideological moderation. Both chambers are headed by ideologically extreme elected leaders, ensuring that the recent impulse away from moderation will continue well into the future. This state of affairs in no way reflects the public at large.

In today's politics, then, the president best reflects the public's will—although imperfectly so. Presidents do not need to take account of public opinion on all issues and at all times. Yet in this era of partisan and ideological polarization, only the president must appeal to a broad cross section of voters. Recent presidential elections have been extraordinarily competitive, with the winner decided by a swing constituency that is ideologically moderate. Because most Americans are moderate, the president is more representative of the public than the Senate or, especially, the House of Representatives.

PARTY POLARIZATION IN CONGRESS

Perhaps the most important development in American politics in the last two decades has been the marked ideological polarization of the two major parties, especially in Congress. No matter the measure, it is clear that Democrats are becoming increasingly liberal and Republicans, at an even faster rate, are becoming increasingly conservative.

Figure 6-1 shows this change in the House using a measure called DW-NOMINATE scores. Devised by Keith Poole and Howard Rosenthal, these scores track the voting records of members of the House of Representatives over time. Each member gets a NOMINATE score for every two-year term based on the extent to which his or her voting record was conservative or liberal. Very liberal members receive very low scores, very conservative members receive very high scores, and more moderate members receive scores in between.

Sorting the Republican and Democratic members into their party caucuses reveals how remarkably ideologically distinct the parties are. Since the early 1970s, the parties have been moving apart at a breakneck pace. For example, in

Figure 6-1

Distance between Average Members of House Party Caucuses, 1967–2009

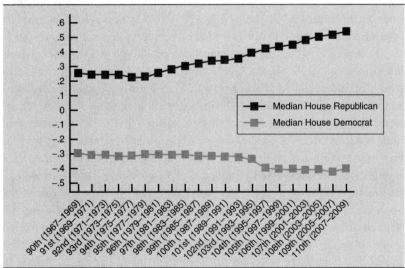

Source: DW-NOMINATE scores are available at http://voteview.com/dwnomin.htm.

the Ninetieth Congress (1967–1969) the average Republican member was about 0.25 points from the ideological center and the average Democratic member was about 0.30 points from the center, or about 0.55 points from each other. By the 110th Congress (2007–2009), the difference between the parties had increased to nearly 0.95 points, almost twice as great. Most of the polarization has taken place since the mid-1980s. Unlike the late 1960s and early 1970s, the average Republican member is now significantly further to the right than the average Democratic member is to the left.

Not only is the "average" member of the House increasingly extreme, congressional leaders are often even more so, which, in turn, has probably accelerated the parties' continued movement apart. Not many years ago, leaders tended to come from the ideological center of each party. For example, for most of the 1980s the House minority leader was Robert Michel, R-Ill., who had a DW-NOMINATE score that placed him in the middle quartile of his party. The majority leader, Jim Wright, D-Texas, was another moderate. His NOMINATE score placed him at the exact median of his party when he first became its leader. These ideological "middlemen" made certain that the caucuses did not stray too far to the left or to the right. When the Republican Party seized control of the House after the 1994 elections, they started a trend of electing more ideologically extreme leaders. For example, Tom DeLay and Richard Armey, both of Texas, took important roles in the GOP leadership despite being in the most extreme 3 percent of their party. The Democrats followed suit when Nancy Pelosi, one of the more liberal members of her caucus, started her meteoric rise up the leadership ladder, ultimately becoming Speaker in 2007. As a result, increasingly extreme parties in Congress are being led by even more extreme party leaders.

The reasons for this change are many. The most important is that the once solidly Democratic South is now a Republican stronghold. In the 1950s, Republicans controlled only a tiny number of seats in what is today among the most conservative regions of the country. During that period, the large number of conservative southern Democrats in Congress ensured that their party remained quite moderate to counterbalance the party's conservative southern and progressive northern wings. But when the Democratic Party championed civil rights in the 1960s, it sparked a fundamental realignment in American politics. During the next three decades, the Democratic Party fell into disfavor in the South and was dislodged by an even more conservative southern GOP. In 1994 Republicans won more than 50 percent of the House districts in the eleven states of the former Confederacy for the first time. In the 2000 election, they upped that percentage to 63 percent. Although that percentage dropped to 55 after the second of two consecutive dismal election cycles for Republicans in 2008, members from these eleven states made up fully 40 percent of the

Republican House delegation in the 111th Congress (2009–2011). No longer, then, did liberal Democrats need to take account of a substantial conservative wing, while the Republican caucus came increasingly under the control of elements from among the most ideologically extreme regions of the country.

Meanwhile, a similar, although less dramatic, change was taking place in the Northeast. Traditionally, the New England and Middle Atlantic states have been liberal, but they did elect a fair share of liberal Republicans to Congress. In the decades after the civil rights revolution, these liberal northeastern Republicans were in large measure replaced in Congress by even more liberal northeastern Democrats. In fact, the GOP failed to win even a single House seat in New England in 2008. The results of these regional shifts have been fewer members of Congress who are ideologically in tune with the other party and thus two parties that are ideologically much more homogeneous.

The political reform movement that followed the Vietnam War and the Watergate scandal in the 1960s and 1970s also contributed (unwittingly) to this trend toward more ideologically extreme parties in Congress. Campaign finance laws passed during this period were intended to minimize the role of sometimes corrupt party organizations. Indeed, initially the new streams of money opened by the Federal Election Campaign Act of 1974 provided candidates the freedom to govern in less party-centered ways. As time passed, however, elections were dominated by a disproportionate number of ideological activists whose chief desire was to implement policy objectives—a desire that ran counter to that of members produced by the old patronage-driven boss system. Because patronage depended on winning elections, party bosses tended to choose ideological moderates as candidates. The new breed of candidate values ideological outcomes more than patronage.

In the House, redistricting has also hastened the trend toward ideologically extreme parties in Congress. In its 1962 *Baker v. Carr* decision, the U.S. Supreme Court ruled that congressional districts must be of approximately equal population, and it called on each state to redraw its congressional districts after every decennial census to reflect changes in population. After the 1990 and 2000 censuses, redistricters took full advantage of great advances in computer technology to protect incumbents from competition. The original concern about redistricting was that the majority party in each state would attempt to maximize its partisan advantage by drawing districts so that the other party could not compete. The more recent concern has been that redistricting officials from both parties would collude to protect as many incumbents from interparty competition as possible.

The latter concern is well founded. Although always high, the reelection rate of House incumbents is often stratospheric. In 2004 only nine incumbents tasted defeat (two in primaries, seven in general elections). And even in 2008, an electorally volatile election year, only 23 of the 404 incumbents who ran for reelection lost (4 in primaries and 19 in general elections). Moreover, only a small handful of races are usually even close. The benchmark for a marginal district (one that can be won by either party) is that the winning candidate triumphs with less than 55 percent of the two-party vote. In 2004 a mere 8 percent of races were marginal, and the average House incumbent won with 70 percent of the vote. In fact, sixty-two House races featured no major-party competition at all. Open-seat races—those with no incumbent running—are ordinarily the most competitive. Yet in 2004, only five of the thirty-two open-seat races were won by the party opposite that of the retiring member, historically a very low percentage. Even with sweeping Democratic gains in both 2006 and 2008, which made some seemingly safe Republican districts more uncertain, competition in a general sense was not much greater. In 2008, for example, only 13 percent of the races were marginal, while thirteen retiring Republicans were replaced by Democrats.

Because they face little competition in general elections, House members are not particularly constrained by public opinion. To the extent that real competition may arise in their districts, it is more likely to occur in a primary than a general election. But primary voters tend to be much more ideologically extreme than the electorate as a whole. This fact further reinforces the polarization that is occurring in the House of Representatives.

Although it has not been as stark, the Senate has been undergoing a change similar to that under way in the House for all the same reasons except for redistricting, which does not apply to the Senate. Figure 6-2 provides two snapshots of the Senate's ideological makeup—one taken in 1985 and one taken in 2001. The x-axis in both graphs is the loyalty score awarded to House members by the Americans for Democratic Action (ADA), a liberal interest group. The score represents the percentage of times a senator votes with the ADA on bills it cares about. The y-axis is the score awarded by the American Conservative Union (ACU), a conservative interest group.

Figure 6-2a reveals that in the 1980s some senators in both parties scored about 50 percent, indicating ideological moderation. About half the time they voted with the conservatives and about half the time they voted with the liberals. In fact, some Republican senators appear on the liberal side of the figure and even more Democrats appear on the conservative side. Each party also had a fair number of ideologues, clustered in the upper left-hand and lower right-hand corners of the figure, but the important point is that the distribution of senators in both parties was widely dispersed.

Figure 6-2a

Support for Positions Held by Americans for Democratic Action (ADA) and by American Conservative Union (ACU) by Selected Senators, 99th Congress (1985–1987), First Session

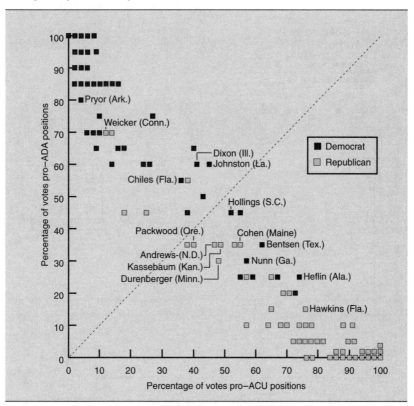

Source: Developed from data appearing in http://www.adaction.org and http://www.conservative.org.

The picture looks much different in the 2000s (Figure 6-2b). Only a handful of senators appear in the center. For every moderate like Ben Nelson, D-Neb., or Arlen Specter, R-Pa., there have been ten ideologues like Trent Lott, R-Miss., and Edward M. Kennedy, D-Mass., who almost always vote conservative or liberal, respectively. Indeed moderates of one party might feel more ideologically in tune with the other party, as was the case in 2009 when Specter switched parties, giving the Democrats 60 votes in the Senate.

If the public were similarly polarized along ideological lines, then Congress's ideological polarization would be representative. The public, however, is not

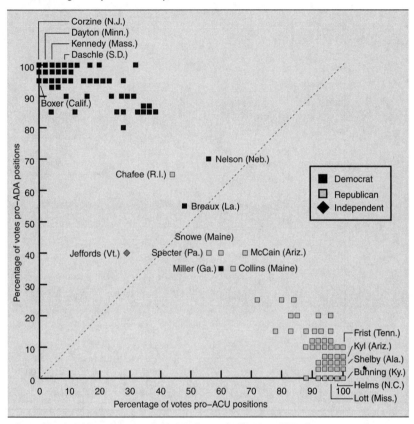

Figure 6-2b

Support for Positions Held by Americans for Democratic Action (ADA) and by American Conservative Union (ACU) by Selected Senators, 107th Congress (2001–2003), First Session

Source: Developed from data appearing in http://www.adaction.org and http://www.conservative.org.

ideological in any meaningful sense of the word. Indeed perhaps the most durable finding from the last fifty years of public opinion research is that Americans know little about politics and thus are unable to organize their thoughts about politics in ideological terms. Individuals' opinions about issues tend to oscillate wildly, which is inconsistent with the notion that their preferences are deeply held.

Americans do not seem to want to think of themselves as ideologues either. Since 1972, the National Election Study has asked Americans to place themselves along a seven-point ideological scale ranging from extremely liberal on one end to extremely liberal on the other. They can also call themselves "liberal," "slightly liberal," "slightly conservative," or "conservative." The midpoint of the scale is labeled "moderate" or "middle of the road." People can also indicate that they have not thought very much about their political position. In the eighteen studies since the question's debut, a minimum of 20 percent of respondents have availed themselves of the "haven't thought much about it" option. Among those who do place themselves on the scale, the most popular choice in all eighteen studies has been "moderate, middle of the road."

In 2008, for example, 22 percent of respondents called themselves moderate, and another 25 percent said they had not thought much about it. In other words, about 50 percent of Americans eschewed the liberal and conservative labels altogether. A combined 21 percent of respondents said they are either slightly liberal (9 percent) or slightly conservative (12 percent). Although most members of Congress are extremely conservative or extremely liberal, only 6 percent of the public thinks of itself as such.

In general, public opinion tends to follow changes in the behavior of leaders. But such a shift has not happened to any meaningful degree with ideological identification. In 1972, for example, only 44 percent of respondents placed themselves in either of the three liberal or three conservative categories. In 2008 that percentage was 53 percent. The difference represents an increase in ideological self-identification, but not one that in any way reflects the increase that has occurred in Congress. The public, by any measure, is centrist. The House and Senate are not.

THE PRESIDENT IS A LITTLE DIFFERENT

Presidents face a different set of political imperatives that make them significantly more representative of the public as a whole than members of Congress (especially in view of its present polarization). Recent presidential elections have been remarkably close, especially in the electoral vote count. George W. Bush's thirty-four-electoral-vote victory in 2004 may have seemed like a landslide compared with his five-electorate-vote victory in 2000, but it was still razor thin by historical standards. Over the last fifty years, the Kennedy-Nixon and Carter-Ford elections produced popular votes that were just as close, but they also produced eighty-four- and fifty-seven-electoral-vote victories, respectively. Only one election in the twentieth century had a closer electoral vote count than the 2004 election—Woodrow Wilson's twenty-three-electoral-vote victory over Charles Evans Hughes in 1916. Although Barack Obama won in 2008 by more than seven percentage points in an election that some think might foreshadow a fundamental shift in the American political system, his electoral college victory was narrower than in either of Bill Clinton's victories and much narrower than those produced by George H. W. Bush in 1988 and Ronald Reagan in 1980 and 1984. No matter how personally popular a candidate is or how unpopular the opposition party might be, many states are simply not up for grabs in early twenty-first-century American politics.

Despite the highly competitive nature of elections at the national level, a large number of states are uncompetitive, which is consistent with the trend toward a polarized Senate. In 1960, when the national popular vote margin was razor thin, only six states gave one candidate a twenty percentage point victory over the other; eighteen states produced a victory margin of less than five percentage points, which is the usual definition of a battleground state. Likewise, the 1976 election, in which Jimmy Carter won a 2.1 percentage point victory in the national popular vote (about the same as George W. Bush's 2.8 percentage point victory in 2004), produced six twenty-plus percentage point blowouts and twenty battleground states. By 2004, however, things had changed. The number of blowouts had increased to seventeen, and the number of states decided by five points or less had dropped to ten. Reflecting Obama's relatively large popular-vote victory, state-level competition was even weaker in 2008. The number of blowout states remained constant at seventeen, but the number of states decided by five points or fewer dropped to a mere six.

And what role do battleground states play in any argument claiming that the president is more representative of the public than Congress? These states are, after all, the ones that both parties know they must win to take the presidency. Presidential candidates spend the bulk of their time trying to carry these states. In both 2000 and 2004, the battleground states were the same: Colorado, Florida, Iowa, Michigan, Minnesota, Nevada, New Hampshire, New Mexico, Ohio, Oregon, Pennsylvania, and Wisconsin. And, even though many of these states turned out to be easy victories for Obama in 2008, both campaigns still targeted them along with emerging battlegrounds like North Carolina, Indiana, and Virginia. For the most part, these are moderate states with heterogeneous electorates that require presidential candidates to appeal to the political center.

Most battleground states fall into two categories. Half of them are in the Rust Belt and the upper Midwest—that is, those states that run without interruption from Pennsylvania in the east to Iowa and Minnesota in the west. Each of these states has a significant labor movement, and all but Iowa have a major urban center; both of these characteristics favor Democrats. But each also has large rural and suburban populations, which tend to favor Republicans. The other cluster of battleground states is in the Southwest: Colorado, Nevada, and New Mexico. All three have strong Republican traditions but also, increasingly, large Latino populations. Although Bush increased the Republican share of the Latino vote in 2004, this is still a strongly Democratic constituency as evidenced by

Obama winning the group by better than two to one in 2008. Moreover, the growth of the Latino population is also increasing the heterogeneity of these states, which, in turn, is contributing to their political moderation.

Another indication of the moderation of these states can be found in their choice of senators. After the 2008 elections, only twelve states currently had one Democratic and one Republican senator, a clear sign that their voters are comfortable voting for both conservatives and liberals. Five of the six states in which the presidential election in 2008 was decided by five points or less (Missouri, Florida, Ohio, Indiana, and North Carolina) have split party delegations, and three others with split delegations (New Hampshire, South Dakota, and Iowa) had the presidential election decided by between five and ten percentage points. In the face of such moderation in these battleground states, the president is compelled to tout policies that bridge the partisan divide.

In addition, as shown in the previous section, most Americans, when considering the nation as a whole, are moderate and nonideological. A president who fails to account for this factor runs the risk of alienating a large chunk of the public. Indeed George W. Bush, a president who often catered to his religious conservative base on domestic and foreign policy, provides a good example of the pitfalls of a president who comes to be perceived as too ideological. It is not surprising in this polarized time that the difference between Democrats and Republicans in their approval ratings for President George W. Bush was the largest difference in the history of polling, which dates to the 1930s. Most Republicans loved him, and almost all Democrats hated him, particularly after the government's sluggish response to Hurricane Katrina. Importantly, however, the broad ideological middle grew to dislike him as well, which was central to understanding his historically low approval ratings during his final two years in office. It is also noteworthy that President Obama made ideological moderation and bipartisanship a centerpiece of his campaign, suggesting that his campaign understood the important disconnect between an ideologically moderate mass public and a polarized Washington. Electorally safe individual members of Congress, especially in the House, need not make such overtures.

CONCLUSION

Presidential candidates face a different electorate than most members of Congress face. House members' districts tend, by nature, to be relatively homogeneous, and redistricting has made them more so. Thus members have little incentive to embrace ideological moderation. Indeed, because the competition House members face is potentially greater in primaries, ideological extremeness is almost a virtue. Senators have moved toward one ideological pole or the other as well. Some states with especially heterogeneous populations do elect moderate senators, but they make up only a small minority of states. This relatively small group of truly moderate states is, however, decisive in determining who wins presidential elections. Thus presidential candidates must tailor their messages and policies to appeal to the moderate voters in these moderate states.

CON: Richard J. Ellis

The notion that the president is the truest or most authentic representative of the American people is an old one, dating back at least to Andrew Jackson. Its enduring appeal rests in large part on the American people's habitual distrust of politicians, parties, and legislative bodies. Members of Congress are typically denigrated as parochial or in the pocket of powerful interests, corrupt and out of touch with the people who sent them to Washington, D.C. The chief beneficiary of this deeply ingrained skepticism of Congress is the president.[1]

To be sure, the president's claim to being the most authentic representative of the people rests on more than Congress bashing. It also stems from the fact that the president is the only government official selected by all American citizens. Members of Congress are elected in contests open only to a small fraction of the American people: those who reside in a particular state or electoral district. But the question is not whether the president is a truer representative of the nation than a senator from Rhode Island or a representative from Georgia, but rather whether the president more authentically represents the American people than do the political deliberations of 535 representatives selected from every part of the nation.

One does not have to look hard to find some of the many ways in which the will of the people—or at least the will of the majority of the people—may be frustrated in a legislature. The legislative structure provides a plethora of veto points whereby intense, well-organized minority interests can prevent action from being taken on a piece of legislation. Indeed, the halls of Congress are littered with apparently popular proposals that never made it out of committee, or that made it out only in a hopelessly watered-down form. Further attenuating the connection between voter preference and congressional output is the power of incumbency. High name recognition coupled with attentive constituency service and massive fund raising can help to insulate a member of Congress from shifts in popular opinion. And when districts are redrawn to make incumbents' seats safer still, Congress's responsiveness to public opinion drops even further.

It is right, then, to reject the assumption that Congress will automatically and accurately mirror voter preferences. That the legislative process often distorts the popular will is indisputably true. In fact, to some extent it intentionally thwarts majority preferences—the filibuster is but one example. But it does not follow from this observation that the president more accurately represents the will of the people. Indeed, the president is, in many ways, less representative of the people than is Congress.

How can that be? After all, the president is elected by the people. If the people do not like what the president is doing in their name they can throw the rascal out of office. This observation has an intuitive appeal, but it makes certain assumptions about voter behavior that turn out often not to be justified. In particular, it assumes that voters, first, know the candidates' stands on issues, and, second, vote on the basis of the candidates' issue positions.

But even when voters have strong views on issues, they often have a difficult time connecting those issues to the positions taken by the candidates. In 2000, for example, George W. Bush made tax cuts the centerpiece of his campaign, yet polling data collected by the National Annenberg Election Survey found that only 60 percent of respondents identified Bush as the candidate who favors "the biggest tax cut." And when asked whether Bush or his Democratic opponent, Al Gore, favored using the Medicare surplus to finance tax cuts, only 51 percent of respondents identified this as the position of candidate Bush.[2] If people do not know what a candidate's issue positions are, they cannot use their vote to express their issue preferences.

President Bill Clinton had the same problem, particularly when he took centrist positions. A 1998 poll showed that although nearly seven in ten respondents knew that Clinton supported a woman's right to have an abortion, only about one in four knew that Clinton had not promoted a universal system of national health insurance. A mere 13 percent knew that Clinton had signed welfare reform into law. Even when offered only two choices, fewer than a quarter knew (or guessed correctly) that the Clinton administration opposed the international treaty banning land mines. And it was not that people were not following politics: 93 percent could correctly identify White House intern Monica Lewinsky. But when it came to identifying the president's issue positions, particularly those in which he tacked to the center, voters failed miserably.[3]

And, of course, in presidential elections much more is at stake than issue positions. Voters are encouraged to think about the candidate's character and experience. Most Americans probably want voters to think about a candidate's temperament before deciding on whether that person should possess the power to destroy the world many times over. But casting a vote based on character and experience, however sensible, weakens the connection between the vote and support for issue positions. The more that character matters, the less the vote for president can tell us about the policy preferences of voters.

Finally, even if voters were perfectly informed about the issues and the candidates' positions on those issues, and voted entirely on the basis of those positions, there would still be reason to question whether a president's programmatic agenda represented the will of the people. Claims that the president has a mandate from the people are inherently implausible because, as political scientist Raymond E. Wolfinger reminds us, there are many issues but only one vote.[4] In other words, even in a hypothetical environment of informed, purely issue-oriented voters (an environment that does not exist today and has never existed in the past), a president's electoral victory reveals little about the issue preferences of the electorate. Only if these perfectly informed issue voters arrange their issue preferences in ideologically consistent packages that are identical to those of the candidate would candidate choice reflect voters' issue preferences. In the real world, presidential candidates are about as likely to win in spite of their issue positions as because of them.

In short, presidential election results are an unreliable indicator of public opinion on any given issue. The fact that a candidate is elected president says next to nothing about what issue positions voters favor or the issues they care about most. The only halfway reliable way to know what voters prefer is to poll them. Thus even though the president is elected by all the people, the president is not any more likely than Congress to represent voter preferences. The difference is that media pundits and Washington insiders regularly make the mistake of assuming that presidents have electoral mandates to pursue particular policies, whereas the same mistake is rarely made when those same people talk about Congress.

The real test, then, is whether the president or Congress actually pushes policies that are closer to the views of the public. One might think presidents would move closer to the views of the people in an effort to boost their popularity and gain reelection. But do presidents in fact single-mindedly seek to boost their popularity? Are they single-mindedly focused on reelection? And is their behavior significantly different in this respect from that of members of Congress?

Even if it is assumed that presidents single-mindedly seek reelection, this motivation is more likely to lead them to keep the economy purring than it is to prompt them to adopt particular issue positions. It is a long-standing precept of political behavior that in the general election presidential candidates tack to the center to appeal to the median voter's preference. The electoral college is supposed to accentuate this tendency, because a presidential candidate's attention is necessarily focused on the most competitive states. But is that how presidential candidates really behave? Certainly in 2004 the candidates spent the lion's share of their time in competitive states. But did Bush focus his campaign in Ohio on moderate swing voters? Or did he seek to turn out his evangelical base, just as the Democrats in Ohio countered by turning out their African American base? The fewer the number of undecided voters, the greater is the incentive for presidential candidates to appeal to their base rather than to reach for the middle.

An incumbent president has a particularly strong incentive to pay attention to his partisan base. Since 1970, the only incumbent presidents to be defeated were those who faced stiff primary challenges, from the right if they were Republicans and from the left if they were Democrats. Republican Gerald R. Ford went down to defeat in 1976 after receiving a stern primary challenge from Ronald Reagan; Democrat Jimmy Carter was defeated in 1980 after being pressed to the wire by fellow Democrat Edward M. Kennedy; and Republican George Bush lost in 1992 after having to fend off a bitter primary challenge from Pat Buchanan. The four incumbent presidents who won—Richard Nixon, Ronald Reagan, Bill Clinton, and George W. Bush—faced no serious primary opposition. So even a president who focuses single-mindedly on his reelection would arguably be more concerned with placating his base than appealing to the middle.

Even if one accepts the unlikely premise that the electoral needs of presidents push them toward the political center, that argument would only hold for a first-term president. The Twenty-second Amendment cuts the knot between a second-term president and the people. Second-term presidents may still worry about their popularity, especially if they think it will improve their effectiveness (though the empirical evidence that it does is decidedly mixed), but they have their eyes on a larger agenda: their place in history. Such a president may pursue wise or unwise policies, but those policies will be shaped far more by the views, beliefs, prejudices, and wisdom of the president and his closest advisers than they will be by the views of "the people."

Consider Social Security. When voters were asked in 2003 and 2004 what was the most important problem facing the country, few said the looming crisis in Social Security. Yet after the 2004 election President Bush made Social Security *the* issue facing the country. Moreover, the president's position on the issue—that Social Security should be privatized and that there should be benefit cuts rather than tax increases—was not a position shared by the American people. When polled, the most popular answer with the American people was a modest increase in the level at which income was exempt from Social Security taxes. The president's position represented not the views of the people; it represented his own views and those of his advisers and some vocal Republican activists.

By contrast, members of Congress, even quite conservative members from relatively safe seats, were much more in tune with the concerns and anxieties of the American people. When members went back to their districts to talk about the president's plan, they encountered real voters with real concerns, and they immediately transmitted those anxieties back to Washington. When members of Congress held town hall meetings to talk about Social Security, they were not the carefully scripted, invitation-only affairs favored by the Bush administration. Rather, they were open to all comers, and so were louder, angrier, and more skeptical. In these meetings were heard the discordant notes of democracy, notes that the representatives of the people carried back to the capital.

Of course, presidents—even second-term presidents—look at polls. But they use polls less to make policy than to sell policy. For example, focus groups and internal polls prompted the Bush administration to stop talking about the privatization of Social Security and to talk instead about "personal accounts." Polls drove the packaging, but they did not change the policy. In short, presidents pay attention to polls not in order to follow the public's will but to mold it.[5]

Moreover, democratic responsiveness is often not even regarded as a virtue in presidents. Presidents who try to tack to the center or pay too much attention to public opinion polls are viewed as either weak or untrustworthy ("Slick Willy"). Presidents who stand by their convictions, even when those convictions are not shared by a majority of the American people, are praised as leaders with resolute courage and character. And if it is character that matters to voters in choosing a president, then it should hardly be a surprise that presidents do not feel a pressing need to be responsive to voter preferences on issues.

All government, as historian Edmund S. Morgan has rightly observed, "requires make-believe. Make believe that the king is divine, make believe that he can do no wrong or make believe that the voice of the people is the voice of God. Make believe that the people *have* a voice or make believe that the representatives of the people *are* the people. Make believe that the governors are the servants of the people."[6] Make believe that when presidents speak they speak as the voice of the people. Make believe that presidents have mandates from the people to enact policies. Make believe that, as political scientist Clinton Rossiter put it, presidents are "the one-man distillation of the American people."[7] Make believe—this time in the words of Woodrow Wilson—that "when the president speaks in his true character, he speaks for no special interest."[8] Make believe that when presidents act, the people rule. Elections, contrary to what these fictions would have us believe, are primarily events in which Americans choose which few individuals will rule over the rest of them.

The same is true for Congress. But in American politics there is little danger that people will uncritically accept the myth that the voice of the people expresses itself through Congress. Skepticism of politicians in Congress runs deep. Congress is the only "distinctly native American criminal class," jibed Mark Twain. But the presidency poses a qualitatively different challenge. The president speaks with a single voice, and the president claims to speak for all Americans. The news Americans read and see on television is structured around the president's agenda and the president's words. Individual presidents may be unpopular, but Americans are loath to relinquish the fiction that the president speaks for all Americans. The truth, however, is that the president is just an extremely powerful politician whose policies are about as likely to reflect public opinion as not.

To reject the idea that the president is the most authentic representative of the people is to defend not only Congress but democratic politics. It is to insist that 300 million people are more likely to be represented in all their diversity by 535 people than they are by a single person. Deliberations in Congress *are* more rancorous, but that is because Congress, for all its many failings, is a more open, democratic institution than is the modern presidency. Democracy, moreover, is not about finding an "authentic" expression of the people's voice, because "the people" do not have a single voice. Rather, the people make a cacophonous variety of sounds and utterances, and those sounds and utterances are far more likely to be heard in the halls of Congress than they are in the speeches of a president.

7

RESOLVED, presidents have usurped the war power that rightfully belongs to Congress

PRO: Nancy Kassop

CON: Richard M. Pious

War transforms nations and governments. It centralizes power. It elevates state over society, the national government over local and regional governments, and the executive over the legislature. State building in Europe—in countries such as Great Britain, France, and Germany—was a direct result of war and the threat of war. Throughout much of its early history, the United States was blessedly free of the threat of war. Separated from the European powers by a vast ocean, the United States was able to maintain a relatively small military, a weak central government, and a limited executive.

The astute French observer Alexis de Tocqueville correctly diagnosed the political significance of America's isolation from the great powers of Europe.[1] Tocqueville understood that "it is chiefly in the realm of foreign relations that the executive power of a nation finds occasion to demonstrate its skill and strength." The United States that Tocqueville observed in 1831 had "an army that consists of six thousand soldiers" and a navy of "only a few vessels." The president was empowered by the Constitution to "direct the Union's dealings with foreign nations," but the nation had "no neighbors" and "no enemies." From Tocqueville's Eurocentric point of view, the United States was "separated from the rest of the world by the Atlantic Ocean." Rarely, he observed, "do its interests intersect with those of other nations of the globe." The result was that, although "the president of the United States possesses prerogatives that are almost royal in magnitude," he has "no occasion to use" such powers, "and the powers that he has been able to use until now have been very circumscribed."

For Tocqueville, these observations underlined the need to look beyond formal powers and constitutional theories. "The law," he wrote, "allows [the president] to be strong, but circumstances keep him weak." Yet "if the existence of the Union were under constant threat, if its great interests were daily intertwined with those of other powerful nations, the executive power would take on increased importance in the public eye, because people would expect more of it, and it would do more." In other words, if and when circumstances changed to diminish the importance of the Atlantic Ocean as a barrier, then the chief executive of the United States would begin to look more like the strong executives of Europe. Executive power—along with the power of the central government as a whole—would grow. Not for the only time, Tocqueville was prescient.

Of course, the United States did have its wars in the nineteenth century, none more important than the Civil War. But during the Civil War, and even during World War I, the growth in executive power and in the control exercised by the central government was followed by a period of reaction in which nearly all of the powers bestowed on the executive and the central government were dismantled. The executive powers exercised during these wars were justified as extraordinary measures necessitated by a national emergency. It was expected that after the threat passed, the political system would revert to its normal, more decentralized pattern of authority.

At first, it appeared that World War II would follow this venerable American tradition of wartime centralization and peacetime reaction. But the cold war with the Soviet Union changed that pattern. War no longer seemed a temporary state but a permanent condition. Anxiety about the communist threat justified the accretion of executive power. After the Berlin Wall was torn down in 1989 and the Soviet Union collapsed in 1991, it appeared that the pendulum might swing back again. With the nation no longer under threat from communism, expansive executive power no longer seemed essential. Many scholars in the Clinton years and in the opening months of George W. Bush's presidency forecast a weakened presidency and a smaller central government. But the September 11, 2001, terrorist attacks on the United States changed all that. The cold war was replaced by the "war on terror," which, like the cold war, seemed to have no clear beginning or, more important, end point. Anxieties about the threats posed to the nation by hidden enemies were again ubiquitous, the state of crisis seemed permanent. And with these feelings of anxiety about the nation's safety came, as Tocqueville predicted, further increases in executive power.

Whether that increase in executive power is good or bad, and whether it is contrary to the intentions of the framers of the Constitution, are among the subjects of the debate between Nancy Kassop and Richard M. Pious. Kassop laments that Americans have forgotten the wisdom of the framers, who placed the power to "declare war" in the hands of Congress. Pious, by contrast, sees the Constitution (in legal scholar Edward S. Corwin's famous phrase) as "an invitation to struggle" for control of foreign policy. In Pious's telling, it is not that the president has usurped the war power of Congress but that Congress, with an assist from the courts, has essentially handed power over to the president.

PRO: Nancy Kassop

"The Constitution ... is an invitation to struggle for the privilege of directing American foreign policy."[1] So wrote the constitutional scholar Edward S. Corwin in 1957. But the words of the framers of the Constitution are actually clear and unambiguous, leaving little over which to struggle. Article I gives Congress the power to declare war, along with the power to provide for and maintain an army and a navy. Article II designates the president as commander in chief, whose authority, according to Alexander Hamilton in *Federalist* No. 69, "would amount to nothing more than the supreme command and direction of the military and naval forces, as first general and admiral of the Confederacy; while that of the British king extends to the *declaring* of war and to the *raising* and *regulating* of fleets and armies—all which, by the Constitution under consideration, would appertain to the legislature."[2] Thus, as with most of the other shared powers in the Constitution, the lines of authority delineated by the framers for Congress and the president seem clear.

Article II, Section 2, of the Constitution reads: "The President shall be Commander in Chief of the Army and Navy of the United States, and of the Militia of the several States, when called into the actual Service of the United States." That provision gives the president a title, commander in chief, but no specific list of powers that can be exercised in that capacity. It also suggests that the president is not "Commander in Chief" all of the time, but only "when called into the actual Service of the United States." As Hamilton wrote, also in *Federalist* No. 69, "The President will have only the occasional command of such part of the militia of the nation as by legislative provision may be called into the actual service of the nation."[3] Further evidence of Hamilton's understanding that the president's power was to be limited is found in his proposal to the Constitutional Convention (he was a delegate from New York) that the president "have the direction of war when authorized or begun."[4] It is Congress, then, that calls the president into service as commander in chief when it declares war or authorizes the use of force by statute. The framers could not have been clearer: the decision to go to war belongs to the deliberative branch of government, because declaring war is a political decision to move the nation from a state of peace to a state of war. Only then does the president command the troops and conduct military operations.[5] As law professor Louis Henkin has noted, "Generals and admirals, even when they are 'first,' do not determine the political purposes for which troops are to be used; they command them in the execution of policy made by others."[6]

The framers, however, were not blind to the possibility that emergency or exigent situations could arise. Notes from the Constitutional Convention confirm that the delegates' change in wording of Article I—from the power "to make war" to the power "to declare war"—indicated their intention to give the president "the power to repel sudden attacks" without specific statutory authorization from Congress.[7] But this sole exception makes the rule all the more plain: presidents can act on their own *only* in defensive circumstances. Any offensive military action, regardless of size, duration, or purpose, must be authorized by Congress. Offensive versus defensive was the crucial distinction for the framers. However, enforcement of that distinction, at least since the middle of the twentieth century, has been sorely lacking. No delegate at the Constitutional Convention, not even Hamilton, would recognize the power to use military force that presidents have wielded in the international arena since World War II.

Thus at a bare minimum the Constitution requires the following:

1. All offensive uses of military force must be authorized by Congress, either through a formal declaration of war or by specific statutory authorization. In either case, joint action by both branches is required—that is, passage by both houses of Congress and signing by the president.

2. Any independent constitutional authority the president may have to direct the use of military force without Congress's approval must be defensive in purpose—"to repel sudden attacks."

3. The president's status as commander in chief is confined to the authority to conduct military operations when Congress determines, through the mechanisms of a declaration of war or specific statutory authorization, that such operations are warranted.

4. The president's status as commander in chief confers on the president, subject to Congress's authorization, the power to conduct military operations after Congress has identified the location, purpose, scope, and, to the extent possible, anticipated duration of hostilities. Status as commander in chief does not confer a "blanket" or open-ended authority to direct domestic policy, unless Congress has delegated specific emergency powers to the president in connection with the use of military force it already has approved as law.

5. In order for Congress to make effective judgments about whether to authorize the use of military force in any situation, the president and other executive branch officials must make good-faith efforts to supply the legislature with accurate, timely, valid, and, as much as possible, complete information. Congress is at the mercy of the executive branch to

provide it with information. The decisions it makes are only as good as the information it receives.

6. The constitutional requirement that Congress approve the use of military force is not satisfied by the approval of other international bodies, such as the North Atlantic Treaty Organization (NATO) or the United Nations Security Council. When an international body calls for the deployment of U.S. military forces, Congress must first give its approval.

Each of these constitutional requirements has been violated by presidents, with increasing impunity, since the mid-twentieth century. Some presidents have violated more than one of these requirements in a single decision. President Harry S. Truman's decision to send U.S. troops to Korea in December 1950 is the most-cited example of a president ordering troops into combat on the basis of inherent executive authority without any participation by Congress. Truman's action violated all of the items just listed. He sent troops to Korea without either a declaration of war by Congress or specific statutory authorization (No. 1). The purpose of the action was not to repel an attack against the United States, but rather to protect U.S. interests by defending an ally against communist aggression (No. 2). Truman based his decision to employ U.S. forces on his commander in chief authority alone, without any participation by Congress (No. 3). He issued an executive order in April 1952 directing the secretary of commerce to seize privately owned steel mills and operate them under government control, arguing, partly on the basis of his status as commander in chief, that averting a strike and continuing production of steel were essential for the war effort (No. 4). He did not consult with or inform Congress about his ordering of U.S. troops to Korea before announcing his decision to the American public (No. 5). And he cited a United Nations Security Council resolution as justification for sending U.S. forces to Korea (No. 6).[8]

Truman's actions established a precedent for presidents to ignore and bypass what had previously been understood and honored, more or less, as baseline constitutional requirements. Previous presidents had, at times, acted on their own authority. For example, Franklin D. Roosevelt made a destroyers-for-bases deal with Great Britain in 1940, and in the spring and summer of 1941 he sent American forces to Greenland and Iceland. He also ordered U.S. naval ships in the North Atlantic to "shoot on sight" any German and Italian submarines west of the twenty-sixth meridian.[9] Although Roosevelt ordered these actions without congressional authorization, historian Arthur M. Schlesinger Jr. has shown that, for the bases deal, the president did conduct "extensive and vigilant consultation—within the executive branch, between the executive and legislative branches, among leaders of both parties and with the press."[10] Schlesinger concedes that Roosevelt's prewar actions skirted the edge of the president's constitutional authority, but Schlesinger notes that FDR displayed "a lurking sensitivity to constitutional issues," that he "made no general claims to inherent presidential power," and that he "did not assert ... that there was no need to consider Congress because his role as Commander in Chief gave him all the authority he needed."[11]

Thus the shift in constitutional approach from Roosevelt to Truman was significant, if not tectonic. Most important, it signaled a new interpretation of the commander in chief clause as a source of executive authority independent of Congress. Such power, once seized without effective challenge, is unlikely ever to be returned. Congress certainly has made little effort to remedy its loss of constitutional authority to the president.[12]

JUSTIFICATIONS FOR PRESIDENTIAL EXPANSIONISM

To understand how this changed interpretation of presidential authority was justified, one need look no further than a 1966 memo written in defense of the Vietnam War by State Department legal adviser Leonard Meeker.[13] Acknowledging that the president's authority to commit U.S. forces to Vietnam did not depend on constitutional sources alone, because Congress and the SEATO (Southeast Asia Treaty Organization) Treaty had supplemented that authority, Meeker nevertheless offered a sweeping, absolutist view of presidential power based on the commander in chief clause. "Under the Constitution," he wrote, "the President, in addition to being Chief Executive, is Commander in Chief of the Army and Navy. He holds the prime responsibility for the conduct of United States foreign relations. These duties carry very broad powers, including the power to deploy American forces abroad and commit them to military operations when the President deems such action necessary to maintain the security and defense of the United States."[14]

Meeker's argument is a blatant misrepresentation of what the framers intended the commander in chief clause to mean. The framers attached no substantive powers to that title, other than to direct the military once Congress had commanded the president to do so. Only to repel a sudden attack could the commander in chief initiate military action.

Meeker's counterargument is that "in 1787 the world was a far larger place, and the framers probably had in mind attacks upon the United States. In the twentieth century, the world has grown smaller. An attack on a country far from our shores can impinge directly on the nation's security.... The Constitution leaves to the president the judgment to determine whether the circumstances of a particular armed attack are so urgent and the potential consequences so threatening to the security of the United States that he should act without formally consulting Congress."[15] Even if Meeker's "small world theory" is accepted, it does not justify the transfer of constitutional power from Congress to the president. In fact, those who think the Constitution's requirements have been superseded by the press of pragmatic contemporary considerations could begin the process of amending the Constitution to reflect the new realities. Any claim that the power to make war has now been effectively shifted to the president does not automatically make it so or justify it constitutionally.

CONGRESSIONAL EFFORTS TO REASSERT ITS AUTHORITY

Just how far presidents have strayed from the Constitution can be measured in the futile efforts by Congress from time to time to rein in rapacious executives and to reassert "first principles." Those efforts found a voice in the National Commitments Resolution of 1969, a nonbinding "sense of the Senate" resolution expressing that, henceforth, "a national commitment by the United States results only from the affirmative action taken by the executive and legislative branches of the United States Government by means of a treaty, statute or concurrent resolution of both Houses of Congress specifically providing for such commitment."[16] This first attempt by the Senate, at the height of the Vietnam War, to reassert its authority was buttressed by a report of the Committee on Foreign Relations that offered an extensive history and analysis of war making, identifying an unmistakable change after World War II that, by 1969, had reached "the point at which the real power to commit the country to war is now in the hands of the president. The trend which began in the early 20th century has been consummated and the intent of the framers of the Constitution as to the war power substantially negated."[17] The report explained that although the country still believed that Congress had the sole power to declare war, it was also

> widely believed, or at least conceded, that the President in his capacity as Commander in Chief had the authority to use the Armed Forces in any way he saw fit. Noting that the President has in fact exercised power over the Armed Forces we have come to assume that he is entitled to do so. The actual possession of a power has given rise to a belief in its constitutional legitimacy. The fact that Congress has acquiesced in, or at the very least has failed to challenge, the transfer of the war power from itself to the executive, is probably the most important single fact accounting for the speed and virtual completeness of the transfer.[18]

It took another four years after the Senate report and the National Commitments Resolution for Congress to organize itself sufficiently to pass, over President Richard Nixon's veto, the War Powers Resolution in 1973. That joint resolution, which has the force of law, imposed procedural requirements on presidents when they decided to send U.S. military forces into hostilities. Its lofty purpose was "to fulfill the intent of the framers of the Constitution of the United States and insure that the collective judgment of both the Congress and the President will apply to the introduction of United States Armed Forces into hostilities."[19] Thus this resolution enacted into law the "commitment" that the Senate had urged in its report four years earlier. Today, however, after thirty years of experience with presidents refusing to comply strictly with its requirements, many scholars and commentators have concluded that this effort, though well-meaning, has effected little, if any, change in presidential conduct. In short, the law has failed to accomplish its objectives.[20] If anything, it has simply added another set of requirements, in addition to the Constitution's, for presidents to ignore and violate.

In summary, presidents have grabbed Congress's war power for themselves; Congress has not been effective in reclaiming its lost power; and the courts have, at best, most often treated these issues as nonjusticiable, and, at worst, supported presidential usurpation of war powers.[21] The only serious effort to restrain a president's usurpation of Congress's war power was in the 1990 case of *Dellums v. Bush,* in which a federal district court refused to accept President George H. W. Bush's claim that the president alone had the authority to distinguish between military actions that constitute war, requiring congressional authorization, and those that are "only an offensive military attack," short of war, thereby needing no congressional approval.[22] Judge Harold Greene called such a claim "far too sweeping to be accepted by the courts. If the Executive had the sole power to determine that any particular offensive military operation, no matter how vast, does not constitute warmaking but only an offensive military attack, the congressional power to declare war will be at the mercy of a semantic decision by the Executive. Such an 'interpretation' would evade the plain language of the Constitution, and it cannot stand."[23] If that was not enough to demonstrate the court's willingness to protect Congress's power, then a comment further into the opinion should suffice: "To put it another way: the Court is not prepared to read out of the Constitution the clause granting to Congress, and to it alone, the authority to declare war."[24] Unfortunately, Judge Greene never decided the merits of the issue in that case, and so the decision stands as a rare announcement of judicial resolve but without any practical consequence flowing from it.

LEGAL INTERPRETATIONS OF PRESIDENTIAL WAR POWERS IN THE BUSH YEARS

Constitutional interpretations of the commander in chief clause took on a new immediacy and prominence during the George W. Bush administration. In the aftermath of the September 11, 2001, terrorist attacks on the United States, the administration tasked a select group of executive branch lawyers to provide an interpretation of the commander in chief clause to guide the president during a "war on terror." Lawyers from the offices of the Counsel to the President and the Counsel to the Vice President worked closely and secretly with handpicked lawyers in the Office of Legal Counsel in the Department of Justice to produce a series of legal opinions that determined that the president had inherent authority under the commander in chief clause to take whatever actions he deemed necessary to protect the nation during wartime. The opinions gave the president a green light to "override" or brush aside acts of Congress, treaties and other international legal agreements, and constitutional guarantees that stood in the way of his counterterrorism policy preferences.[25]

The first of these opinions, titled "The President's Constitutional Authority to Conduct Military Operations Against Terrorists and Nations Supporting Them," written on September 25, 2001, two weeks after the terrorist attacks, proclaimed the broadest possible interpretation of this clause: "It has long been the view of this Office that the Commander-in-Chief Clause is a substantive grant of authority to the President and that the scope of the President's authority to commit the armed forces to combat is very broad."[26] Absent in that pronouncement was any acknowledgement that (1) there is a robust debate over whether the commander in chief clause is, in fact, "a substantive grant of authority" or, instead, a set of functions the president may exercise after Congress has authorized him to do so; and (2) the "broad" scope of the president's authority knows any limits. This opinion was the first of many that asserted that the president's power to act in wartime was exclusive and absolute.[27]

The public disclosure of these opinions several years after they were written was significant for two reasons. First, the opinions revealed an unprecedented and untenable authority for presidential policies during wartime that permitted, for example, interrogation methods that constitute torture, indefinite detention without habeas corpus guarantees, domestic wiretapping without a warrant, and domestic use of the military for law enforcement purposes, all based in large part on the president's authority as commander in chief.[28] Second, the public learned of the extraordinarily influential role played by the Office of Legal Counsel in its function of interpreting the president's constitutional powers in a way that has binding legal force.[29]

This public release provoked considerable controversy, but the larger point is that the constitutional interpretation on which many of these opinions were based was eventually repudiated and discredited. This repudiation occurred in two memorandums issued by the Office of Legal Counsel in October 2008 and January 2009 as the Bush administration was preparing to leave office and in an executive order issued by the incoming Obama administration on January 22, 2009. The October 2008 memo by the outgoing Bush administration stated that an October 23, 2001, Office of Legal Counsel opinion contained "specific propositions that are either incorrect or highly questionable," and "should not be treated as authoritative for any purpose."[30] The Obama executive order mandated that "from this day forward ... officers of the U.S. government ... may not ... rely upon any interpretation of the law governing interrogation issued by the Department of Justice issued between September 11, 2001, and January 20, 2009."[31] Thus, with a few swift strokes of the pen, both the Bush and Obama administrations rejected the Office of Legal Counsel's earlier interpretation that unlimited presidential authority was inherent in the commander in chief clause.

Although the Bush administration's most extreme and strained interpretations of the commander in chief clause have been repudiated, the president's war powers remain far beyond anything envisioned by the Founders. The distance that presidents have traveled from the Constitution in the last half century to embrace the interpretation that they alone may decide on war is justified by some scholars on the grounds that the Constitution's allocation of war powers is an eighteenth-century anachronism that no longer makes sense in the twenty-first century.[32] The best answer to that claim is still that of the framers, whose reasons for separating the power to declare war from the power to conduct it, once declared, are just as valid and relevant today as they were in 1787. Those reasons were, in the words of scholar David Gray Adler, "a deep-seated fear of unilateral executive power and a commitment to collective decision-making in foreign affairs."[33] If the dangers of war in the twenty-first century are more consequential than ever before, that is all the more reason to ensure that the decision to enter a war is made by more than one person and with the benefit of the deliberative process that governs all of the important decisions the United States makes as a nation.

CON: Richard M. Pious

The Constitution is silent or ambiguous on many issues, and nowhere is this more of a problem than on the question of how war powers are to be exercised. The debates at the 1787 Constitutional Convention did not settle the issue. The framers had before them a proposal that gave Congress the power "to make war." Delegate Charles Pinckney proposed instead giving the power to the Senate, because it would be "more acquainted with foreign affairs" and smaller in size than the House of Representatives. Fellow South Carolinian Pierce Butler suggested vesting the war power in the president, "who will have all the requisite qualities, and will not make war but when the nation will support it." George Mason of Virginia spoke against "giving the power of war to the executive, because [the executive is] not safely to be trusted with it." Fellow Virginian James Madison and Elbridge Gerry of Massachusetts moved to insert "declare" instead of "make," thereby leaving the executive "the power to repel sudden attacks." That change was agreed to by seven states with two opposed and one absent. Delegates from all ten states present voted down a proposal by Butler to give the legislature "the power of peace, as they were to have that of war." The president was to be "Commander in Chief of the Army and Navy of the United States, and of the Militia of the several States, when called into the actual Service of the United States." George Washington of Virginia, Alexander Hamilton of New York, and Gouverneur Morris of Pennsylvania preferred to leave language incomplete or ambiguous, with presidential powers underdefined, because once in office they intended to exploit the silences and ambiguities of the Constitution in order to expand those powers.[1]

What can one conclude from the debates at the convention? Only that Congress has the power to declare war, and thus can turn a state of peace into a state of belligerency with another nation. But because presidents can repel invasion on their own authority, the power to "make" war or otherwise make use of the armed forces is not reserved to Congress alone but is a concurrent responsibility of the president and Congress. Beyond these principles nothing is clear. Some commentators argue that no language in the Constitution prevents the president from using force and making war and that many framers would have approved of presidential war making. Others argue that the intent of the framers was to have Congress participate in all decisions involving the use of force. Trying to parse meaning from the literal language of the constitutional text and the statements made by delegates in 1787 will not resolve the debate. A better way is to consider the precedents in American history: How have presidents exercised war powers without a congressional declaration of war? And how have Congress and the federal courts responded?

WAR POWERS: THE LIVING CONSTITUTION

Of the more than two hundred occasions on which the United States has committed armed forces abroad, Congress has declared war only in five: the War of

1812, the Mexican-American War in 1846, the Spanish-American War in 1898, World War I in 1917, and World War II in 1941. Of the early presidents, George Washington used forces without any congressional declaration to clear the Ohio Valley of American Indians; John Adams ordered the navy into action under congressional prodding in an "undeclared" naval war against the French; and Thomas Jefferson used the navy and Marine Corps against pirates harassing American shipping in the Mediterranean Sea. Later presidents used the military to intervene on behalf of American settlers in Florida, Texas, California, and Hawaii. Once America became a world power, armed forces were used to defeat insurgents in the Philippines.

When presidents used force to topple regimes (Grenada in 1982, Iraq in 2003) or safeguard them from being toppled by others (South Korea in the 1950s and South Vietnam in the 1960s), no declaration of war was made by Congress. Since the start of the cold war in the 1950s, Congress has not declared war in any of the major hostilities that have seen the involvement of hundreds of thousands of U.S. troops. Presidents made the decision for peace or war, and Congress used its powers of appropriation, its power to draft or otherwise raise the armed forces, and its other war powers to back the executive, a pattern of behavior known to the courts as "joint concord."

Congress can even express its support retroactively. For example, at the beginning of the Civil War Abraham Lincoln did not call Congress into session (it was not scheduled to meet until December 1861), and he took many actions on his own prerogative, including raising military forces, calling state militias into federal service, sending funds from the Treasury to encourage western Virginia to secede from the Confederacy, and sending naval forces south to enforce federal law. Lincoln then called Congress into special session and informed it that the actions he had taken did not go beyond the scope of the war powers of the national government. This formulation begged the question of whether he had gone beyond the powers assigned to the executive by the Constitution. The congressional response was neither to repudiate his actions nor to impeach him for overreaching. Instead, Congress passed an appropriations act that retroactively legitimized all the actions he had taken in the war. In the *Prize Cases* (1863), the Supreme Court considered whether Lincoln's proclamation ordering a blockade of southern ports had been legal before Congress met and "ratified" it.[2] The Court ruled that no declaration of war was required in a civil conflict. The justices held that any decision to use force in a civil conflict could be made by the president and that federal courts would be governed by his decision. Finally, the Court observed that even if the president had erred in acting alone, the act passed by Congress ratifying his actions would "cure the defect."

Presidents Grover Cleveland and Theodore Roosevelt extended presidential war powers to include "international police powers." They argued that the president's duty to "take care that the laws be faithfully executed" extended to the treaty obligations of nations and the canons of international law. Harry S. Truman extended the police powers and fused the president's powers as commander in chief with the new U.S. obligation to enforce the United Nations Charter's provisions against aggression. Article 51 of the charter recognizes the right of self-defense against aggression and the right of collective security. Article 53 permits regional security pacts and organizations to repel aggression. When Truman sent troops to South Korea in the summer of 1950 to repel an attack from the North, the State Department claimed that a UN Security Council Resolution calling on nations to repel the aggression was an obligation to be met by the president without any need for a declaration of war by Congress. In taking these actions, Truman ignored the United Nations Participation Act of 1946, which requires congressional approval of U.S. collective security efforts under the UN. But instead of protesting, Congress acquiesced, though in this instance it was clear that Truman went beyond its intent and that of the framers.

Presidents also have argued that the North Atlantic Treaty Organization (NATO), Southeast Asia Treaty Organization (SEATO), and Organization of American States (OAS) collective security treaties are self-executing and give the president the right to use the armed forces to protect allies. By contrast, Congress interprets treaty provisions that every nation will act "in accordance with its constitutional processes" to mean that a declaration of war would be required. In consenting to these treaties, the Senate has "agreed to disagree" with the president's interpretation, leaving the president with a free hand to act.

During the cold war, Congress signaled support for presidential use of armed forces in two different ways. In the confrontations in 1955 with communist China in the Formosa Strait, in 1962 with the Soviet Union in the Cuban missile crisis, and in 1964 with North Vietnam in the Gulf of Tonkin incident, Congress passed resolutions in which it would "approve" and "support" possible presidential military actions. In the two more recent conflicts with Iraq, the Persian Gulf War of 1991 and the Iraq War of 2003, Congress went much further, passing joint resolutions (with the force of law) that specifically authorized the president to use armed forces against Iraq. For all intents and purposes, these resolutions were the functional equivalent of declarations of war. Why, then, were they not declarations? Because Congress, in passing them, hoped to send a final signal to Iraq that it must agree to a diplomatic resolution of the crisis or else hostilities would ensue. If the intent of the framers was to require that the president obtain advance congressional consent to a decision to authorize hostilities, then in both conflicts with Iraq the president complied with that obligation.

WAR POWERS AND THE JUDICIARY

Through much of American history, the federal courts did not shy away from ruling on the merits of war powers cases and occasionally checking presidential prerogative. During and after the Vietnam War, however, the federal courts invoked a series of procedural hurdles in order to evade decisions on the substantive issues, thereby leaving the president with a free hand to take military actions without congressional assent.

In *Luftig v. McNamara* (1967), a draftee argued that the secretary of defense, Robert McNamara, had no legal authority to send him to Vietnam because Congress had not declared war.[3] The district court held that judges were precluded "from overseeing the conduct of foreign policy or the use and disposition of military power: these matters are plainly the exclusive province of Congress and the executive." However, in *Berk v. Laird* (1970), although the government argued that absent a declaration of war the president possessed all war powers, a federal appeals court rejected that claim, because it would reduce the congressional power to declare war to "an antique formality."[4] The court held that joint action by Congress and the executive was required. In *Orlando v. Laird* (1971), a court of appeals dealt with the question of whether there must be a declaration of war to satisfy the "joint concord" standard.[5] Orlando argued that the president had placed Congress in an impossible position, because once the war escalated, Congress could hardly refuse appropriations or draft legislation. The court disagreed, finding that "[t]he Congress and the executive have taken mutual and joint action" in prosecuting the Vietnam War from the very beginning. It pointed to the Gulf of Tonkin Resolution whose "broad language ... clearly showed the state of mind of the Congress and its intention fully to implement and support the military and naval activities" of the president. In *Massachusetts v. Laird* (1971), an appeals court found that Congress had amply participated in the Vietnam War in the form of appropriations and selective service extensions.[6] Although the court held that the Constitution requires the "joint participation of Congress in determining the scale and duration of hostilities," it rejected the argument that a declaration of war was required to satisfy the joint concord standard, observing that no language in the Constitution says that Congress must declare war before supporting war. Most important, the court held that it would not decide which institution had what war power, but rather would accept the legality of war powers exercised by the national government when the president and Congress were held to be acting in joint concord.

Even after Congress repealed the Gulf of Tonkin Resolution (thereby ending joint concord in prosecuting the Vietnam War), a federal appeals court ruled in *Da Costa v. Laird* (1971) that the repeal did not change the fact that when the war began Congress had acquiesced in executive actions and had supported them.[7] "It was not the intent of Congress in passing the repeal amendment to bring all military operations in Vietnam to an abrupt halt," the court held. Instead, the court saw repeal as part of the process of Vietnamization of the war that had been started by the president, and it claimed that the war involved "mutual action by the legislative and executive branches." This claim, however, was quite a stretch, considering that the Nixon administration had opposed the repeal measure. Nevertheless, the court ruled that Congress and the president, not the courts, would decide how the war would wind down. Then it added a bit of dicta (language not needed for the decision), observing that "if the executive were now escalating the prolonged struggle instead of decreasing it, additional supporting action by the legislative branch over what is presently afforded might well be required." Yet in 1973, after the president escalated the war to put pressure on the North Vietnamese to negotiate an end to the war, the court did not find that the escalation required any "additional supporting action" by Congress. The court backed down from its earlier holding in *Da Costa* about escalation, and now it claimed that there was a "lack of discoverable and manageable judicial standards" and that "judges, deficient in military knowledge[,]" could not make decisions about whether a specific military operation constituted an escalation of the war.[8] By the end of the Vietnam conflict, the practical effect of judicial rulings on war powers cases was to provide the executive with great flexibility in the exercise of war powers.

THE FAILURE OF THE WAR POWERS RESOLUTION

In response to these court decisions, Congress passed in 1973 the War Powers Resolution (WPR) over President Nixon's veto. The WPR required the president to consult Congress in every possible instance before sending armed forces into either hostilities or a situation in which hostilities might be imminent; he was to report to Congress within forty-eight hours of doing so and every six months thereafter. It also required the president to withdraw forces if within sixty days he had not received from Congress a declaration of war, specific authorization, or an extension of the sixty-day period. He also was to withdraw forces if Congress, by concurrent resolution, required him to withdraw them. In such instances, he was given thirty days to execute the withdrawals.

Every president from Nixon to George W. Bush has denied that the WPR is constitutional. Moreover, they have sabotaged the resolution by failing to consult with Congress prior to the introduction of forces (they provide briefings instead) and by issuing one- or two-page "reports" that they say are consistent with the WPR but not in compliance with it. For example, in 1982 Ronald Reagan signed a measure Congress had passed extending his time period under the WPR, but in his signing statement he insisted that the legislature could not set conditions on his use of the armed forces. Congress, for its part, has turned a blind eye to case after case of presidential nonfeasance or misfeasance involving the WPR. In 1987, in the midst of a crisis with Iran over American-flagged Kuwaiti shipping in the Persian Gulf, Congress gave up entirely on trying to make the WPR a vehicle for joint decision making and instead used the more traditional authorization after the fact. During the crisis, 110 unhappy members of the U.S. House of Representatives contended that the Reagan administration had ignored the reporting requirements of the WPR by using U.S. naval vessels to escort the Kuwaiti tankers and engage in combat with Iranian mine-laying vessels. They then asked a federal court to rule that a report had been required months before. The judge not only refused to rule on the suit, but also observed that the very constitutionality of the WPR could not be assumed.

In both wars against Iraq, and in the intervening hostilities in the Balkans, the war powers of Presidents Clinton and both Bushes were left unscathed after judicial challenges. In *Dellums v. Bush* (1990), fifty-three members of the House and one senator sought a court order prohibiting George Bush from using armed forces for a war against Iraq in 1990.[9] In that case, Judge Harold Greene held that executive claims of complete war powers were too broad, denied that executive war powers could not be isolated from congressional powers, and further denied that harmonization of war powers was a political question, thereby abandoning two decades of contrary federal court doctrine. But having done so, he then used a new procedural dodge to avoid making a decision: the court could not rule because the case was not "ripe" for decision. "It would be both premature and presumptuous for the court to render a decision … when the Congress itself has provided no indication whether it deems such a declaration either necessary on the one hand or imprudent on the other." Greene would not take choices out of Congress's hands or use judicial injunctive relief absent a showing that it was what Congress itself required under the WPR. The intent of the WPR was that congressional inaction would lead within sixty days to the withdrawal of U.S. forces. But after the *Dellums* decision, it was clear that in the face of congressional inaction the courts would excuse themselves from enforcing the WPR, enabling the president to ignore it.

Even with this latitude, the only recent instances in which a president has engaged in war making without congressional support occurred under Bill Clinton. In 1994 he used war powers to threaten an invasion of Haiti and force out a ruling junta, in spite of the misgivings expressed in several nonbinding congressional resolutions that military operations should be authorized in advance and a subsequent resolution expressing the sense of the Senate that he should have consulted with Congress in advance of threatening force. Clinton relied on a resolution from the UN Security Council calling for regime change in Haiti—even though the Senate later passed a resolution saying that the UN resolution did not constitute authorization for the deployment of U.S. forces. In a second instance, in 1995 Clinton ordered the bombing of Serbian forces fighting in Bosnia without seeking or obtaining congressional authorization. Instead, he relied on NATO's establishment of a no-fly zone. He also did not seek advance congressional approval when he bombed Serbia in 1999 to end its war crimes in Kosovo. His counsel even argued that in the absence of a congressional prohibition, the WPR actually recognized the right of the president to use his own war powers—an argument that turned the intent of the law on its head.

In *Campbell v. Clinton* (1999), a district court concluded that the members of Congress who brought the case challenging the president's actions did not have standing.[10] Congress itself had sent contradictory messages. At first, it voted down a proposed declaration of war against Serbia. It also cast a tie vote in the House on authorizing air strikes, and so the measure failed to pass. But it then voted to fund the bombing and voted down a proposed funding cutoff. Because of this inconsistent congressional activity—part endorsement and part attempted check—the court held that "the President here did not claim to be acting pursuant to the defeated declaration of war or a statutory authorization, but instead 'pursuant to [his] constitutional authority to conduct U.S. foreign relations and as Commander-in-Chief and Chief Executive.'" Ironically, then, because Clinton relied on his own claim of war powers rather than on an action by Congress, the legislators were held to lack standing.

In conducting hostilities against Iraq, both Presidents Bush did not act contrary to the intent of the framers. The elder Bush secured congressional authorization, but he also indicated in a news conference that he reserved the right to act in defense of U.S. interests based on his own prerogatives. Similarly, the younger Bush claimed that a 1998 congressional resolution calling for "regime change" in Iraq could be combined with a 2002 resolution authorizing the use of force against Iraq as a form of "joint concord." In both wars, after receiving congressional authorization, the final decision to attack was made unilaterally by presidents without consulting with or reporting to Congress. And once the fighting began, Congress supported both presidents. In the second Iraq conflict, Congress, by overwhelming bipartisan votes, passed a resolution supporting the troops, and within three weeks it appropriated some $80 billion, in a clear demonstration of joint concord.

George W. Bush also claimed he had an international mandate to proceed against Iraq, but here he played fast and loose with the wording of a UN resolution warning Iraq of "serious consequences" if it did not allow inspections for weapons of mass destruction. After the resolution was passed, three of the five permanent members of the UN Security Council issued a statement saying that a further resolution authorizing the actual use of force would be required, but Bush disagreed. Later, when the administration failed to obtain an explicit Security Council authorization for the use of force, Bush asserted that the United States had the sovereign authority to use force to assure its own national security. Still later, the president pledged on the 2004 campaign trail that he would never ask the United Nations for a "permission slip" before using force.

The federal courts, citing passage of the prior congressional resolution, held once again that war powers involved a political question. In *Doe v. Bush* (2003), active duty service personnel, their parents, and some members of the House sought a preliminary injunction to prevent Bush from initiating war against Iraq.[11] They argued that, by passing the resolution, Congress had unconstitutionally delegated to the president its power to declare war. The court, however, declined to rule, claiming that the issue was nonjusticiable. It also held that there was evidence of joint concord, because Congress had called for regime change and had authorized hostilities.

CONCLUSION

Since the nation's earliest years, presidents have used the military on their own prerogative, making decisions to use force unilaterally and obtaining congressional support after the fact. For their part, since the start of the cold war the courts have been reluctant to rule on "boundary questions" between the president and Congress, preferring to find evidence of "joint concord." Any attempt to try to hold the president to an ambiguous (perhaps nonexistent) constitutional standard is ultimately to engage in fruitless speculation about whether a presidential use of force goes beyond the framers' intent. The real issue is not that presidents have made war without the consent of Congress—for the most part they have obtained that consent either before or after using the armed forces in major hostilities—but rather that Congress has failed to insist that presidents follow the collaborative mechanisms of the War Powers Resolution before making these decisions and that judicial decisions have left presidents free to do so.

In the final analysis, the issues in debates over presidential war making do not really involve legitimacy—such as whether the president followed proper procedures, or whether he made a decision that was lawful and constitutional—although they are often presented that way by critics. Criticisms of the president's war power usually stem from disagreements with a particular presidential action. These questions about the viability or wisdom of the policy, rather than attempts to parse original intent from limited debates and vague constitutional clauses, are the ones that really matter.

8

RESOLVED, fighting the war on terrorism requires relaxing checks on presidential power

PRO: John Yoo

CON: Louis Fisher

"Are all the laws, but one, to go unexecuted, and the government itself to go to pieces, lest that one be violated?" That was the question Abraham Lincoln posed in the message he delivered to a special session of Congress on July 4, 1861, a message that sought to justify the extraordinary actions he had taken during the preceding three months without congressional approval. He had suspended habeas corpus and held rebel leaders without trial in military prisons, he had blockaded southern ports, and he had called out 75,000 troops to suppress the rebellion and enforce federal laws. His actions, "whether strictly legal or not," he told Congress, had been thrust upon him by "public necessity." Fighting a civil war, Lincoln was telling Congress, required relaxing the normal constitutional checks on executive power.

Lincoln's sentiments echoed those Thomas Jefferson had expressed in a letter he penned not long after leaving the White House. "Strict observance of the written laws," Jefferson acknowledged, "is doubtless *one* of the high duties of a good citizen, but it is not *the highest*." Jefferson continued:

> The laws of necessity, of self-preservation, of saving our country when in danger, are of higher obligation. To lose our country by scrupulous adherence to written law, would be to lose the law itself, with life, liberty, property and all those who are enjoying them with us; thus absurdly sacrificing the end to the means.

These principles, Jefferson explained, did not apply to "persons charged with petty duties, where consequences are trifling, and time allowed for a legal course." For the vast majority of people in the vast majority of situations, obedience to the law was a solemn duty. But those few who "accept of great charges" must "risk themselves on great occasions, when the safety of the nation, or some of its very high interests are at stake." This is how Jefferson justified the Louisiana Purchase to himself and others: his "transgression of the law," he insisted, was warranted by the "great ... advantage" it brought to the security and prosperity of the nation.

The belief that emergencies require extraordinary grants of power to the executive is as old as representative democracy itself. In *The Second Treatise of Civil Government*, written in 1690, John Locke explained that "since in some governments the lawmaking power is not always in being, and is usually too numerous, and so too slow, for the dispatch requisite to execution; and because also it is impossible to foresee, and so by laws to provide for, all accidents and necessities that may concern the public," it was necessary that there be "a latitude left to the executive power, to do many things of choice which the laws do not prescribe." This power "to act according to discretion, for the public good, without the prescription of the law, and sometimes even against it, is that which is called prerogative."

In insisting, then, that the normal checks on executive power needed to be temporarily relaxed to respond effectively to the murderous attacks of September 11, 2001, George W. Bush and his administration were invoking an idea with a distinguished pedigree. But the "war on terror" is different from past wars or emergencies in that it is more difficult to envision what victory looks like. The Civil War came to an end when the armies of the North defeated the armies of the South; World War II finished when the Allied armed forces defeated the armed forces of Germany and Japan. An indefinite war on terrorism raises the question of whether temporary grants of executive power will become permanent enhancements of executive power.

John Yoo and Louis Fisher offer radically different answers to the question of whether the war on terror requires the nation to relax constraints on executive power. Yoo, who served in the Justice Department's Office of Legal Counsel between 2001 and 2003, agrees with President Bush that a "new kind of war" and a "new kind of enemy" require new executive powers. It is foolish, Yoo suggests, to cling to outdated assumptions and practices in the face of terrible dangers that the framers could not possibly have envisioned. Fisher contends, however, that combating terrorism makes it even more important to adhere to the checks on executive power that have served the nation so well in the past. The framers' system of checks and balances, Fisher argues, were constructed for exactly those occasions when executive officials proclaim or seize upon national crises or emergencies to expand their power.

PRO: John Yoo

An American president faces war and finds himself hamstrung by a Congress that will not act. To protect the national security, the president orders actions that seem to violate statutes, invoking his powers as commander in chief. He is criticized for usurping dictatorial powers, placing himself above the law, and threatening to "break down constitutional safeguards." Commentators exclaim that the Constitution "does not give the President carte blanche to do anything he pleases in foreign affairs."[1] Senators and scholars denounce the policies as illegal and unconstitutional.

Is this President George W. Bush choosing to use harsh interrogation measures on high-ranking al-Qaeda leaders and wiretap suspected terrorists' communications without a warrant? Possibly.

But these particular attacks on presidential power occurred in the years preceding American entry into World War II. Many believed that President Franklin D. Roosevelt was violating the Neutrality Acts by sending destroyers to Great Britain in exchange for British bases. Upon hearing the news of FDR's deal, Princeton political scientist Edward Corwin wrote: "why may not any and all of Congress's specifically delegated powers be set aside by the President's 'executive power' and the country be put on a totalitarian basis without further ado?"[2] Corwin, the leading constitutional law scholar of his day, scoffed at the attorney general's claim that the president's commander in chief powers provided the authority to take such steps to protect the national security. It was "an endorsement of unrestrained autocracy in the field of our foreign relations, neither more nor less."

Throughout American history, times of crisis have called forth broad uses of presidential power, episodes invariably accompanied by loud protest that the president has arrogated monarchical powers. Yet history portrays such moments as times of challenge and presidential greatness. In the darkest depths of the Civil War, Abraham Lincoln invoked his powers as commander in chief to issue the Emancipation Proclamation and free the slaves of the Confederacy, acting wholly without the approval of Congress and in the face of contrary statutes. Then and since, critics have asserted that the Emancipation Proclamation violated the Constitution's protections for private property (in the *Dred Scott* decision, the Supreme Court had found slaves to be property). Lincoln took extraordinary measures to raise and fund an army without appropriations, used military force against the seceding states, suspended habeas corpus, and instituted military trials for civilians working with the Confederacy. Critics assailed him for seeking "absolute power" by acts "subversive of liberty and law, and quite as certainly tending to the establishment of despotism."[3] Civil liberties did suffer, but Lincoln led the Union through the terrible crises of secession, slavery, and civil war.

WAR WITH AL-QAEDA

The war on terrorism provokes similar criticism today, even though its unconventional nature underscores, more than ever, the need for a vigorous and flexible executive. On September 11, 2001, al-Qaeda operatives hijacked four commercial airliners and used them as guided missiles against the World Trade Towers and the Pentagon. Resisting passengers brought down a fourth plane apparently headed toward either the Capitol or the White House. The attacks disrupted air traffic and communications and caused about three thousand deaths and billions of dollars in losses. Both the president and Congress agreed that the attacks marked the beginning of an armed conflict between the United States and the al-Qaeda terrorist network.[4] Indeed, al-Qaeda's September 11 attacks amounted to a classic decapitation strike designed to eliminate the political, military, and financial leadership of the country.

Al-Qaeda is not a nation-state, nor is it an alter ego supported by a nation-state. As a non-state actor, al-Qaeda does not have a territory or population, nor does it seek to defend or acquire any specific territory. Its operations are also unconventional and, as strategic analysts like to say, asymmetric. Al-Qaeda soldiers do not wear uniforms, nor do they operate in conventional units and force structures. Rather, their personnel, material, and leadership move through the open channels of the international economy, and they are organized in covert cells. Al-Qaeda does not seek to defeat the enemy's regular armed forces on the battlefield; instead, it seeks to achieve its political aims by launching surprise attacks, primarily on civilian targets, using unconventional weapons and tactics such as placing concealed bombs on trains or using airplanes to commit suicide attacks. Victory for al-Qaeda does not come from defeating the enemy's forces and negotiating a political settlement, but from terrifying an enemy's society and coercing it to take desired action.

Another factor distinguishes the war against al-Qaeda from previous wars. In previous modern conflicts, hostilities were limited to a foreign battlefield while the American home front remained safe behind the two oceans. In this conflict, the battlefield can be anywhere, and there is no strict division between the front and home. The September 11 attacks themselves, for example, were launched by foreign forces within the United States. While American territory has witnessed foreign attacks in the past, most notably the attack on Pearl Harbor, the September 11 attacks constituted the first major attack on the continental United States by a foreign enemy since the War of 1812.

Like previous wars, an important dimension of the conflict with al-Qaeda has occurred abroad, where the U.S. armed forces and the intelligence agencies have played an offensive role aimed at destroying the terrorist network. But unlike previous conflicts, the war against al-Qaeda also has a significant domestic dimension. The initial salvo was launched by al-Qaeda operatives from within the United States, and al-Qaeda shows no lessening in its efforts to pull off another attack within the United States on the scale of September 11.

THE PRESIDENT'S POWER TO RESPOND

What is unconventional is not the exercise of presidential power in response to a dire threat to national security, but the nature of the struggle itself. The framers of the Constitution created an executive branch with a unitary design and broad authority precisely so it could respond to the demands of war. Structurally, a branch headed by a single person can process information more easily, analyze the situation and make decisions faster, and implement policies decisively and vigorously. In contrast, Congress's large numbers create severe transaction costs that prevent it from organizing and acting quickly, and the courts act slowly and address only issues that arise as a case or controversy over federal law. "Decision, activity, secrecy, and dispatch will generally characterize the proceedings of one man, in a much more eminent degree, than the proceedings of any greater number," Alexander Hamilton reminds us in *Federalist* No. 70, "and in proportion as the number is increased, these qualities will be diminished."[5]

The virtues of decisiveness, secrecy, and speed are at a premium during the unpredictable high stakes of war; hence, the framers vested the president with the executive power of commander in chief so he could marshal the nation's military with speed and decision to defeat its external foes. "Of all the cares or concerns of government," Hamilton wrote, "the direction of war most peculiarly demands those qualities which distinguish the exercise of power by a single hand."[6] "The direction of war implies the direction of the common strength," he continued in *Federalist* No. 74, "and the power of directing and employing the common strength forms a usual and essential part in the definition of the executive authority." To avoid the "mischiefs" and "dissensions" that would arise from multiple commanders, the framers vested the power to conduct war—the commander in chief power—in a single president.[7]

Thus, war naturally shifts power to the executive branch. This insight can be traced at least as far back as Alexis de Tocqueville. In his classic, *Democracy in America,* he observed that the presidency was a relatively weak office because the armed forces were tiny, the oceans protected the nation from Europe, and no natural enemies sat along its borders. "The President of the

United States possesses almost royal prerogatives, which he has no opportunity of exercising; and the privileges that he can at present use are very circumscribed. The laws allow him to be strong, but circumstances keep him weak." But that would change as America grew, Tocqueville predicted. It is in foreign relations "that the executive power of a nation finds occasion to exert its skill and its strength." If the national security of the country "were perpetually threatened, if its chief interests were in daily connection with those of other powerful nations," Tocqueville continued, "the executive government would assume an increased importance in proportion to the measures expected of it and to those which it would execute."[8] The more unconventional and unprecedented the challenge of a specific war, such as the war on terrorism, the more our constitutional system will demand the flexibility, decisiveness, and speed that only the executive branch possesses.

HISTORICAL CONSIDERATIONS AND THE WAR ON TERRORISM

Every president since World War II has consistently argued that the Constitution's commander in chief power gives him the right to use force abroad to protect the nation's security and interests. Presidents have consistently refused to acknowledge the constitutionality of the 1973 War Powers Resolution, and several have violated its terms. In these situations, Congress has often recognized the president's right to use force, as it did in its 2001 Authorization to Use Military Force and its acquiescence in the numerous presidentially led interventions abroad. Even the case of *Youngstown Steel Sheet & Tube v. Sawyer,* much beloved by supporters of congressional authority, does not take away the president's powers abroad.[9] *Youngstown* held that the regulation of the steel mills in wartime remained within Congress's power to legislate on domestic affairs. It did not address the president's authority over the armed forces during war, nor did it address the scope of the commander in chief's power to set military strategy or tactics, direct the military, or gather intelligence. *Youngstown* even acknowledges that if Congress attempts to limit presidential action, the executive could prevail by relying on "his own constitutional powers minus any constitutional powers of Congress over the matter."[10]

The Bush administration's claims of executive authority in the war on terrorism fall into the tactical and strategic decisions appropriate to the commander in chief. Commanders have long set the standards for the capture and treatment of enemy prisoners. The executive branch has played the leading role in the development of the laws of armed conflict, and it is up to the president and military commanders to decide how to enforce them. The Lincoln administration issued the first code of the laws of war. The Wilson administration found that unrestricted submarine warfare was a casus belli. FDR approved the strategic bombing of Germany and Japan, even when hundreds of thousands of civilians were killed—a position put on stark display by President Harry S. Truman's decision to drop the atomic bomb. President Ronald Reagan refused to adopt an international agreement extending the Geneva Conventions to irregular fighters because it would have given terrorists the same status as regular troops. Congress has power over the funding and creation of the military and the authority to pass laws for the "Government and Regulation of the land and naval Forces," but it has never sought to prevent the president from making critical decisions about the best means to prevail on the battlefield.

Even the Bush administration's domestic pursuit of al-Qaeda terrorists, while controversial, has followed the example of past presidents confronted with enormous security challenges. The military has detained hundreds of al-Qaeda terrorists at Guantanamo Bay without access to civilian courts and has established military commissions to try dozens of them for war crimes. Bush designated several U.S. citizens and permanent resident aliens as enemy combatants and ordered their detention without criminal trial. This policy is consistent with presidential actions in the Civil War and World War II. President Lincoln ordered the detention of 12,000 American citizens without criminal charge (not to mention the many more Confederate prisoners of war who, under Lincoln's theory of the war, remained American citizens) for assisting the Confederacy and deprived them of the right to seek a writ of habeas corpus.[11] And FDR ordered Nazi saboteurs (two were American citizens) arrested on American territory to be detained without criminal charge and tried by military commission.

What has changed has not been presidential policy, but the Supreme Court's decisions. In the Civil War, the justices refused to review the detentions and military trials until the conflict was over;[12] in World War II, the Court upheld military trial and detention in *Ex parte Quirin*.[13] Today, the Supreme Court has sought to extend habeas to broader classes, such as non-U.S. citizens held outside the United States at Guantanamo Bay, and the Congress and the president have joined together to overrule them.[14] Most recently, for the first time in American history, a majority of the Court refused to obey the president and Congress and held that enemy prisoners, captured abroad and held abroad, have the right to seek release from the federal courts, a decision that could interfere with the conduct of the war.[15]

Electronic surveillance is yet another area where, the claims of critics to the contrary, the tactics in the war on terrorism fall within the practice of previous presidents in wartime. President Bush ordered the interception, without a warrant, of electronic communications involving suspected terrorists coming into or out of the United States.[16] The warrantless Terrorist Surveillance Program does not seek information to use in convicting terrorists; it only intercepts communications that would allow the intelligence agencies or armed forces to take action to prevent an attack against the United States. Although the Supreme Court has never decided whether a warrant is required in such situations, every lower federal court has found in favor of presidential power. As a special federal intelligence court said in upholding the constitutionality of the Patriot Act in 2002, every federal appeals court to address the question has "held that the President did have inherent authority to conduct warrantless searches to obtain foreign intelligence information."[17] The FISA (Foreign Intelligence Surveillance Act) Appeals Court did not even feel that it was worth much discussion. It took the president's power to do so "for granted" and observed that "FISA could not encroach on the President's constitutional power."[18]

Again, Bush's tactics in the war on terrorism were not unprecedented, but instead relied on past presidential practice. Every chief executive from Woodrow Wilson to Jimmy Carter similarly ordered, without a judicial warrant, the interception of electronic communications thought to be related to national security threats from abroad.[19] FDR went so far as to order such surveillance (more than a year and a half *before* Pearl Harbor) even though the Supreme Court had recently read an existing federal law to prohibit government interception of electronic communications without judicial approval. Roosevelt claimed that the Supreme Court could not have intended "any dictum in the particular case which it decided to apply to grave matters involving the defense of the nation."[20]

History shows that President Bush's counterterrorism policies have reduced civil liberties less than the policies of his predecessors who also faced war. The United States has always had to balance civil liberties and security interests, and in wartime liberties will be narrowed to give the government broader freedom to win. Unless one wants to prevent the government from making any adjustment in the trade-off between security and liberty, the presidency will be the branch that often must strike that balance in wartime.

CONCLUSION

The war on terrorism provides a cautionary tale about current proposals to rein in executive power. Despite the executive's constitutional powers, Congress always has the ability to counter the president. Trying to force the president to assume less initiative may make the office more comfortable for the risk averse, but it may also prevent the executive branch from rising to the great challenges confronting the nation. After Watergate, Congress embarked on a similar mission by passing statutes to hamstring future presidents. Some had little effect; some had a large one. One of those, the Foreign Intelligence Surveillance Act, required that presidents obtain a warrant from a special federal court before they could pursue domestic wiretapping for national security purposes. The courts and the Justice Department read the law to prohibit sharing intelligence with domestic law enforcement officials. As the 9/11 Commission found, FISA prevented American security agencies from tracking down al-Qaeda agents who had entered the country in the summer of 2001, by prohibiting the Central Intelligence Agency from informing the Federal Bureau of Investigation (FBI) about the identities and photographs of some of the 9/11 hijackers already in the country.[21] Overapplication of FISA also prevented FBI agents from searching the laptop computer of Zacarias Moussaoui, who was arrested at a Minnesota flight school days before the 9/11 attacks.[22] That law was passed with the best of intentions—to prevent another Richard Nixon from ever using the intelligence agencies to harass his domestic opponents. But it also blocked the executive branch from taking the swift action necessary to prevent a devastating attack on the American homeland.[23]

No one wants another Nixon to abuse his powers to attack his political enemies. But the restraints necessary for a risk-free presidency may sap the executive of those unique qualities that allow it to act decisively when the nation's security is at stake. A system that could abort another Nixon could also hamstring another Lincoln or FDR. The flexibility necessary for an energetic executive can lead to bad outcomes as well as the good. For the bad, our constitutional system seems up to the job. It has adequately handled the abusive presidents with political resistance or by forcing them from office. It would be a mistake to attempt to supplement the Constitution's measures for an executive run amok. While the Nixons of American history have cost the nation dearly, the Washingtons, Lincolns, and FDRs have brought the nation much more benefit, including that of national survival. If allowing presidents to exercise their constitutional powers risks executive abuse, it also brings with it the promise of flexibility and energy to meet the challenges of war.

CON: Louis Fisher

The war on terror after September 11, 2001, is unique in some respects. The United States faces new enemies: the Taliban and al-Qaeda. Unlike past wars when America fought against countries like France, England, and Germany, the Taliban and al-Qaeda are non-states. Previous wars came to an end. This one is unlikely to have the enemy surrender at a signing ceremony. Are those conditions unique and thus checks on presidential power must be relaxed?

More than two centuries of experience with presidential wars provide the answer: No. When threats emerge from an enemy, the record is clear that presidential action is more dangerous and ineffective when there are fewer checks. Secrecy and concentrated power in the executive branch lead to incompetent and illegal actions. Whenever constitutional checks are relaxed, threats to Americans are likely to come as much from their own government as from enemies.

A CONSTITUTION FOR PEACE AND WAR

The framers did not write a constitution to function only in time of peace. They had just come through a bitter and costly war with England in gaining their independence. With a small country of thirteen states perched on the eastern seaboard, they might have decided to concentrate power in a president. That option was rejected. They concluded that the country and the United States Constitution would be more secure under a system of separated powers and checks and balances. Although many of their values came from the Enlightenment, including the dignity of the individual and freedom of conscience, they also distrusted human nature and particularly executive officials who had power over war.

James Madison and other framers studied previous military actions. Their attitudes are reflected by John Jay in *Federalist* No. 4. Executives, Jay wrote, "will often make war when their nations are to get nothing by it, but for purposes and objects merely personal, such as a thirst for military glory, revenge for personal affronts, ambition, or private compacts to aggrandize or support their particular families or partisans." The pattern from past military conflicts was sobering. Executives engaged in wars "not sanctified by justice or the voice and interests of [their] people." The wars did not serve the national interest. Instead, they sent millions to their deaths and impoverished the national treasury.

William Blackstone, a British legal scholar of the eighteenth century, placed all external affairs with the executive, including declaring war. The framers broke with that model because they were creating a republican form of government that relied on popular sovereignty rather than monarchical power or the divine right of kings. Of all the powers of military and foreign affairs that Blackstone assigned to the executive (including declarations of war, appointing ambassadors, and making treaties), the framers did not place a single one exclusively with the president. Such powers are either vested in Congress alone (declaring war, authorizing small wars called "reprisals," raising and supporting armies, and making rules for the military) or shared between the president and the Senate (appointments and treaties).

The Constitution reserves to Congress alone the authority to take the country from a state of peace to a state of war. No president challenged that principle until President Harry Truman went to war against North Korea in 1950 without ever coming to Congress for approval. Presidents before that time recognized that they needed to come to Congress for a declaration or authorization.

REPRESSING CHECKS AND BALANCES

When war begins, presidents try to exploit military operations to limit checks and balances. The first such test came in 1798 after Congress, in a series of statutes, authorized war against France; it was called the Quasi-War because there was no formal declaration and the conflict remained a naval war, not a land war. In the midst of this emergency, President John Adams and Congress agreed to pass a number of laws shifting power to the executive branch. One piece of legislation was the Sedition Act. Fines and prison terms awaited any U.S. citizen or alien who wrote or said anything about Congress or the president deemed to be "false, scandalous and malicious." Citizens and aliens were not allowed to "defame" those political institutions or bring them into "contempt or disrepute." Nor could they "excite" any hatred against them or "stir up" sedition and resist federal laws or any presidential effort to implement them.

In short, the First Amendment freedoms of speech and press were to be subordinated to the supposed needs of war. Any criticism of government could be punished. The principle of self-government was now replaced by a government pitted against the sovereign people. Critics of the legislation warned that government would be seen not as a protector of the people but as the enemy of the people. Even though most of the newspapers in the country supported the Adams administration, any newspaper considered out of line was subject to prosecution for merely expressing opinions, no matter how well grounded in fact or reason.

Individuals prosecuted and convicted under the Sedition Act were later pardoned by President Thomas Jefferson. Congress passed legislation condemning the statute as "unconstitutional, null, and void" and appropriated funds to reimburse whoever had been fined under the statute. The bill helped to cripple the Federalist Party. Instead of a party known for upholding constitutional principles, its new reputation was that of a party hostile to popular government, public debate, free press, civil liberties, and immigrants. Within a matter of decades the Federalist Party passed out of existence.

The Civil War marked another threat to civil liberties. When the war began in April 1861, President Abraham Lincoln took a number of emergency actions, including withdrawing funds from the Treasury Department without an appropriation, placing a blockade on the South, raising a militia, and suspending the writ of habeas corpus. Yet Lincoln never claimed the prerogatives associated with the English king or any of the powers recognized by Blackstone. When Congress came back into session, Lincoln sent a message explaining what he had done, whether "strictly legal or not." Lincoln conceded that he exercised not only the powers available to him under Article II of the Constitution but also powers available to Congress under Article I. For that reason, he asked Congress to pass legislation that would retroactively authorize what he had done. In passing that statute, lawmakers understood that Lincoln did not have constitutional authority to take the actions he did. His frank admission that he acted outside his powers and that he needed congressional authority helped to preserve the Constitution. He never claimed that he could exercise the war power free of checks and balances.

When the United States entered World War I, President Woodrow Wilson and Congress decided once again to subordinate individual rights to national power. Legislation in 1918 covered seditious utterances. Whoever willfully spoke, wrote, or published "any disloyal, profane, scurrilous, or abusive language" about the form of the U.S. government, the Constitution, U.S. military forces, or the U.S. flag could be fined and sent to prison for twenty years. Rose Pastor Stokes was convicted for saying, "I am for the people and the government is for the profiteer." States passed their own sedition laws. Joseph Gilbert of Minnesota was sent to prison for commenting, "We were stampeded into this war by newspaper rot to pull England's chestnuts out of the fire."

A federal judge in 1920 attempted to resist efforts by government to prosecute citizens who spoke their minds: "Far worse than the immediate wrongs to individuals that [sedition laws] do, they undermine the morale of the people, excite the latter's fears and produce distrust of political institutions."[1] Punishing citizens for expressing their opinions created doubts about the sufficiency of law and authority. As the judge noted, heavy-handed and abusive actions by government "incline the people toward arbitrary powers, which for protection cowards too often seek, and knaves too readily grant." Under such conditions, he warned, the people "cease to be courageous and free, and become timid and enslaved."

After 9/11, some states reflected on their treatment of those who had opposed World War I. In May 2006, for example, Montana governor Brian Schweitzer issued pardons for seventy-five men and three women who were convicted under its sedition law during the First World War. He told their descendants: "Across this country it was a time in which we had lost our minds."[2]

Initially, the Supreme Court during World War I upheld efforts by the government to punish opponents of the war. In *Schenck v. United States* (1919), Justice Oliver Wendell Holmes concluded that antiwar circulars constituted "a clear and present danger" that Congress had a right to control. He reasoned that "in many places and in ordinary times the defendants in saying all that was said in the circular would have been within their constitutional rights." For Holmes, in time of war those rights disappeared and the country had to rally around the government. He offered the following analogy: "The most stringent protection of free speech would not protect a man in falsely shouting fire in a theatre and causing a panic."[3] But falsely shouting fire in a crowded theater to produce panic has nothing to do with circulating a leaflet that expresses an opinion about a war.

THE NEED FOR CHECKS

Writing for the *Harvard Law Review* in June 1919, Zechariah Chafee Jr. defended the right of citizens to criticize government in time of war.[4] He argued that the First Amendment declared a national policy that supported broad public debate on national issues. There were two separate interests. One was the individual's interest in speaking out on public policy. The other was society's interest in hearing criticism about the commitment of funds and troops to a war. To Chafee, criticism from members of the public was not seditious. It was a citizen's duty. The war clauses of the Constitution could not be used "to break down freedom of speech." It was a mistake to think that in time of war the Bill of Rights could be safely placed on the shelf until the emergency was over. After the government decides to exercise military force, "there is bound to be a confused mixture of good and bad arguments in its support, and a wide difference of opinion as to its objects." To sift truth from falsehood, government had to be subject to cross-examination by the public. Otherwise, war can easily be "diverted to improper ends, or conducted with an undue sacrifice of life and liberty, or prolonged after its just purposes are accomplished." For all those reasons, Chafee said it was a "disastrous mistake to limit criticism to those who favor the war."

In a later decision, *Whitney v. California* (1927), Justice Louis Brandeis offered a powerful defense of free speech, free press, and civil liberties in time of war.[5] The framers who "won our independence by revolution were not cowards. They did not fear political change. They did not exalt order at the cost of liberty." The purpose of government is to inspire individual thought and encourage public participation. The framers believed that "freedom to think as you will and to speak as you think are indispensable to the discovery of political truth." Public discussion was a political duty. The framers understood that political order could not be secured "merely through fear of punishment or its infraction; that it is hazardous to discourage thought, hope and imagination; that fear breeds repression; that repression breeds hate; that hate menaces stable government." The framers believed in the power of reason and public discussion and opposed "silence coerced by law—the argument of force in its worst form."

PRESIDENTIAL DECEPTION AND INCOMPETENCE

The record of the United States during the Quasi-War with France, the Civil War, World Wars I and II, the Korean War, the Vietnam War, and the period after 9/11 underscores the damage that government will do to individual rights and constitutional liberties when acting in the name of national interest. Too often the national interest is a euphemism for the political interest of a president and the president's party, based largely on the mistaken belief that a "great president" must be a war president. The experiences of Harry Truman in Korea, Lyndon B. Johnson in Vietnam, and George W. Bush in Iraq provide abundant evidence that costly and needless wars damage the president, the president's party, the United States, and regions of the world subject to U.S. interventions.

The Bush administration went to war against Iraq in March 2003 on the basis of suppositions and beliefs about Iraq possessing weapons of mass destruction. All of the administration's claims about mobile labs carrying biological agents, the existence of chemical and biological weapons, aluminum tubes supposedly capable of being used to produce nuclear weapons, Iraq seeking uranium ore from a country in Africa, unmanned aerial vehicles (drones) able to carry biological warfare agents, and Iraq's links to al-Qaeda proved to be utterly empty.[6]

The failure to find weapons of mass destruction in Iraq raises many questions. The Bush administration regularly issued alarming threats without any credible proof. Why were lawmakers and congressional committees unable to understand that executive claims and warnings are not evidence? Trained inspectors should have been sent to Iraq to collect facts before Congress decided to vote on a resolution authorizing war. As it turned out, legislative debate on the resolution, passed in October 2002, was uninformed and superficial, based not on evidence but on various partisan calculations about electoral benefits.

After the Iraq War began, the House Armed Services Committee held hearings on June 18, 2003. By that time it was obvious that Iraq possessed no weapons of mass destruction. When asked how the administration's claims could be so faulty, Deputy Secretary of Defense Paul Wolfowitz replied: "If there's a problem with intelligence … it doesn't mean that anybody misled anybody. It means that intelligence is an art and not a science." But executive officials in the Bush administration consistently treated intelligence as a precise science, not as vague claims of uncertain accuracy. The administration released a national intelligence estimate stating that "Baghdad has chemical and biological weapons." Not had, but has. Not programs, but weapons. No evidence supported the statement. The State Department issued what it called a "fact sheet," but the document was filled with baseless and misleading claims.[7] Appearing before the UN Security Council on February 5, 2003, Secretary of State Colin Powell made the case for war, presenting what he said were "not assertions" but "facts and conclusions based on solid intelligence." The world would later discover that what Powell presented were not merely assertions but untrue assertions.

Although the discussion above focuses on the administration of George W. Bush, a similar critique can be leveled at the Johnson administration and its erroneous statements about the Vietnam War. Just as the Bush administration went to war by arguing that Iraq had weapons of mass destruction, so did the Johnson administration claim in August 1964 that North Vietnam had made "unprovoked" attacks against American ships not once but, two days later, a second time. The attacks were not unprovoked. The United States had been providing assistance to South Vietnamese assaults on North Vietnamese positions. The so-called second attack was questioned at the time, and the National Security Agency (NSA) has recently admitted there was no second attack. NSA had received signals indicating a possible second attack, but after further analysis the agency concluded it received the signals late from the first attack.[8]

The pattern of executive officials resorting to lies and deception about the need for war continues after military operations begin. False reports are released to Congress and the public that claim substantial tactical and strategic successes. For those interested in a compelling account of executive deceit and incompetence, watch former secretary of defense Robert McNamara in *The Fog of War* explain his performance during the Vietnam War.[9] Confident and self-assured announcements about military operations had little to do with information available to executive officials.

There may be a temptation to dismiss what the framers said about the war power. It has been argued that the eighteenth-century model of checks and balances has no application to contemporary threats of nuclear war and terrorists wielding weapons of mass destruction. Under those pressing conditions, advocates of executive power claim that traditional legislative and judicial checks must be put aside. The false, costly steps toward war in 1964 and 2002 are recent reminders that the framers properly understood that executives are not to be trusted with the war power. The democratic process requires careful deliberation before committing the nation to war. The continuing capacity of executive officials for deception and incompetence makes checks and balances of ever greater importance.

9

RESOLVED, presidential signing statements threaten to undermine the rule of law and the separation of powers

PRO: Peter M. Shane

CON: Nelson Lund

When the colonists drew up their list of grievances against King George in the Declaration of Independence, their first complaint was that "he has refused his Assent to Laws, the most wholesome and necessary for the public good." Yet a decade later, when drawing up the new constitution in Philadelphia, the framers decided to give a veto power to the president, albeit in a qualified form. Only a few delegates—Alexander Hamilton, James Wilson, Gouverneur Morris—favored granting the president an absolute veto, but the convention very nearly required a vote of three-quarters of both houses to override a presidential veto. Only in the Constitutional Convention's final days, by a narrow 6-4 vote, did the delegates consent to lower the override threshold from three-quarters to two-thirds.

James Madison (as well as George Washington) had been among the delegates who objected to this late change. Madison insisted that a three-quarters override would be necessary to "check legislative injustice and encroachments." The diminutive Virginian shared Wilson's fear that the gravest threat to the new American government would come not from executive aggrandizement but from the "legislature swallowing up all the other powers." Madison and his allies may have lost the battle but they won the war. Since the Constitution's ratification more than 220 years ago, Congress has succeeded in overriding a president's veto on only 110 occasions. That is, only about 7 percent of the nearly 1,500 presidential regular vetoes have been overridden. And that leaves out of the equation the more than 1,000 pocket vetoes that presidents have issued in the nation's history—which Congress cannot override.

At first, the veto was used sparingly. Washington vetoed only two bills and Adams and Jefferson none at all. In the nation's first half century the regular veto was exercised on only thirteen occasions and the pocket veto ten times—with Andrew Jackson accounting for about half of these vetoes. Since the Civil War, however, every president except James Garfield and Warren Harding, neither of whom served even a single term, has issued at least as many vetoes as Jackson did.

As use of the veto increased, so too did legislative efforts to override the president's veto. John Tyler, dubbed "His Accidency" by detractors, was the first president to have a veto overridden. Congress roughed up the ineffective Franklin Pierce, overriding five of his nine vetoes. But that was kid-glove treatment compared with what Congress handed out to Andrew Johnson, whose twenty-one vetoes were overridden an astounding fifteen times. Pierce and especially Johnson were anomalies, however. For the rest of the nineteenth and twentieth centuries, presidents fared very well in sustaining their many vetoes. Only one president who served during this 130-year time span had a success rate of less than 75 percent: Richard M. Nixon, whose twenty-six regular vetoes were overridden on seven occasions, or 27 percent of the time.

If the pattern of the modern presidency is many vetoes and few overrides, then the George W. Bush presidency is a puzzle. During his first term George W. Bush never vetoed a bill, not a regular veto or even a pocket veto. In his second term, particularly after 2006 when Democrats gained control of the Senate and the House of Representatives, Bush began to wield the veto more often, but at the end of his two terms Bush had used the pocket veto only once and the regular veto on only eleven occasions. One has to go all the way back to Warren G. Harding, who served for only two and one-half years, to find a president who issued fewer vetoes than Bush. And, equally striking, one has to go back to Andrew Johnson's presidency to find a president who was less successful than Bush in sustaining his vetoes—four of Bush's eleven regular vetoes (36 percent) were overridden by Congress.

What accounts for the Bush anomaly? Of course, a large part of the reason that Bush did not use the veto in his first term was that his party controlled the Senate and House. But that is not the whole story. After all, Jimmy Carter issued thirty-one vetoes during his time in the White House even though his party controlled both houses of Congress. Similarly, Lyndon Johnson had a Democratic Senate and House but still vetoed thirty-one bills. Perhaps part of the reason that Bush relied less on the veto is that he discovered an alternative to the veto: the presidential signing statement. During his eight years in office, Bush issued 161 signing statements that challenged more than a thousand statutory provisions; 70 percent of these signing statements came in his first term.

The Constitution calls upon the president to explain a veto, but it is silent about what a president should do when signing a bill; it neither requires nor forbids a president from issuing a signing statement. The origins of this practice can be traced all the way back to the early nineteenth century, but it was only in the Reagan administration that signing statements began to be seen as a way for the president to shape the way the law would be interpreted, at least by executive officials if not judges. Not until George W. Bush's administration, however, did this practice generate widespread public comment, including a sharply critical 2006 report by an American Bar Association (ABA) task force that concluded that signing statements posed "a serious threat to the rule of law."

Nelson Lund and Peter M. Shane agree that Bush made unprecedented use of the signing statement, but they differ on whether this development is healthy or pernicious for American democracy. Lund takes to task the ABA task force report for its faulty constitutional analysis and insists that signing statements, properly understood, are neither unconstitutional nor dangerous. Shane, in contrast, like the ABA, views heavy reliance on signing statements as bad for both representative democracy and the rule of law. Whatever side one takes in this debate, it is a safe bet that future presidents will be reluctant to relinquish such a promising source of power and control.

PRO: Peter M. Shane[1]

When presidents veto legislation that Congress enacts, the Constitution obliges the president—as long as Congress or its clerks are available to receive presidential messages—to return that legislation "to that House in which it shall have originated" along "with his Objections."[2] In contrast, when the president signs proposed legislation into law, he is not required to say anything. The only constitutionally compelled presidential expression is his signature. Presidents, however, most often do speak about legislation they are approving. Usually presidents provide written messages touting the benefits that the legislation is projected to achieve. These are statements of no legal significance and not much importance otherwise.

Signing statements, however, may also state a president's policy reservations with respect to aspects of the new law. On occasions that were relatively rare—until the administration of George W. Bush—presidents even used signing statements to indicate doubts about the constitutionality of particular provisions of the newly enacted statutes they were signing. In such cases, presidents typically state that they will implement or interpret the statutory provisions in question to minimize the perceived constitutional difficulties. In some instances, presidents even say they will simply ignore the statutory provisions they take to be unconstitutional. It is this group of signing statements—signing statements that assert the partial unconstitutionality of what the president is signing and authority to ignore or reinterpret the law—that threaten to undermine the rule of law and the separation of powers.

The threat to the rule of law comes in two forms, one fairly mechanical and one more subtle but far more critical. To understand the mechanical problem, we have to focus on the numbers involved. By one scholarly count, the total number of statutory provisions to which presidents objected on constitutional grounds between the administration of James Monroe and the beginning of the first Reagan administration was 101.[3] The advent of the Reagan administration marked a significant increase in the frequency of the device plus a dramatic departure in terms of its intended institutional significance. Attorney General Edwin Meese persuaded the company that publishes new laws also to publish the president's signing statements. The signing statements were intended to become, as one report explained, "a strategic weapon in a campaign to influence the way legislation was interpreted by the courts and Executive agencies."[4]

During the course of two administrations, President Reagan issued seventy-one signing statements that objected to or unilaterally reinterpreted one or more statutory provisions he was signing into law.[5] In a single term,

President George H. W. Bush issued 146 such statements.[6] Most of the Bush objections involved the president's asserted foreign policy powers although many reflected the administration's full embrace of unitary executive theory and some of the more expansive claims of presidentialist constitutionalism. President Clinton used the signing-statement device also: his 105 signing statements raising constitutional objections[7] exceeded the record of President Reagan although Clinton's number was more modest than the record of President George H. W. Bush. In terms of robust presidentialism, however, none of these three presidents can compete with the record of the George W. Bush administration. In his first six years in office, President George W. Bush raised nearly fourteen hundred constitutional objections to roughly one thousand statutory provisions; this was more than three times the total of his forty-two predecessors combined.[8]

When presidential signing statements proliferate to this degree, they become unmanageable as a source of legal guidance. First, it is a fair guess that government lawyers rarely consult signing statements in deciding what a statute means because the statements have no clear legal status. Their relevance is likely to be episodic, if not wholly random. Second, because they are frequently conclusory, even cryptic, they hardly provide a source of legal reasoning from which separation of powers law can emerge in any orderly way. Typical signing statements offer no actual legal argument or reference to legal authority for the claims being asserted. Finally, many recent statements are quite obviously inflected with the political philosophy of a particular president, rather than law.

In an obvious gesture toward critics who argued that George W. Bush hugely abused the signing-statement prerogative, President Barack Obama, on March 9, 2009, issued a memorandum appearing to limit the use of signing statements to exceptional circumstances.[9] He promised to "act with caution and restraint, based only on interpretations of the Constitution that are well-founded." He then directed executive agencies as follows:

> To ensure that all signing statements previously issued are followed only when consistent with these principles, executive branch departments and agencies are directed to seek the advice of the Attorney General before relying on signing statements issued prior to the date of this memorandum as the basis for disregarding, or otherwise refusing to comply with, any provision of a statute.

In other words, he effectively told agencies: Don't act on the basis of my predecessors' constitutional qualms without approval by the Attorney General.

The problem is, however, that on March 11, 2009, President Obama signed into law the Omnibus Appropriations Act of 2009, accompanied by an Obama signing statement raising constitutional concerns of his own about numerous provisions. He wrote, for example:

> Sections 714(1) and 714(2) in Division D prohibit the use of appropria-tions to pay the salary of any Federal officer or employee who interferes with or prohibits certain communications between Federal employees and Members of Congress. I do not interpret this provision to detract from my authority to direct the heads of executive departments to super-vise, control, and correct employees' communications with the Congress in cases where such communications would be unlawful or would reveal information that is properly privileged or otherwise confidential.[10]

It is, of course, entirely obscure what operational significance the presi-dent's second sentence has. It seems utterly superfluous. But, if we assume that President Obama's signing statements are somehow intended to affect admin-istrative action of some sort, they will raise an obvious question when read in conjunction with President Obama's March 9 directive. That is, does the presi-dent now intend that agencies act upon *his* signing statements *without* having to consult the attorney general? And, if President Obama has a Republican suc-cessor, might that president issue a presidential order directing agencies to treat Republicans' signing statements as authoritative but not, without consultation, the Democrats' statements? A system of legal pronouncements that presump-tively alters with every change in the party identification of the incumbent president would not be a system of law at all.

Presidents might well promise to avoid this consequence by issuing signing statements only rarely and based only on the clearest and most persuasive understandings of constitutional law—legal theories that presumably every administration would endorse. Statements so confined would be very rare, and President Obama's statement on signing statements suggests something like such a limitation (even as he arguably departed from it). But, as I discuss below, President Bush's signing statements frequently fell short of this standard, and there is no obvious mechanism for effectively limiting presidents to the prom-ulgation of signing statements that might satisfy an "exceptional circum-stances" test. The only restraint possible—and one we desperately need—is a change in executive branch legal culture that cuts against gratuitous assertions of hypothetical presidential authorities.

But, putting aside the fact that signing statements have now become a burgeoning and largely unmanageable mass of obscure, politicized, and con-clusory quasi-legal objections to legislation, the second way in which signing statements threaten the rule of law runs much deeper. And to see this point, it must be recognized that the efflorescence of signing statements during the

George W. Bush administration was no accident. It is really not plausible that, between 2001 and 2006, Congress acted in constitutionally offensive ways three times more often than all the Congresses that came before, put together. Nor was President Bush facing a hostile Congress. For the first two of these years, Republicans held a majority in the House of Representatives; they were one vote short of control in the Senate. For the latter four years, Bush partisans controlled both houses of Congress. Bush was thus not pushing back against any genuine institutional threat to executive power.

Instead, the Bush administration sought to take advantage of the fact that there is virtually no formal legal or other institutional check on the content of signing statements. The president and his lawyers used signing statements in order to fabricate a body of official documents that might lend credence to an audacious and largely unsupportable theory of expansive executive power. No president wants to appear to claim to be above the law. The president's lawyers want to have some text to hold up as authoritative legal support for any claim of executive authority. Constitutional text, statutes, and judicial opinions are the pieces of paper that usually serve this kind of function. Unfortunately for our most aggressive supporters of presidential authority, the Constitution is ambiguous, at best, on the nature of executive power. Congress enacts very few statutes that embody anything like congressional ratification for the executive branch's most prodigious ambitions. Few judicial opinions support what I call the "presidentialist" view of the Constitution because separation of powers disputes are rarely litigated, and the courts have not been receptive to extreme presidentialist claims of executive authority. There were thus no cases to cite with anything like strong support for many of President Bush's most frequently asserted claims, and there was frequently strong contrary authority. Thus a pressing need existed for the executive branch to manufacture its own legitimating documents, formal pieces of paper that seemed to sanction the president's expansive assertions of unilateral power.

Two examples crystallize just how bizarre were some of the president's claims. Consider first the president's signing statement for the 2006 Postal Accountability and Enhancement Act.[11] That act amends the law describing an agency called the Postal Regulatory Commission. As amended, this rather undramatic law now reads as follows:

> The Postal Regulatory Commission is composed of 5 Commissioners, appointed by the President, by and with the advice and consent of the Senate. The Commissioners shall be chosen solely on the basis of their technical qualifications, professional standing, and demonstrated expertise in economics, accounting, law, or public administration, and may be removed by the President only for cause. Each individual appointed to

> the Commission shall have the qualifications and expertise necessary to carry out the enhanced responsibilities accorded Commissioners under the Postal Accountability and Enhancement Act. Not more than 3 of the Commissioners may be adherents of the same political party.[12]

In signing the act, the president objected to this provision as one of two in the act that "purport to limit the qualifications of the pool of persons from whom the president may select appointees in a manner that rules out a large portion of those persons best qualified by experience and knowledge to fill the positions."[13] He then went on to state that the executive branch would construe these provisions "in a manner consistent with the Appointments Clause of the Constitution."[14] In other words, President Bush wanted to go on record as objecting to this innocuous statute as a violation of his power to nominate and appoint officers of the United States, and he said he would read the law in some unspecified manner that would be consistent with his authority.

Putting aside constitutional issues for a moment, what exactly could the president be thinking here? The statute invites the president to nominate new commission members "on the basis of their technical qualifications, professional standing, and demonstrated expertise in economics, accounting, law, or public administration." What "large portion of those persons best qualified by experience and knowledge" could possibly be excluded by this requirement? Because Congress's specifications are so broad and commonsensical, there is no plausible objection to be made that Congress's new version of the law compromises the public interest in a serious way.

The strangeness of the president's insistence is all the more apparent, however, if one considers the institutional context. The statutory qualifications for postal rate commissioners are legally unenforceable. If the president fails to nominate someone meeting the statutory standards, no one can sue him. Senators might decline to confirm a nominee they believe falls short of the statutory standard, but senators are entitled to reject any nominee for any reason they want, so this hardly leaves the president worse off. Objecting to a statutory specification of qualifications in this context amounted to nothing but pointless swagger. It was really to say to Congress, "I, the president of the United States, am offended, constitutionally speaking, that you think I even have to listen to you with regard to the qualifications of potential officeholders. It is irrelevant that this office operates directly to fulfill Congress's constitutionally vested authorities with regard to interstate commerce and the post."

Many of President Bush's constitutional objections fell within areas about which presidents are usually protective. Of the nearly 1,400 objections lodged in signing statements between 2001 and 2006, 84 mentioned potential interference with commander in chief powers, 144 mentioned interference with his constitutional authorities regarding diplomacy and foreign affairs, and another 183 pointed to alleged violations of the president's constitutional authorities to withhold or control access to information to protect foreign relations or national security, sometimes mentioning also the president's power to protect executive branch deliberative processes or the performance of the executive's constitutional duties.[15]

Even in these traditional contexts, however, the substance of the president's objections was often extreme and hypertechnical. My second example of presidential bizarreness is this: A statutory provision Bush thought in conflict with his commander in chief powers would put limits on the number of Defense Department civilian and military personnel who could be assigned to the Pentagon's Legislative Affairs office.[16] According to the president, Congress "cannot constitutionally restrict the authority of the president to control the activities of members of the armed forces, including whether and how many members of the Armed Forces assigned to the office of the Chairman of the Joint Chiefs of Staff, the combatant commands, or any other element of the Department of Defense shall perform legislative affairs or legislative liaison functions."[17] In other words, putting to one side the highly debatable proposition that the president is beyond congressional regulation in the use of the armed forces for bona fide military purposes, President Bush would actually have Americans believe that he has unlimited authority to determine how many soldiers and sailors it takes to lobby Congress.

Going beyond these somewhat astonishing claims in areas of traditional presidential concern are hundreds of claims in wholly novel areas. The president, for example, objected to 214 legally imposed reporting requirements as interfering with his constitutional authority to recommend measures to Congress.[18] Apparently, President Bush believed that the president's entitlement to speak personally to Congress entails a prohibition on Congress demanding any other reports or recommendations from the executive branch. This is a historically baseless argument. As our original secretary of the Treasury, Alexander Hamilton—the most pro-executive of the framers—clearly found himself as responsible for filing reports with Congress as to the president.[19] Any constitutional infirmity in the requirement of executive reports to Congress is entirely a figment of the contemporary presidentialist imagination.

In his first six years in office, President George W. Bush lodged 346 objections based on Congress's alleged interference with the president's control over the "unitary executive."[20] Many of these assertions seem to be merely "piling on" with regard to other, narrower objections. But others were distinctively rooted in an imagined presidential authority to direct personally the discretionary activity of every member of the executive branch on any subject, regardless of what the law prescribes. For example, one statutory provision to which the president objected on "unitary executive grounds" is Section 115 of a 2002 "Act to Provide for Improvement of Federal Education Research, Statistics, Evaluation, Information, and Dissemination and for Other Purposes."[21] The act creates the Institute of Education Sciences within the Department of Education, to be run by a director and a board. Section 115 requires the director to propose institute priorities for board approval. The president of the United States, of course, has no inherent constitutional power over education. Yet, executive branch lawyers seem to imagine that it somehow violates the separation of powers either to allow the director to recommend priorities or for the board to decide on those priorities without presidential intervention. In a similar vein is a "unitary executive" objection to a statutory provision requiring the secretary of agriculture to consider, in preparing the annual budget for the Department of Agriculture, the recommendations of an advisory committee on specialty crops.[22] Although the law does not require the secretary actually to implement those recommendations but merely to take them into account, the president implicitly believes that the president has inherent authority to forbid subordinates from giving any weight whatever to public policy input from any source other than the White House.[23]

The point here is not just that the content of these statements is legally insupportable. The very proliferation of such statements threatens the rule of law because they embody a kind of unchecked institutional ambition that feeds on itself. *Presidential signing statements in this extreme volume are both a reflection of and encouragement to a psychology of constitutional entitlement within the executive branch.* They are intended as a form of discipline within the executive branch, signaling that, to be a part of this team, all administrators must subscribe to the theory that our Constitution envisions a presidency answerable, in large measure, to no one.

There is thus a direct link between signing statements on topics as mundane as specialty crops and the dangerously irresponsible "lawyering" that attended the Bush administration's handling of Guantanamo and warrantless wiretapping. Official declarations of the theory of unilateral authority that fuels the president's stance on obscure matters helps to maintain the attitudes—the norms of governance—that lead to other, more consequential claims of unilateral executive authority. An important function of the George W. Bush signing statements was that they served as reminders to administration members, and especially to administration lawyers, of how the president wanted the administration to behave: claim maximum power, concede minimum authority to the other branches. Again, this is not the rule of law, but its opposite.

This is most profoundly how the proliferation of signing statements threatens the rule of law and the separation of powers. The repeated utterance of the president's imagined immunity to both important and obscure forms of congressional regulation cannot help but shape executive branch behavior by inducing allegiance to norms of hostility to external accountability. Unless confined to relatively rare instances where presidents are standing up for bedrock, well-established principles of executive authority, signing statements embody both a disregard for the institutional authorities of the other branches—especially Congress—and too often a disregard for the necessity to ground legal claims in plausible law. Presidents should curtail their use.

CON: Nelson Lund[1]

In 2006, a task force of the American Bar Association declared that presidential signing statements—especially those issued by George W. Bush—threaten "the rule of law and our constitutional system of separation of powers."[2] Although the ABA report was signed by several prestigious members of the elite legal establishment, its position is analytically untenable and irresponsibly hyperbolic.

The key conclusion in the ABA report is that a president violates the Constitution when he announces that he regards some provision in a bill he signs as unconstitutional and unenforceable, or interprets the provision in a manner inconsistent with what the report calls "the will of Congress."

The dominating error in the ABA report is the notion that the president has a "constitutional obligation to veto any bill that he believes violates the Constitution in whole or in part," and that he therefore must either veto a bill or enforce all of its provisions. Which part of the Constitution imposes this choice on the president? The ABA report offers two answers, based on different provisions of the Constitution. Neither answer can withstand scrutiny.

PRESENTMENT CLAUSE

The Constitution specifies how a bill may become a law:

> Every Bill which shall have passed the House of Representatives and the Senate, shall, before it becomes a Law, be presented to the President of the United States; If he approve he shall sign it, but if not he shall return it, with his Objections to that House in which it shall have originated [and the veto may be overridden by a two-thirds vote of each House]. If any

> Bill shall not be returned by the President within ten Days (Sundays excepted) after it shall have been presented to him, the same shall be a Law, in like manner as if he had signed it, unless the Congress by their Adjournment prevent its Return, in which Case it shall not be a Law.

This clause offers no support for the ABA's claim that the president has a "constitutional obligation to veto any bill that he believes violates the Constitution in whole or in part." The presentment clause simply gives the president the option of returning a bill with his objections (of whatever nature they may be) for reconsideration, which may result in an override of the veto. He also has two other options. He can sign the bill; or he can do nothing, which has the same effect as signing it except when the so-called pocket veto provision is applicable. The presentment clause does not tell the president which bills to veto. Nor does it say anything at all about the existence, scope, or nature of a president's obligations with respect to the enforcement of enacted statutes (whether they were enacted during his administration or at some earlier time).

The ABA, however, claims that a president's refusal to enforce unconstitutional provisions in statutes that he has signed is actually an illegal line-item veto, that is, a decision by the president to veto part of a bill while signing the rest of the bill into law. The report is correct that the president has no authority to exercise a line-item veto. Similarly, the president is not permitted to repeal statutes unilaterally. But an announcement that the president will not enforce a provision because he regards it as unconstitutional is not the same as a veto.

Most significantly, other legal actors (including the courts and future presidents) may disagree with the president's interpretation of the Constitution. They will then treat the provision as valid, and enforce it. This cannot happen with a bill that the president has vetoed (unless, of course, his veto was overridden by Congress). For the same reason, a president's refusal to enforce statutes that he believes are unconstitutional is not the same as repealing them.

TAKE CARE CLAUSE

The ABA's second effort to justify its denunciation of signing statements is based on the constitutional provision requiring the president to "take Care that the Laws be faithfully executed." According to the ABA, "[b]ecause the 'take care' obligation of the President requires him to faithfully execute all laws, his obligation is to veto bills he believes are unconstitutional."

Once again, the ABA has confused questions about the president's obligation to execute the laws with the question of whether he is obligated to veto bills he believes are unconstitutional. The take care clause says nothing at all about an obligation of the president to veto any bill. In addition, the ABA fails to recognize that the Constitution itself is one of the "Laws" that the president is obliged to execute. The take care clause does not purport to determine what the president should do when one law (such as a statute) conflicts with another (such as the Constitution). That is an important question, but it is not answered by the take care clause.

THE PRESIDENT AND THE COURTS

For these reasons, the ABA is wrong to claim that the Constitution imposes a rule requiring the president to "veto any bill he believes would violate the Constitution in any respect." Not only is this rule absent from the Constitution, it is silly. And the ABA seems to realize that it cannot work. In a somewhat confusing passage, the report acknowledges that there may be exceptions to the ABA's rule. One example mentioned in the report is a bill that contains "insignificant [though unconstitutional] provisions in omnibus emergency-relief or military-funding measures, enacted as Congress recesses or adjourns, [that] would seem not to merit a veto."

Another exception that shows the unworkability of the ABA's rule involves the persistent inclusion by Congress of unconstitutional provisions in its bills. The report admits that Congress includes unconstitutional provisions in many bills and suggests that presidents may be free to sign some of these bills and treat the unconstitutional provisions as nullities. The report, however, confines this exception from its "veto or enforce" rule to a narrow class of unconstitutional provisions, namely those that the courts have already said are unconstitutional.

Some such exception would certainly be necessary to salvage the ABA's rule from unworkability. But why should this exception apply only in cases where the courts have already declared a certain type of statute unconstitutional? Or, in other words, why should presidents be obliged to enforce unconstitutional statutes that have not yet been litigated? The report explains: "Definitive constitutional interpretations are entrusted to an independent and impartial Supreme Court, not a partisan and interested President. That is the meaning of *Marbury v. Madison.*"

Perhaps because of this faith in judges, the ABA is extremely offended by the thought that the president might have what the report calls "the last word" on which statutes will go unenforced because they are unconstitutional. But whatever the reason for the report's statement, it is wrong.

First, the Constitution nowhere says that "[d]efinitive constitutional interpretations" are entrusted to the Supreme Court, and the Constitution nowhere says that the Supreme Court must always get "the last word" about the meaning of the Constitution. Furthermore, there is no reason at all to assume that judges are more impartial and disinterested than presidents when it comes to deciding how much power they think the Constitution gives them. If anything, the self-evident fact is that Supreme Court justices are *not* impartial angels incapable of overreaching with respect to their own power. Like presidents, judges may sometimes be able to get away with exercising powers the Constitution does not give them. But the mere fact that some people claim that the Constitution gives them final authority doesn't make it so. That goes for judges, just as it does for presidents.

In any event, the ABA is wrong about the famous Supreme Court decision in *Marbury v. Madison*, which nowhere made the sweeping claim to judicial supremacy attributed to it by the report. If anything, *Marbury* actually undermines the ABA's attack on presidential signing statements. That case held that the Supreme Court is authorized to refuse to enforce unconstitutional statutes. The most logically powerful argument in *Marbury* for that conclusion is this: faced with a conflict between the Constitution and a statute, courts have no choice except to give effect to the more authoritative of the two laws, namely the Constitution. That logic applies to the president every bit as much as it does to the Supreme Court.

Significantly, however, nobody on the Supreme Court has ever actually accepted all the implications of *Marbury*'s logic. Any justice who did so would have to conclude that conflicts between the Constitution and judicial precedent must always be resolved by giving effect to the Constitution, not the precedent. After all, if statutes enacted by the people's representatives are always trumped by the Constitution, it would seem to follow by inexorable logic that mere judicial opinions must also be trumped by the Constitution. According to the Constitution itself, the "supreme Law of the Land" includes the Constitution, statutes enacted pursuant to the Constitution, and treaties. Conspicuously absent from the list is any mention of judicial opinions.

In practice, the Supreme Court has developed a very complex and flexible approach to the exercise of constitutional review. There is almost nobody who would seriously maintain today that courts are obliged by the Constitution to enforce unconstitutional statutes. But it is also true that very few would seriously maintain that courts are *always* obliged to strike down statutes they think are unconstitutional, even in the face of thoroughly settled judicial precedent.

Presidents take the same general approach that the Supreme Court has taken, and properly so. In principle, presidents always have the option of refusing to enforce or comply with statutes they consider unconstitutional. But they are not obliged to ignore or defy *every* such statute. And the same goes for Congress. The Constitution nowhere imposes on the legislature an obligation to relentlessly impose its own constitutional views on other branches of government.

POLITICAL SELF-RESTRAINT

One might think that leaving the president, the Supreme Court, and the Congress with concurrent authority to decide on the meaning of the Constitution is an invitation to constitutional crises and ultimately to chaos. History demonstrates that this is not so. With respect to who gets "the last word" on the meaning of the Constitution and other laws, the simple fact is that each branch of government sometimes gets the last word, and sometimes does not.

The Supreme Court, for example, has all kinds of devices by which it avoids trying to become the last word on all constitutional questions. These include many doctrines under which the justices frequently decline to issue any decision at all, as well as countless rulings that give the so-called political branches broad discretion in exercising various constitutional powers.

Like the courts, presidents have also sought to minimize conflicts with the other branches. Over the years, for example, the president's legal advisers in the Justice Department have developed an elaborate internal jurisprudence that largely adheres to Supreme Court precedents. That jurisprudence displays some independence from the views of the judiciary, especially with respect to matters directly touching on the president's institutional interests, such as the scope of his executive authority. But the jurisprudence is memorialized in written legal opinions that take judicial decisions very seriously and treat them as dispositive on many issues. In addition, the interpretive techniques—such as the practice of interpreting statutes so as to avoid constitutional difficulties—whose use has sometimes generated controversy in both these Justice Department opinions and presidential signing statements are generally borrowed directly from the Supreme Court.

It is important to keep in mind that these Justice Department legal opinions are purely advisory so far as the president is concerned. The president is free to ignore or overrule them, and presidents sometimes do just that. Perhaps most important, presidents have not felt compelled to exercise every right they believe they have, or that the Justice Department tells them they have. There is a fundamentally important distinction between claiming the authority to do something and actually doing it.

George W. Bush himself grasped the difference, and perhaps better than some of his supposedly more sophisticated critics. That much, at least, is suggested by the following extemporaneous comment during a public press conference at which he was asked about one of his most controversial signing statements:

> I signed the appropriations bill with the McCain [anti-torture] amendment attached on because that's the way it is. I know some have said, well,

> why did he put a qualifier in [the signing statement]? And one reason why presidents put qualifiers in is to protect the prerogative of the executive branch. You see, what we're always doing is making sure that we make it clear that the executive branch has got certain responsibilities. Conducting war is a responsibility in the executive branch, not the legislative branch. But make no mistake about it, the McCain amendment is an amendment we strongly support and will make sure it's fully effective.

We all need to keep President Bush's commonsense point in mind when evaluating alarmist rhetoric like that found in the ABA report. Bush may have used his signing statements to *articulate* a relatively expansive view of presidential power somewhat more aggressively and systematically than his predecessors did, especially in connection with national security matters. But how much of this was limited to expressing his administration's constitutional views, and how much of it led to actual defiance of statutes? When I did a detailed study of the George H. W. Bush administration's jurisprudence of presidential power, I found that the first Bush had been quite aggressive in publicly claiming constitutional authority and extremely *timid* about actually exercising the powers he claimed to have. Could the same thing have been true of his son, George W. Bush?

After the Democrats took control of Congress in 2007, they directed the Government Accountability Office to conduct a study of the Bush administration's treatment of statutory provisions to which the president had objected in his signing statements. The most striking result of this research project was the GAO's inability to find evidence that the Bush administration failed to comply with even a single statutory provision as a result of objections articulated in a presidential signing statement.[3]

Like many others who study the Supreme Court, I think it has often misinterpreted the Constitution, sometimes badly and even inexcusably. I also disagree with a number of interpretations of the Constitution set forth in Justice Department opinions and presidential signing statements. And I believe that Congress has passed more than a few unconstitutional statutes, some of which have been signed by presidents and upheld by the Supreme Court. There is lots of room for reasonable debate about these issues, and about such questions as how much deference each branch of government should give to constitutional decisions reached by the others. But such debates are not usefully advanced either by the ABA report's shoddy legal analysis or by its hysterical claim that President Bush's signing statements constituted a threat to "the rule of law and our constitutional system of separation of powers."

Suppose that a president really did seriously abuse his power by, for example, systematically using dishonest interpretations of the law as a fig leaf for efforts to approximate the exercise of an unconstitutional line-item veto or to suspend valid existing statutes by executive fiat. That might trigger a truly serious constitutional confrontation, and if it did there can be little doubt about which branch would have the last word. Congress, after all, still has the power of impeachment.

In fact, Congress has been very cautious about using this power to enforce its interpretations of the Constitution, and the impeachment of Andrew Johnson suggests why. He was accused of violating the Constitution by refusing to comply with a statute that interfered with his control over the military. Many decades later, in *Myers v. United States* (1926), the Supreme Court decided (and correctly so, I believe) that the statute was an unconstitutional infringement on the president's legitimate authority. Johnson's trial in the Senate may also serve as a useful reminder of what a real constitutional crisis looks like. Had he been convicted and removed from office, what the ABA calls "our constitutional system of separation of powers" might indeed have been profoundly altered.

THE FUTURE OF SIGNING STATEMENTS

Those who signed the ABA report no doubt found President Bush's constitutional views highly offensive, and they no doubt strongly disagreed with his policies on national security and other matters. But offending your political opponents, or an organized interest group like the ABA, is not quite the same as threatening the rule of law and the separation of powers.

Even if one assumes that Bush was wrong about some of the specific statutory provisions that he claimed were unconstitutional, it does not follow that these mistakes posed any real danger to the Republic. Fortunately, President Barack Obama has refused to be stampeded by the ABA and other critics of Bush. While hinting that he intended to use signing statements more cautiously than his predecessor, Obama announced on March 9, 2009, that they "serve a legitimate function in our system, at least when based on well-founded constitutional objections." Two days later, Obama issued a signing statement objecting to numerous provisions in an appropriations bill and declaring that he would either ignore them or interpret them to be consistent with his own views of his constitutional authority. As this book went to press, Obama had issued several more such signing statements, all of which contained constitutional objections just like those that Bush had been excoriated for raising.

If the ABA's overwrought attack on signing statements has any significance at all, perhaps it is this: by crying wolf about President Bush, the ABA and the prestigious authors of its report have made it less likely that they will be taken seriously if they ever have occasion to warn the nation about a genuine threat to the constitutional order.

10

RESOLVED, the president has too much power in the selection of judges

PRO: David A. Yalof

CON: John Anthony Maltese

Few issues have engendered more controversy in Washington in recent years than the selection of federal judges. Republican president Ronald Reagan's nomination of Robert H. Bork to the Supreme Court in 1987 provoked a bitterly partisan debate between anti-Bork liberals and pro-Bork conservatives. In the end, the Democratic-controlled Senate voted Bork down. Reagan's Republican successor as president, George H. W. Bush, sparked an even fiercer firestorm when he nominated Clarence Thomas, a conservative, to the Court in 1991. Amid charges and countercharges about Thomas's alleged sexual harassment of law professor and former employee Anita Hill, the Senate confirmed him by the narrowest majority of any Supreme Court nominee in history, 52-48. When Bill Clinton, a Democrat, became president in 1993 and the GOP took control of Congress in 1995, Republican members of the Senate Judiciary Committee defeated many of Clinton's appellate court nominations by refusing to send them to the full Senate for a vote. Although Republican George W. Bush enjoyed a Republican Senate for most of his time as president, Democratic senators were able to defeat or delay several of his court of appeals nominees by threatening or launching filibusters. Bush managed to win Senate confirmation of two Supreme Court nominees, John G. Roberts Jr. and Samuel A. Alito Jr., but only after succumbing to political pressure to withdraw the nomination of White House counsel Harriet Miers. Barack Obama's first choice for the Supreme Court, Sonia Sotomayor, was both hailed and attacked as the first Latina in history to be nominated.

These controversies over judicial nominations have stemmed mainly from the bitter ideological partisanship that characterizes contemporary politics, with conservative Republicans and liberal Democrats fighting fiercely about a whole range of issues. Such "polarized politics" has been aggravated by the frequency of divided government, in which one party controls the presidency and the other controls Congress, as well as by the willingness of the federal courts to wade into controversial issues such as abortion, school prayer, and affirmative action. In such a climate, seats on the Supreme Court and the thirteen federal courts of appeals are prizes worth fighting about.

The roots of the fights over judgeships, however, extend deep into the Constitution. Although the framers gave federal judges life tenure in order to remove them from partisan politics once they were on the bench, they entrusted the process by which these judges are appointed to intensely political actors. Specifically, the framers mandated that the president "shall nominate, and by and with the Advice and Consent of the Senate, shall appoint" judges to the federal courts. In other words, the power of judicial selection is a shared power that can be exercised only if both branches cooperate. The Senate cannot "nominate" anyone to serve on a federal court. Nor can the president give a nominee the constitutional "Consent" necessary to make someone a judge.

Does the president have too much power in the selection of federal judges? Although David A. Yalof says yes and John Anthony Maltese says no, both agree that much hinges on the meaning of the other crucial word in the Constitution's judicial appointments clause: "Advice." Specifically, did the framers want the president to seek advice from the Senate before making a judicial nomination, or did they intend to restrict the Senate's advisory role to the postnomination phase of the judicial selection process?

PRO: David A. Yalof

The late senator Strom Thurmond, a Republican from South Carolina, used to tell law school audiences a story that reveals just how far the theory of separation of powers sometimes strays from its actual practice. On October 23, 1987, the U.S. Senate rejected President Ronald Reagan's nomination of Judge Robert H. Bork to replace Lewis F. Powell Jr. on the Supreme Court. Within days of that defeat, the president's second choice for the post, Judge Douglas H. Ginsburg, withdrew his name from consideration amid allegations that he had used drugs while a Harvard Law School professor. By all accounts, Reagan, then a lame-duck president soon to be entering his final year in office, should have been at the nadir of his power to influence the appointment process. That is precisely the moment that Thurmond, then the ranking Republican on the Senate Judiciary Committee, chose to pay Reagan a visit at the Oval Office. As Thurmond told it, he had wanted to convince the president to nominate his close friend, U.S. Court of Appeals Judge William Wilkins of South Carolina, to the high court. Thurmond told President Reagan that it might be a good idea to put a southerner on the Court—after all, Powell was a southerner, and his retirement had left the high court without a justice from that region of the country. But Reagan apparently had settled on his own third choice for Powell's seat, and even from this relatively weak political position he was not about to let Thurmond or any other senators share in the decision-making process. Thurmond even recalled Reagan's quick retort to his pleas for Wilkins: "You're from South Carolina and you want Willie Wilkins on the Court. But I'm from California, and the next Supreme Court Justice will be Anthony Kennedy of California." So much for senatorial advice and consent. With the help of Thurmond and other Senate Republicans, Kennedy was quickly confirmed and sworn in as the next associate justice just a few weeks later.[1]

In the modern appointment process, presidential arrogance is business as usual when selecting federal judges and Supreme Court justices. Indeed, up through President George W. Bush, chief executives tended to choose their high court nominees without giving most senators the privilege of even a cursory consultation beforehand.[2] Even leading senators from the president's own party may discover the name of the president's nominee only a short time before everyone else. With its constitutional advice function a virtual dead letter, can the Senate fall back on its power to withhold consent for Supreme Court nominees? In theory, that power remains, but in practice it is only rarely exercised. For all the attention given to the nomination debacles of Bork, Ginsburg, Clarence Thomas, and, most recently, Harriet Miers, of those four only Bork was actually rejected by a vote of the Senate (Ginsburg and Miers withdrew, and Thomas was confirmed). In fact, between 1932 and 2009 only three of forty-five Supreme Court nominees have been rejected in an actual Senate vote on the merits of the nomination.[3]

Nor can senators find much consolation in the appointment process for the federal district and appeals courts, the venue in which senatorial advice has traditionally received its due. The era in which senators confidently instructed the White House whom to nominate for federal judgeships in their home states is long gone. Recent presidents have dominated the lower-court selection process, reducing senators from their own party to the status of well-respected advisers, on a par with important interest groups and other significant presidential constituents. Despite this shift in practice, Senate resistance to presidents' more objectionable nominees remains muted. Although Senate Democrats' resistance to President George W. Bush's lower-court appointments was unprecedented in one respect—the Senate minority leadership resorted to the filibuster time and time again to oppose ideologically extreme candidates—in raw numbers Democrats outright blocked fewer than 20 of Bush's 373 lower-court judicial nominees with a filibuster or negative vote. How did the presidency come to enjoy such a stranglehold over judicial selections? Some of the chief executive's increased leverage in this area mirrors the growth of presidential power as a whole during the twentieth century. Yet there is something especially disconcerting about the growth in the president's power to appoint judges. In foreign affairs, the nation, arguably, must speak with a unified voice. But lively dialogue between the nominating institution (the president) and the advising and consenting institution (the Senate) hurts no one, save those nominees whose credentials are so thin that they stand little chance of surviving more intense forms of review.

THE FOUNDERS AND THE JUDICIAL APPOINTMENT PROCESS

Judicial appointments were a hotly debated subject at the Constitutional Convention in 1787. The initial efforts to vest the appointment authority in the executive were soundly defeated. A proposal by James Madison, delegate from Virginia, to give the president the power to appoint judges "unless disagreed to" by two-thirds of the Senate was rejected, because it would tip the balance too far toward the executive. Proposals to have the Senate make all appointments enjoyed the support of a majority of delegates for nearly two months, but that plan was eventually discarded. In the end, the convention settled on a shared arrangement between the two branches. The final scheme of presidential appointment with the Senate's advice and consent was eventually approved as a way to create a mutually dependent process.

One noted scholar contends that by separating the act of nomination from the act of appointment (the Constitution says that the President "shall nominate, and by and with the Advice and Consent of the Senate, shall appoint …"), the framers meant to keep the Senate's advice and consent out of the nomination phase.[4] Such an interpretation would effectively merge the advice and consent functions into one: if the Senate must wait until after the president has submitted a nomination to advise, what difference is there between advising the president that a nominee will be rejected and actually rejecting the nominee with a formal vote? The framers would never have identified a separate advice function if they did not intend that function to have real influence in the nominating process.

The Constitution gives no specific criteria to guide the selection of justices, but this absence of criteria does not mean that the president was expected to have unlimited authority over the selection process. Consider the views of New York delegate Alexander Hamilton, perhaps the foremost advocate among the founders of a strong executive. In *Federalist* No. 77, Hamilton argued that Senate influence over presidential appointments was intended to provide a formidable check on the chief executive: "If by influencing the President be meant restraining him, this is precisely what must have been intended." At the same time, in *Federalist* No. 76 Hamilton assumed that the Senate would only rarely reject a president's nominees—after all, why would the Senate routinely reject candidates who emerge from a process in which the Senate offers significant assistance in the first place?[5]

In the early years of the Republic, the Senate quickly learned to practice what the founders preached. Although only one of President George Washington's nominees to the high court was rejected, that rejection was based on the Senate's *political* objections to the nominee, a clear rebuke to the notion that the Senate was intended to be merely a screening mechanism to ensure the minimal competence of judges. When, in 1795, Washington nominated John Rutledge of South Carolina to be chief justice, Rutledge's credentials were impressive, including previous service on the Supreme Court as an associate justice. But Rutledge had openly opposed ratification of the Jay Treaty with England, and he had urged Washington not to sign it. That stand put Rutledge squarely at odds with the Federalist majority in the Senate, which rejected his nomination 10-14. President Washington may have been disappointed by this turn of events, but he never openly challenged the Senate's power to reject his nominees on political grounds. Because he had acted as president of the Constitutional Convention, Washington knew firsthand that the appointment authority had been granted to two branches rather than one.

THE ADVICE FUNCTION

For much of U.S. history, presidents have sought senators' advice on judicial appointments, and not just because the words of the Constitution encouraged them to do so. Involving senators at an early stage in the process was smart politics—it invested senators in the appointment process, thereby creating critical allies for the confirmation stage. Many senators were also knowledgeable Washington insiders, and most presidents valued their advice. Thomas Jefferson even relied on House and Senate members to scout out potential Supreme Court nominees. When Associate Justice Alfred Moore of North Carolina retired in 1804, Jefferson looked to two members of the South Carolina congressional delegation, Sen. Thomas Sumter and Rep. Wade Hampton, to help him find a replacement. Presidential–Senate dialogue over judicial nominees continued into the early twentieth century. For example, in 1902 Republican senator Henry Cabot Lodge of Massachusetts championed Oliver Wendell Holmes for a seat on the Supreme Court.

By contrast, presidents today rarely seek senatorial advice on Supreme Court vacancies. Modern presidents up through George W. Bush mobilized their administrations to identify and research prospective nominees behind the scenes, and senators learned about the shortlist of nominees only at the tail end of the process, after the president and his advisers have already performed most of the more critical vetting functions. On the rare occasion that the president publicly seeks advice, the process often entails meaningless consultations between presidential aides and senators about a decision that has already been made. For example, Chief of Staff Howard Baker insisted, even after Robert Bork became President Reagan's clear choice to fill a Court vacancy, that White House officials go through the charade of meeting with key senators and asking their advice about an artificial list of "potential nominees." Some observers believe that President Bill Clinton leaned heavily on senators for advice before making his two Supreme Court nominations: Stephen G. Breyer and Ruth Bader Ginsburg. In truth, however, in undertaking selection of nominees by trial balloon the Clinton White House floated names not only to senators but also to the public at large. In one instance, environmental groups were as influential as Senate Republicans in discouraging Clinton from nominating Interior Secretary Bruce Babbitt. Certainly, the Senate enjoyed no special privileges as an adviser in the process.

Even more dramatic changes have occurred in the lower-court appointment process, and once again senators have seen their opportunities to exert influence over such appointments sharply reduced. In the nineteenth century, such judgeships were mostly a matter of senatorial patronage. Well into the twentieth century, presidents continued to defer to senators—particularly those of the president's own party—on nominees to judgeships in their states. Indeed, that practice continued up until the 1970s. A president who violated this norm by nominating his own candidate over the objections of the home state senator risked seeing that nomination permanently buried by the Senate Judiciary Committee. That was precisely the fate suffered by William B. Poff, President Gerald R. Ford's nominee for the federal district court in Virginia. Senator William Scott, R-Va., preferred another candidate, and he made his views known to the president. When Ford boldly went ahead with Poff's nomination, the Senate Judiciary Committee, though run by the Democrats at the time, tabled the nomination in deference to their Senate colleague from the other party.[6]

Of course no amount of deference to home state senators would keep the White House from exercising free rein over all the seats on the U.S. Court of Appeals for the D.C. Circuit, now widely recognized to be the second most powerful court in America. Meanwhile, in the other lower courts presidents during the last quarter century have been increasingly willing to disregard the preferences of home state senators. President Reagan, for example, insisted that Republican senators identify three individuals for every judicial vacancy, and he required that those names meet his administration's stringent ideological criteria.[7] His successor in office, George H. W. Bush, continued this practice. At the end of the twentieth century, the rising use of "blue slips" by senators—a blue slip was in effect a veto over judicial appointments in a senator's state— allowed them to reassert some of their authority, but it did not result in a greater advisory role for the Senate.

In summary, today presidents control the choice of Supreme Court and D.C. Circuit Court nominees. For all other courts, senators play an active, if somewhat curtailed, role in the nominating process. The judicial appointment process now in place seems a far cry from the shared dialogue imagined by the framers.

THE CONSENT FUNCTION

Although senators' advisory function has been reduced substantially, the Senate can theoretically exert considerable leverage by withholding consent for the president's judicial nominees. In practice, however, the Senate only rarely exercises that right. In his award-winning book, *The Selling of Supreme Court Nominees,* my debate partner John Anthony Maltese speaks of the "increasingly contentious nature of recent confirmations."[8] Political scientist Mark Silverstein notes that in 1968 the politics of judicial confirmations underwent an abrupt transformation as "the presumption respecting presidential control was honored more in the breach than in the observance."[9] Yet what has the Senate gained in this supposedly new era of relative parity between the branches? As noted earlier, since 1932 only three Supreme Court nominees have been rejected outright by the Senate, and thirty-eight have been confirmed (four others withdrew before the Senate voted). Meanwhile, fifteen of the last eighteen nominees have been confirmed. Compared with those in the nineteenth century when one in four Supreme Court nominees was rejected, institutional relations in the modern era seem downright cooperative.

Changes in the procedures for confirmation have contributed to Senate deference to the president. Nominees appeared at public confirmation hearings for the first time in 1925, but such appearances did not become routine until 1955.[10] Yet instead of clarifying matters for senators considering a possible challenge, public confirmation hearings have made evasion and obfuscation by nominees the norm. As Maltese notes, "Most nominees have refused to discuss cases with members of the Judiciary Committee."[11] Judge Antonin Scalia's refusal in 1986 even to comment on such a well-settled precedent as *Marbury v. Madison* made a near mockery of the proceedings. The exception was Robert Bork in 1987, and, by all accounts, his willingness to wrestle candidly with all the hot-button issues of the day contributed mightily to his appointment's undoing. Three years after the Bork fiasco, nominee David H. Souter deftly ducked pointed questions about his position on *Roe v. Wade*; in doing so, he denied potential conservative and liberal critics of his nomination any real ammunition with which to defeat him.

Even in an era of greater openness and transparency, nominees continue to obfuscate in their confirmation hearings with few or no repercussions. In 2005, Bush's nominee to become chief justice, John G. Roberts Jr., refused to yield any ground to Democratic senators eager to learn of his specific views on whether *Roe v. Wade* should be reversed. As a nominee for associate justice in January 2006, Samuel A. Alito Jr. was confronted with a "personal qualifications statement" he had submitted decades earlier when applying to be an assistant attorney general under President Ronald Reagan. Alito had forthrightly declared on the form that the Constitution "does not protect the right to abortion"; responding to outrage expressed by Sen. Charles E. Schumer, D-N.Y., and others, the nominee volunteered only that he would "respect stare decisis" and the "judicial process." Alito's willingness to fall back on such vague platitudes did not derail his confirmation prospects.

Another obstacle in the path of concerted Senate resistance to a president's judicial nominees has been the marked increase in partisan polarization. In the past, senators from the president's party would sometimes refuse to go along with a proposed Supreme Court nomination. For example, eight Senate Republicans opposed Robert Bork for the Supreme Court in 1987. Yet just four years later, the only Republican senator remaining from that octet to oppose the controversial nomination of Clarence Thomas was Sen. James M. Jeffords of Vermont, the same senator who bolted the Republican Party once and for all in 2001. Senators from the president's party have learned that in this current era of partisan polarization, the political cost of voting against the president's nominee can be very high indeed. Consider the case of Democratic senator Zell Miller of Georgia, who became a pariah within his own party for consistently voting in favor of Republican president George W. Bush's policies and for supporting every one of Bush's lower-court nominees. By August 2004, Miller remained a Democrat in name only. He was even invited to deliver the keynote address to the Republican Party's national convention in New York City. By contrast, on the other side of the aisle moderate Republican senators Olympia Snowe and Susan Collins of Maine avoided the same fate, offering President Bush steadfast support for nearly all of his most ideologically conservative nominees. In fact, not one Republican senator voted against either of Bush's two Supreme Court nominees, while a combined sixty-four votes were cast against them by Senate Democrats. Because of the increased political costs of defection, it is a rare occasion indeed when senators choose to cross their own party leader in the White House.

On one recent occasion, senators from the president's own party *did* make themselves heard to a degree in the appointment process. In October of 2005, some conservative Republican senators, including Sam Brownback, R-Kan., helped to convince President Bush of the need to withdraw his second nominee for the high court, Harriet Miers. Miers, they felt, lacked a reliably conservative track record and was creating a serious split within the president's conservative base of support. Yet those senators pressing for her withdrawal were hardly acting from a position of strength. Minority Leader Harry Reid, D-Nev., had already offered his open support for Miers, and several Republican senators, including John Cornyn, R-Texas, still supported the controversial nominee at the time of her withdrawal. Thus Brownback and Miers's other detractors were most fearful that an up-or-down vote on Miers would go in her favor—certainly most headcounts of the Senate at that time indicated that a pro-Miers alliance between Democrats and moderate Republicans offered her more than enough votes to secure her confirmation. Most telling was the fact that key senators from President Bush's own party had been excluded from the decision-making process—how else can one explain their vocal frustration with Miers's candidacy? Thus while the president may occasionally confront resistance in the confirmation process, those occasional flare-ups should not be confused with what should be a truly deliberative appointment process.

At the outset of his presidency, Democratic president Barack Obama's judicial nominees could count on a significant degree of support from the Democratic-controlled Senate. The upper chamber that convened during the 111th Congress included nearly sixty members hailing from Obama's party; a Senate filibuster (by which forty-one senators can deny a vote on any matter) would thus become the principal tool by which Senate Republicans in the minority might offer a roadblock to Obama's judicial nominees. Yet even if Senate Republicans occasionally resort to the filibuster in the current Congress, will the president's domination of the judicial selection process be significantly hindered? During his two terms as president, George W. Bush successfully made 324 appointments to the lower courts. His record of successful appointments thus compares with those of other recent presidents during the modern era: the elder president Bush appointed 187 lower-court judges during his one term as president, and President Clinton made 366 judicial appointments in eight years. Even with the president and the Senate often at loggerheads over the confirmation of federal judges, the wheels keep turning, and most nominees continue to be confirmed. Although the Senate Democratic caucus may well be weakened by the 2010 midterm elections, President Obama's judicial nominees should on the whole expect favorable treatment in a process that is all but dominated by the executive branch.

If anything, the use of extreme tactics such as the filibuster serves as an indication of just how desperate these times have become for senators who wish to fight the president's judicial nominees. That each of the nominees filibustered during President Bush's two terms would have been confirmed in a straight up-or-down vote by the Senate provides further evidence of Senate deference. In American politics today, presidents nominate judges for the federal judiciary, and, with very few exceptions, the Senate obediently confirms those choices.

CON: John Anthony Maltese

What exactly does Article II, Section 2, of the Constitution mean when it says that the president "shall nominate, and by and with the Advice and Consent of the Senate, shall appoint ... Judges of the supreme court"? (By law, the same procedure is used for appointing lower federal court judges.) The Constitutional Convention of 1787 considered and ultimately rejected several different methods of judicial appointment: by Congress as a whole, by the Senate alone, and by the president alone. New York delegate Alexander Hamilton was among the most articulate defenders of the final constitutional language, and his explanation of that language in *Federalist* No. 76 is worth considering.[1]

Hamilton assumed that the Senate would rarely reject nominees put forth by the president. It is "not very probable," he wrote, that the Senate would often overrule the president's nomination. Only when there were "special and strong reasons for the refusal" would the Senate risk placing a "stigma" on a nominee through rejection and thereby call into question "the judgment of the chief magistrate."[2]

What might these "special and strong reasons" be? Could they include a nominee's failure to comply with a "litmus test" of how he or she should vote on particular issues? Anyone seeking to answer these questions must look at the precise wording of the Constitution and consider the intent of those who framed it.

The Constitution says that only the president has the power to *nominate*. As Hamilton wrote in *Federalist* No. 76, the president exercises "his judgment alone" in the act of nomination.[3] Even George Mason of Virginia, who opposed executive appointment of judges, conceded as much in a letter to fellow Virginian James Monroe: "There is some thing remarkable in the Arangement of the Words: 'He shall nominate.' This gives the President *alone* the Right of *Nomination*."[4]

Hamilton argued in *Federalist* No. 76 that the president's power to nominate meant that the "person ultimately appointed must be the object of his preference."[5] Why? Because "one man of discernment is better fitted to analyze and estimate the peculiar qualities adapted to particular offices, than a body of men of equal or perhaps even of superior discernment."[6] This is so, Hamilton said, because "a single well directed man … cannot be distracted and warped by that diversity of views, feelings, and interests, which frequently distract and warp the resolutions of a collective body."[7]

The Constitutional Convention ultimately rejected the legislative appointment of judges largely because the delegates feared that legislative appointments would be subject to intrigue and corrupted by factions. The Virginia Plan had originally proposed that Congress as a whole choose federal judges. When the convention debated that proposal on June 5, 1787, James Wilson of Pennsylvania objected. Experience among the states showed "the impropriety of such appointments in numerous bodies," he said. "Intrigue, partiality, and concealment were the necessary consequences. A principal reason for unity in the Executive was the officers might be appointed by a single, responsible person."[8]

On July 18, the convention considered appointment by the Senate alone. Nathaniel Gorham of Massachusetts argued that the Senate was still "too numerous, and too little personally responsible, to ensure a good choice."[9] He suggested a compromise: presidential appointment subject to the advice and consent of the Senate. James Madison of Virginia, who originally had been wary of executive appointment, conceded on July 21 that the executive would be more likely than any other branch "to select fit characters." He added that requiring Senate consent would check "any flagrant partiality or error" on the part of the president.[10] Madison's interpretation sheds light on what "advice and consent" means. It suggests that the Senate should withhold consent only in exceptional circumstances ("flagrant partiality or error" on the part of the president).

What, then, does the word "advice" in the appointments clause mean? Some scholars have suggested that it gives the Senate broad power to advise the president on whom to nominate. But this view runs counter to Hamilton's position in *Federalist* No. 76. It suggests that the power to nominate is *not* one held solely by the president, but rather is a power shared with the Senate.[11] Such a view conforms neither to a strict reading of the advice and consent clause nor to the intent of the framers. As legal scholar John O. McGinnis has persuasively argued:

> The very grammar of the clause is telling: the act of nomination is separated from the act of appointment by a comma and a conjunction. Only the latter act is qualified by the phrase "advice and consent." Furthermore, it is not at all anomalous to use the word "advice" with respect to the action of the Senate in confirming an appointment. The Senate's consent is advisory because confirmation does not bind the President to commission and empower the confirmed nominee. Instead, after receiving the Senate's advice and consent, the President may deliberate again before appointing the nominee.[12]

In short, the Senate's proper role is limited to offering advice on the nominee presented by the president.

This brings us back to the question: On what grounds should the Senate withhold its consent? When is a nominee "an unfit character" unworthy of confirmation? Hamilton, in *Federalist* No. 76, regards the Senate's power to withhold consent as primarily "a check upon the spirit of favoritism in the President" designed to prevent individuals from being appointed because of "family connection" or "personal attachment."[13] This statement corresponds with Madison's notion that the check be used to prevent "flagrant partiality or error." Some scholars have argued that the Constitutional Convention viewed Senate confirmation as a way of preventing the president from making too many appointments from large states.[14]

The failure of a nominee to pass a "litmus test" imposed by senators who want him or her to rule in cases in certain ways does not rise to the level of "special and strong reasons" for rejection. For one thing, this notion runs counter to the ideal of judicial independence, which the framers took great pains to protect. Moreover, it opens the door to the intrigue and faction that the framers sought to avoid. As noted earlier, Hamilton argued that because the president is best fitted to analyze the qualities necessary for each judgeship to be filled, the person appointed "must be the object of his preference." For senators to reject a nomination on the basis of a litmus test is to substitute improperly their preferences for those of the president.

Imposing such tests, however, is precisely what senators of both parties have done at all levels of the federal judicial appointment process in recent years. Senate opposition led to the rejection or withdrawal of six out of twenty-one Supreme Court nominations from 1968 through 2008 (a failure rate of almost 30 percent).[15] If one omits the unsuccessful renominations of individuals already blocked by the Senate, the rate of failed Supreme Court nominations before 1968 was 17.1 percent (21 out of 123 nominations).[16] For many observers of the Court, the Senate's rejection of President Ronald Reagan's nomination of Robert H. Bork in 1987 was a watershed event. After an intense fight against Bork led by a coalition of some three hundred liberal interest groups, the Democratic-controlled Senate rejected his nomination—not because of any improprieties or lack of qualifications, but because of how Bork might vote on the Court.

The Senate also now plays a more aggressive role in the lower federal court confirmation process. At that level, senators have resorted to procedural tactics to prevent the Senate Judiciary Committee from holding hearings on nominees, as well as to filibusters to keep the Senate from voting on them. Obstruction and delay became common during the administrations of Bill Clinton and George W. Bush. Senators from both political parties succumbed to the powerful grip of interest groups eager to influence judicial decision making. In 1997, for example, the Free Congress Foundation (a coalition of more than 250 conservative pro-family, small-business, victims' rights, and law enforcement organizations) pressured the Republican-controlled Senate to block many of President Clinton's lower federal court nominees. This group's Judicial Selection Monitoring Project claimed that Clinton's judicial appointees had "blazed an activist trail, creating an out-of-control judiciary," and urged that the Senate more closely scrutinize his nominees.[17] In a January 1997 letter to President Clinton and all one hundred U.S. senators, the project promised to "fight judicial activism with whatever tools and resources are legitimately at our disposal."[18] Two months later, House majority whip Tom DeLay, R-Texas, further escalated the rhetoric by suggesting that House Republicans should impeach liberal federal judges.[19]

Such pressure motivated Republican senators to use a procedural tactic called the "blue slip" to block hearings on nominees to federal courts in their states. This move resulted in a major slowdown in the confirmation of federal judges. By the end of 1997, one in ten seats on the federal judiciary was empty. President Clinton declared a "vacancy crisis," saying that the Senate's "failure to act on my nominations, or even give many of my nominees a hearing, represents the worst of partisan politics."[20] Although Republicans eased up on the stall tactics in 1998 after Chief Justice William H. Rehnquist criticized the delays in his 1997 year-end report to Congress, they revived their delaying tactics in 1999 in the hope of a Republican victory in the 2000 presidential election.[21] When Clinton left office in January 2001, forty-two of his judicial nominees remained unconfirmed (thirty-eight of them had never received a hearing). In Clinton's eight years as president, the Senate blocked 114 of his lower-court nominations and confirmed 366.[22] A look back reveals how much more aggressive the Senate had become. A Democratic Senate blocked none of Republican Richard Nixon's lower-court nominations and confirmed 224 during his five and a half years in office (1969–1974). In Ronald Reagan's eight years as president (1981–1989), the Senate blocked 43 lower-court nominees and confirmed 368.[23]

Senate obstruction of judicial nominees continued after George W. Bush took office in 2001. Like Clinton before him, President Bush declared a "vacancy crisis."[24] When Republicans regained control of the Senate after the 2002 midterm elections, Senate Judiciary Committee chair Orrin Hatch, R-Utah, altered the Senate rules to prevent Democrats from using blue slips to block hearings on President Bush's nominees.[25] This tactic spurred Democrats to filibuster nominees.

Is the filibuster an appropriate tool for senators to use to block a judicial nominee? It can be argued that it is not. The filibuster is not a power granted by the Constitution. As political scientists Sarah A. Binder and Steven S. Smith have noted, "Delegates to the convention did not write into the Constitution any procedural protections for Senate minorities."[26] The Senate's original rules are also instructive. These rules did not allow for a filibuster. Instead, they allowed for a simple majority to close debate. A senator would make a "motion for the previous question," and an up-or-down majority vote would follow. Not until an 1806 rules change eliminated "previous question motions" was a filibuster even possible. Even so, Binder and Smith point out, because previous question motions "had not been used as a means of limiting debate, its deletion could not have signaled a commitment to extended debate."[27] Lawyers Martin B. Gold and Dimple Gupta not only concur, but also argue that the 1806 rules change that opened up the possibility of filibusters was "a sheer oversight."[28] Indeed, no filibusters occurred in the Senate until the late 1830s. In 1917 the Senate enacted a cloture rule for ending debate by a two-thirds vote, and in 1975 the Senate changed the rule to a three-fifths vote.

The use of filibusters in the Senate has skyrocketed since the 1960s.[29] Using them to block judicial nominees is a relatively recent phenomenon. A coalition of progressive Republicans and Democrats considered filibustering against President Herbert Hoover's nomination of Charles Evans Hughes to the position of chief justice in 1930, but they decided not to take that path because they did not have the votes to sustain the filibuster.[30] In 1968 Republicans mounted a successful filibuster against President Lyndon B. Johnson's nomination of Abe Fortas to be chief justice (the nomination was withdrawn).[31] But only since 2002 has the practice become commonplace. Senate Democrats used the filibuster to block ten of President Bush's first-term appellate court nominees. In response, Republicans threatened to retaliate with the so-called nuclear option, a tactic that would prevent filibusters of judicial nominees. The Senate averted the nuclear option by agreeing to a compromise that allowed judicial filibusters only in "extraordinary circumstances" and put off until the future any formal changes to the filibuster rule. This issue could, of course, reemerge during the presidency of Barack Obama.

What consequences attend the aggressive role taken by the Senate in the judicial appointment process? Arguably, it has contributed to a confirmation mess. Helped (and spurred) by interest groups, opposition party senators now look for ways to disqualify nominees who do not meet their approval. The result, as law professor Stephen Carter puts it, is often a "bloodbath."[32] Public confirmation hearings and public relations campaigns are designed less to reveal nominees' knowledge and understanding of the law than to highlight their positions on policy issues and to expose embarrassing details of their past. Indeed, the confirmation gauntlet has become a political free-for-all. As the Twentieth Century Fund Task Force on Judicial Selection reported in 1988, the modern confirmation process has become "dangerously close to looking like the electoral process," with the use of "media campaigns, polling techniques, and political rhetoric that distract attention from, and sometimes completely distort, the legal qualifications of the nominee." The task force warned that "choosing candidates for anything other than their legal qualifications damages the public's perception of the institutional prestige of the judiciary and calls into question the high ideal of judicial independence."[33] The prospect of enduring the gauntlet may also discourage potential nominees from engaging in public service. Insiders in the Obama administration suggested at the outset of his administration that they intended to submit moderate nominees to the Senate in an effort to make confirmation wars a thing of the past, but they may find a lasting peace hard to secure.[34]

In light of this recent history, it is difficult to conclude that the president has too much power in the selection of judges. If anything, one could argue that the pendulum has swung in the direction of the *Senate* exercising too much power. Both Presidents Bill Clinton and George W. Bush declared a "vacancy crisis" because they believed senators were misusing their power by obstructing the confirmation process for partisan and ideological reasons. That sounds a lot like what some of the framers sought to avoid: a process corrupted by factions and subject to intrigue.

11

RESOLVED, the vice presidency should be abolished

PRO: Douglas L. Kriner

CON: Joel K. Goldstein

The Constitutional Convention lasted 116 days, from May 25 to September 17, 1787. Not until September 4—day 103—were the words *vice president* recorded as being spoken on the convention floor. The constitutional duties that eventually would be granted to the vice president—presiding over the Senate and, in the event that the presidency became vacant, succeeding to that office—instead had been assigned to a senator chosen by the Senate to serve as its president.

How did the vice presidency come about? The short answer is: as a by-product of the delegates' late decision to create an electoral college. To keep electors from voting exclusively for presidential candidates from their own states, the Constitution required that each elector vote for two candidates from two different states—for president. To make sure that electors cast both of their votes seriously, a consequence was attached to both. In addition to the candidate who received the most votes becoming president, the candidate who received the second-most votes would become vice president.

Off to a good start—the nation's first and second vice presidents, John Adams and Thomas Jefferson, became its second and third presidents—the vice presidency entered a steep downward spiral beginning with the enactment of the Twelfth Amendment in 1804. Under the amendment, instead of voting for two candidates for president, each elector would cast one vote for president and one for vice president. The result was that the vice president lost the status of being, in effect, the second-most-qualified person to be president. Never a powerful office, the vice presidency ceased to be a prestigious one as well.

The decline in the prestige of the vice presidency triggered a century-long decline in the caliber of political leaders who were willing to seek the office: a series of has-beens and never-wases. Only with Theodore Roosevelt's election as vice president in 1900 and his succession to the presidency after William McKinley died in 1901 did the vice presidency begin to regain some of its lost prestige. TR was elected to a full term as president in 1904, a feat accomplished by none of the four nineteenth-century successor presidents (John Tyler, Millard Fillmore, Andrew Johnson, and Chester Arthur). After Roosevelt, however, every successor president but one was subsequently elected in his own right: Calvin Coolidge in 1924, Harry S. Truman in 1948, and Lyndon B. Johnson in 1964. Gerald R. Ford, who lost in 1976, came very close. As the vice presidency gained in stature, prominent political leaders became willing to leave positions such as Senate majority leader and Speaker of the House of Representatives to accept vice presidential nominations, bringing their personal prestige to the office.

Serious questions remain, however, about the vice presidency's usefulness as an institution. In May 1974, six months after Vice President Spiro T. Agnew resigned in disgrace from the office, Arthur M. Schlesinger Jr. published a widely read article in the *Atlantic Monthly,* "Is the Vice Presidency Necessary?" Schlesinger's answer to this question—a clear and decisive *no*—came to seem misplaced when, starting with Walter F. Mondale's tenure as vice president in the Carter administration, the office experienced a renaissance of responsibility and prominence that lasted through Al Gore's vice presidency during the Clinton years.

No one doubted that Richard B. Cheney, Gore's successor, was a highly influential vice president in the administration of George W. Bush. Ironically, however, it was the power that Cheney exercised in the office on behalf of controversial policies, not the office's weakness, that set the stage for renewed consideration of whether the vice presidency should be abolished. In the debate that follows, Joel K. Goldstein defends the office, and Douglas L. Kriner attacks it.

PRO: Douglas L. Kriner

During the constitutional ratification debates, anti-Federalist leader George Clinton wrote that "the establishment of a vice-president is as unnecessary as it is dangerous."[1] For the first two hundred years of the office's existence, Clinton's bombastic warning seemed nothing more than sensationalist hyperbole. Yet almost 220 years later, politico Sidney Blumenthal, reflecting on Vice President Dick Cheney's revolutionary tenure in office, decried the emergence of an "imperial" vice presidency.[2] If told that his office would one day be called "imperial," any prior denizen of the vice presidential mansion would most likely have been flabbergasted. Nevertheless, under Vice President Cheney, who exercised enormous power subject to little oversight or restraint and with little regard for public opinion, the description was apt. Although Cheney's unique blend of skill and ambition fueled his unprecedented power grab, his course of action was made possible by the constitutional structure of the office itself.

Three features of the vice presidency render it a dangerous and undemocratic institution that should be abolished. First, because the vice president's primary constitutional responsibility is to preside over the Senate, the office violates the separation of powers doctrine, creates the possibility for undue executive incursions into the business of the legislature, and emboldens efforts by the vice president as well as the vice president's staff to evade oversight from both the executive and legislative branches. Second, the mechanisms by which vice presidents are first nominated and then elected sharply minimize the public's influence in choosing who will hold the second-highest executive office in the land. Finally, the considerable growth in and institutionalization of the vice president's staff in recent decades greatly exceeds the framers' expectations and vests too much power in an office whose occupants do not contest for their position in their own right.

A VIOLATION OF THE SEPARATION OF POWERS DOCTRINE

Ironically, the office of the vice presidency first appears not in Article II of the Constitution, which lays out the powers of the executive branch, but in Article I, which deals with the legislative power. Indeed, the only specific, enumerated power granted to the vice presidency appears in Article I, Section 3: "The Vice President of the United States shall be President of the Senate, but shall have no Vote, unless they be equally divided." Critics of the vice presidency were quick to declare this a stark violation of the separation of powers doctrine. At the Virginia ratification convention, George Mason expanded on Clinton's fear: "Mr. Chairman, the

Vice President appears to me to be not only an unnecessary but dangerous officer. He is, contrary to the usual course of parliamentary proceedings, to be president of the Senate ... the legislative and executive are hereby mixed and incorporated together."[3] During the Constitutional Convention itself, Massachusetts delegate Elbridge Gerry critiqued the provision even more sharply, lamenting that it "might as well put the President himself at the head of the legislature."[4]

As Richard Neustadt famously observed, the Constitution did not create a separation of powers system but one of "separated institutions sharing powers."[5] Not all legislative power was entrusted to the legislative branch; rather the president, through the veto, was granted an important role in the legislative process. Similarly, the Constitution clearly carved out avenues for legislative influence over some executive functions, such as requiring Senate confirmation for cabinet appointees to the executive branch and Senate ratification of international treaties. Yet, the framers did emphasize the importance of keeping the branches separate from and independent of one another. Article I, Section 6, for example, prevents any member of Congress from simultaneously holding an office in the executive branch.

By making the vice president the presiding officer of the Senate, Article I, Section 3 gave the office institutional roles in both the legislative and executive branches. George Mason speculated in 1787 that this failure to keep the two institutions of government separate could sow the seed for subsequent abuse. "I cannot, at this distance of time, foresee the consequences," Mason prophetically warned, "but I think that, in the course of human affairs, he will be made a tool of in order to bring about his own interest, and aid in overturning the liberties of his country."[6]

Throughout American history, a number of vice presidents have sought to leverage their constitutional role as president of the Senate into a position of greater legislative leadership. The nation's first vice president, John Adams, frequently presided over the Senate, addressed its members from the chair, and used his parliamentary skills to influence a number of major issues pending before the chamber. Indeed, in his writings Adams described the role of the vice president as fundamentally legislative in function.[7] Even as late as 1961, former Senate majority leader Lyndon B. Johnson unsuccessfully attempted to retain his position as head of the Senate Democratic Conference after his election as vice president. That said, for most of American history the awkward constitutional construction that made the vice president simultaneously an executive and a legislative officer failed to produce the usurpation of governing authority that Mason feared.

Recent developments, however, render Mason's admonition eerily prescient. In June 2006, Vice President Cheney's office rebuffed a request by the National Archives and Records Administration to conduct an on-site security inspection to ensure the protection and preservation of classified documents pursuant to Executive Order 12958. The vice president argued that his office was not an "entity within the executive branch" and therefore not subject to the terms of the order. Cheney made this claim despite having previously asserted his right as an executive officer to confidentiality with his advisers when he refused to reveal details of his energy task force to public interest groups and congressional committees.[8] The implications of this novel constitutional interpretation go beyond the case of preserving classified records. In a government publication known colloquially as the "Plum Book," Cheney's counsel argued: "The vice presidency is a unique office that is neither a part of the executive branch nor a part of the legislative branch." Cheney's staff repeatedly used this logic to support claims that the office of the vice president was exempt from oversight provisions governing both branches.[9]

Future vice presidents could also exploit the constitutional ambiguities surrounding the office's legislative role to further concentrate legislative authority in the executive branch. For example, even in the face of a strong popular backlash against Cheney's expansion of vice presidential power, Republican vice presidential nominee, Alaska governor Sarah Palin, in the 2008 vice presidential debate plainly interpreted Article I, Section 3 as granting the office considerable legislative power: "I'm thankful the Constitution would allow a bit more authority given to the vice president if that vice president so chose to exert it in working with the Senate and making sure that we are supportive of the president's policies." Palin's statement generated some controversy, yet the governor stood by her position. While Palin acknowledged after the debate that "the vice president, of course, is not a member, or a part of the legislative branch," she added the qualifying phrase "except to oversee the Senate." "That alone," Palin argued, "provides a tremendous amount of flexibility and authority if that vice president so chose to use it."[10] Such an interpretation plainly opens the door for even further usurpations of legislative authority by the executive branch.

As a result, the violation of the separation of powers doctrine created by the vice presidency's very structure is not merely of philosophical consequence; rather, it also has bolstered attempts to evade both executive and legislative oversight and it has raised the specter of future attempts to centralize even more legislative power within the executive branch.

UNDEMOCRATIC MECHANISMS OF SELECTION AND ELECTION

When defending the vice presidency from George Mason's attacks at the Virginia ratification convention, James Madison specifically emphasized the office's direct electoral tie to the American people: "The consideration which recommends it to me is, that he will be the choice of the people at large."[11] Madison was referring to the original text of Article II, Section 1, which provided that each member of the electoral college must vote for two persons for president, one of whom was not from the elector's home state. The individual with the largest number of votes, provided it was a majority, became president; the runner-up became the vice president. In theory, this selection procedure provided a direct link between the public and the vice presidency because the vice president was the public's second choice for president.

In practice, however, the early emergence of political parties quickly led to the creation of presidential tickets with both a candidate for president and for vice president. The Twelfth Amendment, which was ratified in the wake of the electoral college tie between Thomas Jefferson and his vice presidential candidate Aaron Burr during the election of 1800, changed the process to reflect this new partisan reality. The parties would nominate a candidate for president and one for vice president, and electors would cast separate ballots for each office.

The public has virtually no influence in selecting the vice presidential nominees; instead, for most of American history they have been chosen by party leaders. Most vice presidential nominees were selected not because of their stellar leadership credentials or accomplishments in elected office but for more raw political purposes, such as bringing regional or ideological balance to the party ticket or soothing rival factions within the party base.[12] Theodore Roosevelt, for example, was famously placed on the Republican ticket in 1900 to remove him from the New York governor's mansion, where he had aggressively combated the state's machine politics, and to place him in an office where party bosses believed he could do less harm. Since 1940, presidential candidates themselves have selected their running mates; however, for most of this period the single best predictor of an individual's prospects of selection was nothing more significant than the size of the vice presidential hopeful's home state.[13] To this day, the general public has no direct influence over the identities of the vice presidential candidates on the ballot in November.

Perhaps even more alarming is the very limited direct role of popular judgments in selecting who ultimately becomes vice president. In describing the operation of political parties during the old presidential electoral system in which party nominees were picked in the proverbial smoke-filled rooms, political scientist E. E. Schattschneider argued that "democracy is not to be found in the parties, but between the parties."[14] Even though the public had little influence over whom the parties nominated, they could at least choose between the options presented to them in the general election. Of course, Americans do elect the vice president, yet they do so only indirectly by voting for their preferred party ticket. In making this choice, Americans could give great weight to the various options for vice president; however, almost every study of American voting behavior suggests that the public makes its decision primarily based on who is at the top of the ticket. Although every four years media pundits reliably fill the airwaves with speculation about how a vice presidential candidate may help a ticket in a certain state or among a given demographic group, the bulk of the empirical evidence shows that the candidates for vice president have minimal influence on most Americans' electoral decisions.[15] Consequently, vice presidents gain their office on the coattails of the president without ever winning the public's sanction in their own right. The result is that the electoral linkage between the vice president and the public is far weaker than Madison anticipated in 1788.

That the public has such little direct say about who holds the vice presidency in and of itself is troubling. Yet, the ramifications of this state of affairs become even more severe when we remember that nine vice presidents, including five of the eighteen presidents who served during the twentieth century, have succeeded to the presidency upon the death or resignation of their predecessors. Each of these men was nominated through a process insulated from public input and based in large part on raw political calculations. Each gained office without independently contesting it, and each became president and served out the full remainder of his predecessor's term without ever having won a national election in his own right. In denouncing the role of the electoral college in selecting the nation's chief magistrate, George Clinton, himself a future vice president, wrote: "It is a maxim in republics that the representative of the people should be of their immediate choice."[16] Considered in this light, vice presidential succession involves perhaps the clearest possible violation of this principle.

Yet, the troubling normative consequences of vice presidential selection and election do not arise only in cases of succession. In contemporary politics the vice presidency has proved an invaluable stepping-stone to the presidency. Since 1960, every vice president save one who sought his party's nomination received it.[17] The emergence of our current nominating system dominated by media primaries and caucuses has only further intensified the advantages vice presidents enjoy when seeking the presidency. Today, early contests are critically important because they provide the winners with momentum that carries them forward into subsequent primaries.[18] The candidates poised to do well in Iowa and New Hampshire are those who have the name recognition and requisite financial resources to stand out in a crowded field. On both counts, holding the office of the vice presidency gives its occupant significant advantages over any other candidate.[19] As a result, our system fundamentally limits the presidential choices available to the general electorate by granting almost insurmountable advantages to an individual by virtue of that person's holding an office that was not achieved through an independently contested national election. In this way, the vice presidential office is, albeit indirectly, doubly undemocratic.

RUNAWAY GROWTH OF VICE PRESIDENTIAL POWER

Finally, the dramatic growth in influence and governing authority of the vice presidency during the past thirty years only heightens concerns that the officeholder is selected and elected with little input by the American people. From a purely empirical perspective, the institutional transformation of the vice presidency from an office derided by Franklin D. Roosevelt's first vice president, John Nance Garner, as "not worth a warm bucket of spit" to a position of genuine authority during the latter decades of the twentieth century is an impressive accomplishment. Beginning with Richard Nixon's tenure, vice presidents gradually assumed increasing levels of governing responsibility, culminating in Walter Mondale's transformation of the office into something akin to a general partnership in governing with the president.[20] However, from a normative perspective this development has entrusted growing authority to an official with meager direct electoral ties to the public.

In many respects, the evolution of the office has been positive. As expectations for the office have grown among both politicians and the public, the caliber of those seeking the vice presidency has improved, and nominees have felt increased pressure to select running mates who appear "presidential." As a result, the stature and the authority of the office have increased. However, the eight tumultuous years of the Cheney vice presidency make plain how much power a modern vice president can wield and how insufficient are the checks on this exercise of authority.

Vice President Cheney's unparalleled assertions of power were perhaps most prevalent in the realm of foreign affairs. After September 11, 2001, the vice president short-circuited the standard decision-making process to secure quick presidential approval of the November 2001 military order that denied terror suspects access to civilian and military courts and created a system of military tribunals to try them if and when the administration saw fit.[21] Cheney's clandestine exercise of power was so swift and absolute that Secretary of State Colin Powell and National Security Adviser Condoleezza Rice learned of the decision only after the order had been signed. The vice president led the fight to bypass the legal strictures of the Foreign Intelligence and Surveillance Act and to authorize the National Security Agency to wiretap the international communications of U.S. citizens without warrants; Cheney did so without even informing the White House's ranking national security lawyer. Cheney and his advisers played a pivotal role in legalizing "enhanced interrogation techniques" for terror suspects, again without the approval or even knowledge of other key players within the administration, including the secretary of state and national security adviser. Finally, the vice president's office spearheaded the effort to silence critics of the Iraq War, a campaign that publicly culminated in the conviction of Cheney's chief of staff, I. Lewis "Scooter" Libby, for leaking the identity of Central Intelligence Agency operative Valerie Plame Wilson to the press. Moreover, Cheney's unprecedented influence was not limited to the conduct of the war on terror. On a range of domestic issues the vice president frequently played a pivotal role shaping presidential priorities and proposals from energy initiatives to tax policy to environmental policy.[22] In each of these areas, Vice President Cheney wielded extraordinary power unprecedented in American history, and he did so with virtually no constraints on its exercise.

Other executive branch officials whose names never even appear on a ballot can also amass considerable power and exercise undue influence on politics and policymaking. Two factors, however, set the vice presidency apart. First, most top-ranking cabinet and agency officials require Senate confirmation; vice presidents, by contrast, are essentially selected by the president alone, with little opportunity for public influence on the choice.[23] Second, and more important, executive branch officials serve at the pleasure of the president; by contrast, vice presidents can be removed only by impeachment or by the president, who can change running mates when seeking reelection. As a result, congressional and public outrage has frequently been enough to force the resignation of executive officials such as President Bush's attorney general, Alberto Gonzalez, who are perceived to have abused their power. Vice presidents, by contrast, are all but immune from such pressures; for example, despite approval ratings dipping below 30 percent, no amount of public pressure or congressional opprobrium could force Cheney from office.

Defenders of the vice presidency argue that the Cheney years are likely anomalous; future presidents will be loath to devolve so much power to their vice presidential subordinates. This may well be true. However, here Mason's admonition about the unpredictability of future consequences rings most true.[24] The lessons of Cheney's tenure stand as important warnings of what may occur again given the office's insulation from direct popular election and the dearth of institutional checks on potential abuses of power.

ABOLISHING THE VICE PRESIDENCY

In theory, some of these criticisms of the office could be redressed through institutional reform. A constitutional amendment, for example, could address the separation of powers concern and establish that the vice presidency is an executive office subject to oversight by both the executive and legislative branches accordingly. However, the problems caused by the mechanisms of vice presidential selection and election are more intractable. Returning to the system before the Twelfth Amendment could well replicate the result of the election of 1796 and give us a rival president and vice president from competing factions or parties. Such a result clearly undermines coherence and energy in executive governance. In short, there is no simple way to create a vice president genuinely elected directly and personally by the public but who is also committed to the president's program.

The easiest remedy is to abolish the vice presidency. The Constitution should be amended to provide for a caretaker president—perhaps the secretary of state or secretary of defense, who might be best positioned to protect America from any foreign threats until a new president is elected—in the event of the president's death or incapacitation in office. Special elections should then follow within a short, predetermined period of time. A number of potential remedies—all of which do not involve the dangerous mixing of executive and legislative powers inherent in the current system—could be adopted to break a tie in the Senate. Finally, to replace the valuable advisory role that a number of contemporary vice presidents have provided, the president could simply create additional special assistants within the White House staff.

CON: Joel K. Goldstein

The vice presidency should be retained because it fills vital needs in our system of government in a manner superior to any readily imaginable substitute. Our government would be weaker without the vice presidency not only because it would lose the benefits the modern office provides but also because alternative solutions would create new problems.

Three related but often ignored points should be kept in mind when discussing whether the vice presidency should be abolished. First, the test is not whether the vice presidency is imperfect—all political institutions are—or whether those who seek or hold the office sometimes act in an objectionable manner, a measure that would not differentiate the office from other governmental positions that presumably are not in jeopardy. Rather, the question should turn on how the office can reasonably be expected to perform.

Second, those arguing for abolition must show that some better alternative exists to perform the functions the vice presidency serves without causing damage to other aspects of our system of government.

Finally, it is important to discuss the vice presidency as it now exists, not its frail ancestor that was lampooned for most of American history. The modern incarnation of the office bears virtually no resemblance to the vice presidency of the nineteenth century and most of the twentieth. It has been transformed into a more robust institution that makes significant contributions to the American system of government.

The vice presidency became more important in the twentieth century because of changes in other institutions of government. As the role of the national government and the presidency grew during the twentieth century, especially from the New Deal on, the vice presidency was pulled into the presidential orbit. Around 1940, presidential candidates began to wrest control of the selection of their running mates from party leaders, which profoundly changed the relationship between president and vice president. In the aftermath of the New Deal and in the nuclear age, expectations of national government generally, and of the president specifically, increased dramatically. Whereas previously vice presidents had devoted much of their time to presiding over the Senate, beginning in the 1950s that constitutionally prescribed role ceased to engage their attention. Vice presidents, starting with Richard M. Nixon in 1953, migrated to the executive branch and assumed a range of political and executive roles delegated to them by the president. Nixon and his five immediate successors—Lyndon B. Johnson, Hubert H. Humphrey, Spiro T. Agnew, Gerald R. Ford, and Nelson A. Rockefeller—took on a standard set of executive duties—foreign emissary, commission head, legislative liaison, administrative spokesperson, political surrogate.[1] Vice presidents during this quarter century were busier in more different public activities than their predecessors had been; however, they often remained peripheral to high-level decision making in the executive branch.

That changed during the vice presidency of Walter F. Mondale (1977–1981), when the office made its most significant, and apparently permanent, institutional advance. Mondale pioneered a new vision of the vice president as a senior across-the-board adviser to, and troubleshooter for, the president. He obtained important resources for the office, including a White House office, a weekly private meeting with President Jimmy Carter, access to the memorandums and other documents that went to the president, and the right to attend any meeting on Carter's schedule or to see him when he had something to share. Carter and Mondale implemented that vision faithfully and skillfully. Mondale's service demonstrated that the vice president could make important, ongoing contributions in the executive branch.

Mondale left future vice presidents the following legacy—a new model for the vice president, enhanced expectations for the office, and the important resources described above. Mondale's successors all benefited from the greater expectations of the office, retained the resources, and, to varying degrees, imitated the model.[2] George H. W. Bush (1981–1989), for instance, sought to follow the Mondale model. He inherited Mondale's West Wing office, lunched privately with President Ronald Reagan each week, and regularly joined him for meetings. Bush encouraged Dan Quayle (1989–1993) to follow the same pattern. He gave Quayle the same resources and named him chair of the Council on Competitiveness and of the Space Council. Although Bush and Quayle, for different reasons, did not match Mondale's level of influence, Al Gore (1993–2001) apparently did as Bill Clinton's vice president. Gore and Clinton established an easy rapport. Gore became an important voice during the transition and, once in office, acted as Clinton's principal general adviser and assumed significant ongoing responsibilities.

Most observers have concluded that Dick Cheney (2001–2009) exercised more influence than had any of his predecessors. Cheney acted almost as the chief operating officer of the government during the George W. Bush presidency. Bush delegated broad authority to him and relied on Cheney to shape options in many areas for Bush's decision. In the first months of his term, Joe Biden appears to be playing a substantive role in the Barack Obama administration in a manner somewhere between the Mondale and Gore models. He meets with the president regularly, has made important trips abroad, and has assumed responsibility in several crucial areas.

The modern vice presidency makes three important contributions to American government. First, it provides an able presidential successor who has been chosen in an acceptable manner. Second, it makes available to the president as a senior adviser an experienced political figure who is well positioned to view the full range of issues facing the president from a perspective similar to the president's. Finally, it provides the president with a senior constitutional officer to discharge important governmental missions that must be handled at the highest levels, thereby relieving the president of some burdens.

The successor role, though contingent, is critical. As Michael Nelson put it, "[t]he office is most significant, of course, when cocoonlike, it empties itself to provide a successor to the presidency."[3] The Constitution provides that if the president dies, resigns, or is removed from office, the vice president becomes president; if the president is unable to discharge the powers and duties of the office, the vice president acts as president until the disability ends.[4] On nine occasions in our history, presidents have died or resigned before finishing their terms. Moreover, presidents, including James Garfield, Woodrow Wilson, Dwight D. Eisenhower, and Ronald Reagan, have suffered periods of disability, ranging from a few days to many months.[5]

The successor office must be suited to respond to the different contingencies that might create the need for a permanent or temporary transfer of power. Although the contingency of presidential death, which creates a permanent vacancy, more often requires an unanticipated transfer of power, the successor office must also be able to handle the somewhat different and vexing challenges that presidential inability presents when the need for a transfer of power may be temporary and may be disputed. Effective government continuity depends on the availability of an able and accepted successor who is well prepared to assume the presidency without delay and who shares the general outlook of the administration.

Although the successor role is contingent, the other two roles, as adviser and troubleshooter, involve the vice president on an ongoing basis as a contributing member of the administration. Presidents depend on advice, and the quality of their decision making is likely to be shaped by their access to candid counsel from a range of advisers, those with technical expertise and those with political experience. Yet the president's ability to obtain good advice is often compromised. There is a tendency to shield the president from critical assessments or unwelcome news. Moreover, many presidents surround themselves with people who have technical proficiency in particular substantive areas but who lack the political sensitivity and skill that long experience in electoral politics may foster. Even those cabinet officers with political sensitivity understandably tend to become consumed with, and committed to, their departmental priorities and programs. Accordingly, they have neither the time nor the independent perspective to counsel the president more generally. Finally, the modern presidency receives more demands for high-level intervention than one human being can meet. The president needs a person of stature and skill to take on important assignments that must be addressed at a high level but that the president cannot handle personally—conferring with foreign leaders on international trips, meeting with key legislators to win support for a measure, serving as referee to resolve an interdepartmental dispute, negotiating an agreement with parties to a dispute with public implications.

The modern vice presidency has become successful in attracting able political leaders to discharge these three roles of presidential successor, adviser, and troubleshooter. Since 1953, vice presidents have, with few exceptions, been highly skilled and accomplished political figures.[6] Of the twelve men who have served as vice president during that period, ten were clearly presidential timber by virtue of their prior or subsequent public service.[7] Four became president and four suffered the narrowest of defeats.[8] Of the twelve vice presidents, seven won their party's presidential nomination ten times.[9] Five had been legislative leaders in the Senate or House of Representatives.[10] Most vice presidents during this time period were among the ablest political figures of their generation.

The selection process as it has evolved during the past seventy years has increased the likelihood that presidents and vice presidents will be compatible. The presidential candidate, not the party leaders, now selects the running mate and accordingly is in position to choose a compatible partner. In turn, the vice president has reason to be loyal to the person responsible for the elevation to the vice presidency. Whereas relations between some past presidents and vice presidents were notoriously unhappy, vice presidents beginning with Mondale have established very compatible relationships with their presidents and most other key administration officials.

Additional features of the selection process give presidential candidates an incentive to choose able national figures who are plausible presidents. Presidential nominations now are routinely secured months before the convention. The presidential candidates accordingly have time to consider their choice of a running mate in a deliberate and rational way. The selection process presents an important test of the presidential candidates as decision makers. The prolonged public focus raises the stakes of an improvident choice. Presidential candidates hope the vice presidential selection will reflect well on them, and they generally choose accordingly.

Of course, voters cannot vote separately for vice president. The benefits the office provides depend on tying the election of the vice president to that of the president. Yet it is a mistake to conclude that the lack of a separate election deprives the vice president of democratic legitimacy. The vice presidential candidates participate actively in the presidential campaign. They communicate with voters across the country, help shape the campaign debate, and receive significant exposure. On occasion, vice presidential candidates have made a difference in the outcome. Johnson's presence on the 1960 ticket was crucial to John F. Kennedy's victory, and Mondale surely helped Carter prevail, especially in decisive states like Ohio, Pennsylvania, and Wisconsin. Polls suggested that widespread misgivings about the fitness of Governor Sarah Palin to be vice president or president hurt the prospects of Senator John McCain.[11]

When modern vice presidential candidates do not affect the outcome, it is generally because one of two situations exists. When both presidential candidates choose able and broadly acceptable running mates, there is little reason for voters to consider those in the second spot on the tickets. It is not surprising that the choice between Mondale and Bush in 1980 or between Gore and Jack Kemp in 1996 affected few voters. All were highly regarded candidates who were generally compatible ideologically with their ticket partners. Alternatively, when potential swing voters have serious misgivings about a presidential candidate, they are unlikely to support that candidate simply because they like one running mate more than the other. The difficulty occurs when an otherwise preferred presidential candidate chooses a running mate whom the public disfavors. This contingency rarely occurs, Agnew and Quayle being the only modern instances, and those experiences should deter future presidential candidates from selecting running mates who are not seen as being presidential.

Changes in presidential campaigns have created new political institutions and practices that have increased the exposure of vice presidential candidates and accordingly given presidential candidates greater incentive to choose well-qualified running mates. The long and more visible process of vice presidential selection is one, but not the only, relatively new feature that now directs greater attention on the office and the candidates vying for it. Presidential candidates now usually stage a highly visible public rollout of their running mates before their party's national convention, which, by design, focuses attention on that person. Vice presidential debates, which have become a standard feature of every presidential campaign but one since 1976, also place the second candidates in the national spotlight. These new but apparently permanent features of presidential campaigns give vice presidential candidates greater visibility and provide the public an opportunity to measure them. They provide further incentive for presidential candidates to choose impressive running mates. Senator John McCain surely paid a price for his choice of Governor Palin, and that lesson will not be lost on future candidates.

Once in office, modern vice presidents have performed important roles rather than retreating to oblivion as was once the pattern. Every vice president since Rockefeller has had a weekly private meeting with the president. Those since Mondale have had an office in the West Wing, only steps from the Oval Office and sandwiched between the office of the chief of staff and that of the national security adviser. This proximity fosters involvement. Mondale and his successors have spent considerable amounts of time with the president and his other principal advisers, and most have exercised significant influence.

Vice presidents have assumed significant troubleshooting and, in some cases, operational responsibilities. Mondale, for instance, took important substantive foreign missions to China, the Middle East, and Europe and helped secure ratification of the Panama Canal treaties and passage of legislation creating the Department of Education. George H. W. Bush was a skillful and frequent foreign emissary during the Reagan presidency. Quayle ran the Council on Competitiveness, which incubated some of the domestic proposals of the first Bush administration. Gore took charge of Bill Clinton's Reinventing Government initiative, helped direct the administration's environmental and telecommunications programs, and chaired important bilateral commissions with leaders of Russia, South Africa, and Egypt. Cheney's influence and involvement were pervasive, in part because of the unique, and unlikely to be replicated, operational styles of Cheney and President George W. Bush. Bush had previously worked closely with Cheney—Cheney directed Bush's vice presidential selection process in 2000 and the presidential transition of 2000–2001—and Bush delegated an unprecedented amount of operational authority to Cheney. Cheney's control of the transition allowed him to place persons loyal to him throughout the executive branch; once in office, he was not timid in using his broad experience and contacts to shape policy.

There are, accordingly, institutional reasons to expect future vice presidents to have political skill and stature, to be generally compatible with the president, and to be engaged in the administration's work once in office. These common features make the vice president well suited to contribute to American government as adviser, troubleshooter, and successor.

The vice presidency provides a good solution to the problem of presidential succession and inability. The office provides a well-qualified successor who is knowledgeable regarding administration policies and personnel and who generally shares the president's political disposition. The vice presidency accordingly provides substantial assurance of continuity in case of permanent vacancy and makes a transfer of power more likely in response to presidential inability. The vice presidential candidate's participation in the electoral campaign lends legitimacy to the vice president's role as first successor.

The vice president offers several advantages as a senior adviser. The vice president is likely to be an experienced political leader who can offer the perspective of an elected official. Because the vice president generally has no specific department to run, the vice president largely shares the president's perspective; like the president, the vice president can see the entire range of issues facing the administration without departmental bias. Moreover, the vice president often adds a perspective that supplements that of the president's. Five of our six most recent presidents—Carter, Reagan, Clinton, George W. Bush, and Obama—came to the White House with little or no experience in the federal government.[12] In each case, their vice presidents had substantial experience in Washington and often in Congress, too. Mondale, George H. W. Bush, Quayle, Gore, Cheney, and Biden had all served in Congress, all but Bush for at least a decade. Bush and especially Cheney had held important positions in the executive branch.

Finally, the vice president can assume responsibilities that must be handled at the highest levels, thereby relieving some demands on the president's time. Recent vice presidents have helped the executive branch respond to the enormous demands that domestic and international issues place on the president.

The institutional changes in the vice presidency discussed above are interrelated and reinforce each other. The changes in the selection process and election campaigns tend to increase the likelihood that vice presidents will be able people of stature who are compatible with the chief executive. Those attributes, in turn, raise the probability that vice presidents will be put to work after they are in office. Similarly, the enhanced substantive role of the office, especially since Mondale, makes it appealing to talented officials, and the offer of the vice presidency is now rarely turned down when the ticket appears to have a good chance of being elected.

There is every reason to expect the vice presidency to continue to do a good job in its three-part role of providing a presidential successor, senior adviser, and troubleshooter. The changes in selection, election, and vice presidential role appear to have been institutionalized. The pattern of high-level vice presidential involvement since Mondale has created enhanced public expectations for the office that give presidential candidates incentive to choose capable running mates who can help them govern once in office.

The case for retaining the vice presidency is further enhanced by the absence of any appealing alternative. A frequently suggested reform would abolish the vice presidency and have some other officer serve in the interim, pending a special election. This reform would cause more harm than good. Several problems would accompany such a change.

- It would deprive the president of the advice of an experienced political figure who largely shares the president's interest.

- It would divest the president of the help of a high-level troubleshooter.

- The interim successor would lack prior exposure to the full range of issues the president faces.

- The interim successor would have only a remote connection to the most recent national election.

- Our political system is not adapted to holding special elections.

- A special election would impose the prospect of election amid a period of national mourning or an additional transition to a newly elected president in addition to that caused by the unexpected vacancy.

To be sure, vice presidents will not always serve well or meet the standards we would like. The same is true for presidents, cabinet members, senators, and Supreme Court justices, but that fact has not been thought to be an argument for abolishing those offices. The vice presidency has now evolved to a point that it contributes in important ways to the effective operation of the American system of government. Its recent development makes its retention imperative.

RESOLVED, a president's personal attributes are the best predictors of performance in the White House

PRO: Fred I. Greenstein

CON: Stephen Skowronek

Only the most resolute historical determinist would deny that individuals make a difference in history. And yet just as surely, many things are beyond any individual's control. Conditions not of people's own making structure their choices, shape their decisions, and affect their chances for success. On this much all can agree. But truisms are no substitute for political analysis. Can scholars do better at specifying the conditions under which individual attributes matter in politics?

One of the most influential efforts to do better was James David Barber's 1972 landmark study *The Presidential Character: Predicting Performance in the White House.*[1] Barber insisted that character matters a great deal, but the book's originality lay in its effort to categorize character types and to use those types to predict presidential performance.

Character, for Barber, was "the way the President orients himself to life." Barber identified two key dimensions of character: (1) a president's activity level in office and (2) whether the president "gives the impression he enjoys his political life." Those who are active and enjoy their political life are "active-positive" presidents. Such presidents have high self-esteem and an ability to draw flexibly on different styles of leadership, depending on the situation and the president's goals. These are the presidents who are most likely to be successful. Those most likely to fail spectacularly are the "active-negative" presidents, who compensate for low self-esteem with compulsive activity. Active-negative presidents, according to Barber, work hard with little sense of enjoyment. Because their political actions are animated by personal demons, they become personally invested in policies. When those policies falter, they are likely to feel personally threatened and are thus reluctant to make concessions or corrections. Persevering rigidly in a failed policy is the hallmark of the active-negative president.

Barber's prediction that Nixon's active-negative character would cause his downfall gave his ideas a celebrity status rarely achieved by political science theories. *Time* magazine featured Barber's theory, and some presidential candidates put the book on their reading lists (Jimmy Carter claimed to have read it twice). Political scientists greeted Barber's work with more skepticism, asking searching questions about its validity. Do the measures of activity level and attitude toward the job correspond with the psychodynamic patterns and personality needs that Barber identifies? Was Nixon's self-destruction really a product of psychological rigidification? Was Herbert Hoover's rigidification a result of character or of ideology? Where is the line between principled adherence to one's views and unhealthy rigidity? And can that distinction be made without involving one's own political values?

Whether Barber's theory is useful or not, he deserves credit for understanding that, if individual attributes are to predict performance, the infinite variety of human behaviors must be reduced to a manageable number of types. If every president is viewed as entirely unique, then one can never hope to learn from the past. Prediction requires theory, which, in turn, requires simplification.

Stephen Skowronek's seminal 1993 book *The Politics Presidents Make* has the same sort of theoretical ambitions that animated Barber's *Presidential Character*.[2] Like Barber, Skowronek generates a fourfold typology from two dimensions. But whereas Barber's aim was a theory of character, Skowronek's is a theory of political regimes. Barber hoped to generalize about individuals. Skowronek wants to simplify the types of situations presidents face.

Skowronek identifies two crucial situational dimensions: (1) whether the president is affiliated with the dominant regime, or governing coalition, and (2) whether the regime is resilient or vulnerable. A president's chance of success, Skowronek argues, depends on the president's place in "political time"—that is, in the cycle of regime formation and decay. A president affiliated with a regime that is vulnerable—think of Herbert Hoover or Jimmy Carter, both of whom were saddled with faltering economies—has little prospect for success. Although the failure of such presidents is not predetermined, the political deck is stacked against them. By contrast, presidents who come to power opposed to a vulnerable regime—think of Franklin D. Roosevelt and Ronald Reagan, Hoover's and Carter's successors, respectively—are in the best position to remake the political order. Their success is not guaranteed, but they have greater opportunities for success than most presidents do. Personal qualities still matter, but, according to Skowronek, success and failure are often attributed wrongly to character and skill when the credit or blame really belongs to the situation the president faced.

In his widely read *The Presidential Difference,* Fred I. Greenstein resolutely defends the importance of understanding a president's personal attributes: political and communication skills, organizational capacity, cognitive style, as well as emotional intelligence.[3] Unlike Skowronek (and Barber), Greenstein shuns simplifying typologies. The result is a less parsimonious theory, but readers can decide whether it is a less useful way of understanding or even predicting presidential performance. The debate between Skowronek and Greenstein prompts us to ask not only how much individual attributes matter but also how scholars of the presidency should build theories that will enable us to apply the lessons of presidencies past to the prospects for presidencies yet to come. This is not merely an academic question; the nation's ability to elect successful presidents in the future may depend on the answer.

PRO: Fred I. Greenstein

> The President is at liberty, both in law and conscience, to be as big a man
> as he can. His capacity will set the limit.
>
> —Woodrow Wilson, 1908

From George Washington's decision to buy time for the new nation by signing the less-than-ideal Jay Treaty with Great Britain in 1795 to George W. Bush's order of a military intervention in Iraq in 2003, the matter of who happens to be president of the United States has often been of critical importance. The most telling illustration of the difference a White House occupant can make comes from the nuclear age. In October 1962, President John F. Kennedy learned that the Soviet Union had secretly installed in Cuba ballistic missiles that were capable of striking much of the United States. His advisers were split between those who favored using peaceful means to induce the Soviets to withdraw their missiles and those who called for an immediate air strike on the missile sites, an act that almost certainly would have triggered a nuclear war. If Kennedy had chosen a violent option, the result could have been catastrophic.

The impact of personal qualities on presidential job performance is a variable, not a constant. Some political contexts point so compellingly toward a particular course of action that virtually any president would react to them in the same manner. It is difficult to conceive of a White House incumbent who would not have responded militarily to the September 11, 2001, attacks on the World Trade Center and Pentagon. Other contexts leave wide latitude for personal attributes to have an effect. It was not preordained that Bush would order an invasion of Iraq. If Al Gore had been elected in 2000, it is unlikely that he would have taken that action.

In what follows, I examine a target of opportunity for studying the difference a president makes—the early chief executives. These men served at a time when it was up to them to give meaning to the Constitution's sketchy description of their responsibilities. As a result, the conduct of the presidency was strongly influenced by the personal qualities of the incumbent chief executive. I begin by considering the first three presidents—George Washington, John Adams, and Thomas Jefferson—and conclude by considering the sixth and seventh presidents—John Quincy Adams and Andrew Jackson.[1]

THE FOUNDATIONAL PRESIDENCY OF GEORGE WASHINGTON

George Washington had already been acclaimed throughout the British colonies for his exploits in the French and Indian War two decades before the

United States declared its independence. Such was Washington's esteem that he was unanimously elected to high positions four times—commander in chief of the Continental Army in 1775, president of the convention that framed the Constitution in 1787, and for two terms as chief executive in 1789 and 1792.

Washington was acutely aware that his every presidential action was likely to establish a precedent. Shortly after his inauguration on April 30, 1789, he consulted with his associates on protocol and other matters. Pointing out that "many things which appear of little importance in themselves ... may have great and durable consequences from their having been established at the commencement of a new general Government," he asked whether it would be "advantageous to the interests of the Union" for him to tour the states "in order to become acquainted with their principal Characters and internal Circumstances, as well as to be more accessible to numbers of well-informed persons, who might give him useful informations and advices on political subjects." He decided that he would do so.

In the late summer of 1789, Congress established the organs of the new government. But before then, there was a development that cast doubt on whether Washington or Vice President John Adams would be in charge of those bodies. In mid-June, Washington became ill from a large and painful growth that had developed on his thigh. He ran a high fever, and it was feared that he would die. He gradually recovered, however, and in October departed on a twenty-eight-day tour of New England. This and his later tour of the southern states helped impart his towering prestige to the new nation.

One of Washington's goals was to establish a sound financial system. Another was to resolve outstanding issues with Great Britain. His administration dealt with the nation's financial needs by guaranteeing payment of the interest on the national debt and establishing a national bank and system of taxation. It addressed relations with Britain by negotiating the Jay Treaty, which fostered trade between the two nations and provided for the arbitration of boundary disputes with Canada. There was an outpouring of opposition to the Jay Treaty because it did not meet some of the American demands, but Washington's public esteem enabled him to carry the day.

In 1792, war erupted between revolutionary France and Great Britain. There was pressure from Federalists to support Britain and Republicans to side with France. Washington refused to involve the fledgling nation in an overseas military conflict, however, and he issued a proclamation declaring the United States neutral. In 1794, residents of the Pennsylvania frontier refused to pay a federal tax on distilled spirits. Washington dispatched troops to put down the Whiskey Rebellion and personally led the first stage of the advance. The insurrection evaporated as the federal government demonstrated it had the power to enforce its laws.

No president made as much of a difference as Washington. No one else in the new nation had his capacity to legitimize the nation. It once was held that Washington was indispensible for who he was but not for what he did. It is now recognized that he was fully in charge of his presidency although his influence was not always visible because he exercised it through intermediaries such as Representative James Madison and Secretary of the Treasury Alexander Hamilton. Without Washington as president there might not be a United States of America today.

JOHN ADAMS: ABSENTEE PRESIDENT

It would be difficult to imagine two more different presidents than George Washington and John Adams. Washington radiated authority, even in his commanding appearance. Adams was unimposing. He was short, pudgy, and susceptible to seemingly unprovoked rages. Adams has been called "self-righteous," "irritable," and "contentious." Benjamin Franklin described him as "always an honest man, often a wise one, but sometimes, and in some things, absolutely out of his senses."

John Adams was one of the nation's most politically inept presidents. One of his errors was retaining the cabinet he inherited from Washington; he was seemingly unaware that three of its members were secretly taking signals from his political enemy, Alexander Hamilton. Another was removing himself from the capital for extended periods. Adams spent more than one-third of his presidency at his home in Massachusetts or on his way to or from it. His absences from the capital made it necessary for members of his cabinet to go their own ways, which they sometimes did, often in different directions.

The overriding concern of the Adams presidency was an undeclared naval war between the United States and France, which was an offshoot of the larger war between France and Great Britain. At the time Adams took office, the French had begun seizing American ships to prevent them from supplying Britain. Adams asked Congress to vote funds for a military buildup, but he also dispatched a peace delegation to France. In March 1798, the delegation reported that France had refused to receive it. Moreover, the delegation had been approached by French agents who requested a bribe to arrange a meeting with the French foreign minister, a demand the outraged Americans rejected. Adams forwarded the report to Congress, substituting the letters XYZ for the names of the French agents.

The XYZ Affair triggered an outpouring of patriotic indignation. Adams was showered with messages of public support to which he replied with such assertions as "Providence may intend [war] for our good, and we must submit.

That is a less evil than national dishonor." His rhetoric led many to conclude that he was preparing the nation for war. Early in 1799, Adams stunned the political community by announcing without prior warning that he intended to resume peace negotiations with France. Adams then departed for a seven-month stay in Massachusetts. On his return, he dispatched a peace mission to France, and in September 1800 the mission reached an agreement with the French that ended the conflict. Before word crossed the Atlantic, Adams had been defeated for reelection by Thomas Jefferson.

The stubbornly impolitic John Adams provides an example of an incumbent who was psychologically ill-suited for the presidency. Adams's presidential performance suffered from a contentiousness that made him difficult to work with, his failure to control his cabinet, and his propensity to remove himself from the seat of government. He was the first, but far from the last, chief executive whose cognitive strengths were undermined by his emotional weaknesses.

By the time Adams became president, the new American nation was solidly institutionalized. That would not have been the case if the illness that afflicted Washington in his second month as president had been fatal and Adams had succeeded him in the early months of the new political system. If that had occurred, it is uncertain whether the United States would have survived.

THOMAS JEFFERSON AND THE ART OF GOVERNANCE

Thomas Jefferson was a complex and contradictory figure. He was an advocate of economy who spent lavishly on personal luxuries. He also was an eloquent spokesman for the equality of man but owned many slaves. And as secretary of state in the Washington administration, he subsidized an anti-administration newspaper, but denied it. Jefferson also was an inventor, architect, Enlightenment thinker, and republican theorist. One might expect to find little in the way of political skill on the part of a chief executive who was steeped in the life of the mind, but Jefferson was a gifted politician, especially under the favorable circumstances of his first term.

In contrast to Adams, Jefferson appointed a loyal, well-qualified cabinet. He was also an able practitioner of personal politics, who entertained members of Congress at small dinners where he plied them with fine wine and food and urbane conversation to win them over. Jefferson's political skill helped him bridge the separation of powers. His public stance was that he did not involve himself in the business of the legislative branch, but he exercised great behind-the-scenes influence on Capitol Hill, even drafting bills and arranging for members of Congress to introduce them but telling them not to reveal that he was their author.

Jefferson's political skills enabled his administration to achieve an ambitious first-term agenda that included eliminating domestic taxes and reducing the federal debt and the size of the armed forces. Jefferson's crowning achievement was buying the huge Louisiana Territory from France, an acquisition that doubled the size of the nation. Because he believed in a strict construction of the Constitution, Jefferson considered calling for a constitutional amendment to authorize such a purchase. But when it became evident that Napoleon's offer might not wait, he dismissed his ideological scruples as "metaphysical subtleties" and signed off on the politically popular purchase.

Jefferson's second term was vastly different from his triumphant first term. After an interlude of peace, war broke out again between Britain and France. Each of the great powers sought to prevent the United States from supplying the other. In addition, the British boarded American ships to remove alleged deserters from the Royal Navy and force them back into service. This practice rankled Americans, but the British viewed it as necessary to prevent a hemorrhage of trained seamen in a time of war.

Jefferson's republican ideology, which had led him to reduce the size of the armed forces, also led him to oppose war as an instrument of statecraft. As a result, he responded to the attacks on American shipping by instituting the embargo of 1807, which confined American vessels to port. Jefferson was convinced that if Britain were denied trade with the United States it would alter its policies. The main effect of the embargo, however, was to damage the American economy, especially in areas that relied on trade. Although the embargo was politically costly for Jefferson, he persisted in it, enforcing it with repressive measures that were inconsistent with his values.

Entire books have been written on Jefferson's enigmatic personality. This much is certain: He was a gifted political pragmatist *when he chose to be.* But he had a darker and less pliable side. Jefferson's flexibility was evident when he put aside his constitutional scruples in order to acquire the Louisiana Territory. The other side of his psyche manifested itself in his rigid adherence to a counterproductive embargo. His political skill made his first-term successes possible, and his ideological blinders contributed to his second-term failures.

THE POLITICAL INCOMPETENCE OF JOHN QUINCY ADAMS

John Quincy Adams's public service began at age fourteen, when he served as an aide to the American minister in Russia. It ended at age eighty, when he died after suffering a stroke on the floor of Congress. During the course of his career, Adams was minister to the Netherlands, Prussia, Russia, and Great Britain; helped negotiate the end of the War of 1812; was secretary of state;

and capped his career with seventeen years of post-presidential service in the House of Representatives. Adams has been widely praised for his courage in advancing unpopular views as a member of Congress and for his effectiveness as a diplomat, but he was one of the least-effective presidents in American history.

Adams brought many of his presidential difficulties upon himself. He became chief executive in 1824 after running second to Andrew Jackson in an election that had to be resolved in the House of Representatives because none of its four candidates had a majority of the electoral vote. The necessary votes to make him the winner were supplied by Speaker of the House Henry Clay. Adams then took the politically disastrous action of naming Clay as his secretary of state. Jackson charged that there had been a "corrupt bargain" with Adams, firing the opening salvo in the next presidential campaign. From then on, Jackson's supporters did what they could to deny Adams a record of accomplishment.

In his first message to Congress, Adams proposed an array of policy departures that would have been visionary for a landslide winner rather than a minority president who had finished a distant second in the popular vote. Included was a program of public improvements; a national bankruptcy law; and the establishment of a department of the interior, a national university, and an astronomical observatory. Adams's ambitious program might have been taken seriously a century later in the period of positive government, but it was widely held in his time that the best government is the least government.

Adams's program was met with a mixture of indifference and opposition. A politically able president might have moderated his proposals, established priorities, and set about building support for the measures he deemed most important. It was not in Adams's character, however, to make such adjustments. In 1826, Jackson's supporters won control of Congress. In 1828, Adams's opponents compounded his difficulties by enacting a prohibitively high tariff. Adams was aware that the measure would embarrass him politically, but he signed it on the principle that the veto should only be used to strike down legislation on constitutional grounds. Adams was also handicapped by his refusal to cultivate political support and to discharge members of his administration who were working against him.

John Quincy Adams resembled his father in being ill suited for leadership in a democracy. But he differed from the senior Adams in that he was marked by rigidity rather than passivity. The younger Adams was an archetypical political purist who lacked the capacity to bend to political realities and do what was called for to get results.

ANDREW JACKSON: FORCE OF NATURE

Andrew Jackson was a barely educated frontier general who nevertheless succeeded in redefining the role of the chief executive. Jackson established a precedent for conceiving of the presidency as a policy-making institution rather than an office principally responsible for carrying out the will of Congress. He also anticipated the modern practice of making extensive use of advisers and aides. And he transformed the veto from a rarely used instrument for negating unconstitutional measures to a means of influencing public policy, vetoing more bills than his predecessors combined.

The defining episodes of Jackson's presidency were the nullification crisis and the bank war. The nullification crisis was triggered by the claim of southerners that states have the right to declare federal laws null and void within their boundaries. In 1832, a South Carolina convention voted to invalidate a pair of tariffs that had an adverse economic effect on the South and to secede from the Union rather than allow them to be enforced in the state. Jackson responded with a combination of threat and conciliation. He signed a bill that authorized him to use military power to enforce the collection of tariffs, but he also assented to a measure that provided for tariff reduction. South Carolina repealed its nullification of the tariffs.

The Bank of the United States was originally created as part of the financial reforms of the Washington administration. Jackson's confrontation with it was slow in developing, but by its conclusion the United States no longer had a central banking system and would not have one until the passage of the Federal Reserve Act in 1913. Jackson had a frontiersman's distrust of banks and credit. In January 1832, the bank's strong-willed president, Nicholas Biddle, requested that its charter be renewed even though it had four more years to run. Biddle and his congressional allies reasoned that Jackson would not dare attack a perceived pillar of the economy in an election year.

Congress granted Biddle's request, but Jackson vetoed the action, denouncing the bank in a blistering veto message. His veto was sustained. Jackson then withdrew the government's funds from the Bank of the United States, which went bankrupt before long. Jackson once declared that the bank was trying to kill him, but that he would kill it. In doing so he destroyed an institution that in the view of many economic historians played a constructive part in stabilizing the economy.

Like George Washington, Andrew Jackson brought exceptional force of character to the conduct of the presidency although he often lacked our first president's sense of political prudence. He fought a war against the national bank that many of his close advisers had counseled against as being far too risky.

Had a Democrat like Martin Van Buren been in office there almost certainly would have been no bank war. Jackson's uncompromising stance against nullification played better with the New England opposition than it did with his own Democratic constituency, but Jackson persevered nonetheless. Throughout his presidency, Old Hickory plunged without hesitation into the political fray, foreshadowing the presidencies of the twentieth and twenty-first centuries in which the chief executive is the central political actor in the nation.

THE PRESIDENTIAL DIFFERENCE

The American presidency has been described as a chameleon that takes its color from the personality of the president. The observation is particularly apt for the presidency in its infancy when incumbents were painting on a largely empty canvas. Faced with the ambiguities of the Constitution, these men imposed their personal proclivities on their jobs.

Some of the early presidents—most notably Washington, Jefferson, Jackson—had personal qualities that were conducive to placing their stamp on the nation's policies and politics. Others—especially John Adams and John Quincy Adams—were ill suited for the demands of presidential leadership. Presidential success and failure has many causes, but among the most important are the skills, judgment, temperament, and other personal qualities the chief executive brings to the office.

CON: Stephen Skowronek

When a president succeeds, Americans' natural inclination is to laud the special talents and skills he brought to the office; when things go wrong, they look for personal missteps and character flaws. There is something comforting in these judgments, for they sustain confidence in the office of the presidency no matter what the experience of the particular incumbent holding power at the moment. So long as performance is tied to the personal attributes of the individual president, success is always a possibility; it awaits only the right combination of character and skill. So long as the presidency is a true test of the person, its incumbents are free to become as great as they can be.

Much of what is written about the presidency reinforces these conceits. Typically, analysis of presidential leadership begins by describing an office that all presidents have shared, a position defined by constitutional arrangements that have undergone remarkably little change since 1789. To this is added the trappings of modernity—new governing responsibilities imposed on the office in the wake of the Great Depression and World War II and new resources made available to it. These responsibilities and resources distinguish the leadership situation shared by all presidents after Franklin D. Roosevelt from that of all their predecessors. Setting things up this way, the analysis holds the demands and capacities of the office constant over the latter half of the twentieth century and presents leadership as a problem of how best to apply the resources of the modern presidency to the responsibilities of the modern presidency. In effect, each modern incumbent becomes a new source of insight into what attributes of character and skill work best, what strategies are most effective, what it takes to measure up.

In fact, however, the political demands on incumbents and the leadership capacities of the office of the presidency vary considerably from one administration to the next, and much of what is taken to be evidence of personal flaws and leadership skills can be accounted for by paying closer attention to the particular relationships established between the presidency and the political system by each incumbent in turn. To see how, we first need a clear idea of these changing relationships, and that, in turn, entails thinking about presidential history a bit differently. Rather than set the modern presidents apart from the pre-moderns to treat them as a separate and coherent group, we will need to compare them individually with counterparts in earlier periods. By making better use of the whole history of presidential leadership, we can better assess the contextual conditions under which great leaders typically arise and identify the limitations on leadership possibilities imposed by less fortuitous circumstances.

The alternative history I have in mind charts change in American politics through the recurring establishment and disintegration of relatively durable political regimes. This regime-based structure of American political history has been widely observed by political scientists and historians alike. It demarcates the rise and decline of Federalist nationalism between 1789 and 1800, of Jeffersonian democracy between 1800 and 1828, of Jacksonian democracy between 1828 and 1860, of Republican nationalism between 1860 and 1932, and of New Deal liberalism between 1932 and 1980. Each of these regimes can be identified with the empowerment of an insurgent political coalition whose reconstruction of basic governing arrangements endured through various subsequent configurations of party power. Just as America's fragmented constitutional system has made sweeping political change rare and difficult to achieve, it has worked similarly to perpetuate the ideological and programmatic commitments of the few insurgencies that have succeeded. To this extent at least, the regime structure of American political history may be considered a by-product of the constitutional structure of American government. It is manifest today in the persistence of the conservative regime ushered in by Ronald Reagan in 1980.

Looking over the course of each of these regimes suggests a number of typically structured relationships between the presidency and the political system, and thinking about the modern presidents in these terms places each of them in a unique analytic relationship with the presidents of the past. I do not mean to suggest that regime formation and decay are processes external to presidential leadership; on the contrary, I mean to show that the active intervention of presidents at various stages in these processes has driven them forward. What I am suggesting is that we try to understand the political demands and challenges of presidential leadership as variables mediated by the generation and degeneration of these political orderings, and that we reverse the standard analytic procedure by holding personality and skill constant and examining the typical political effects of presidential action in the differently structured political contexts characteristic of the U.S. constitutional system.

THE POLITICAL STRUCTURES OF PRESIDENTIAL LEADERSHIP

Each regime begins with the rise to power of a new political coalition out to construct and legitimize alternative governing arrangements and to recast relations between state and society in ways advantageous to its members. These coalitions will then attempt to extend their claims on power by elaborating and modifying their basic agendas in ways that are responsive to new political demands and changes in the nation at large. Once they are established, however, coalition interests can have an enervating effect on the governing capacities of these regimes. An immediate and constant problem is posed by conflicts of interest within the dominant coalition. The danger here is that attempts to elaborate the coalition's political agenda in ways responsive to new governing conditions will focus a sectarian struggle, weaken regime support through factional disaffection, and open new avenues to power for the political opposition. A longer-range, and ultimately more devastating, problem is posed by changes in the nation at large that throw into question the dominant coalition's most basic commitments of ideology and interest. The danger here is that the entire political regime will be called into question as an inadequate governing instrument and then repudiated wholesale in a nationwide crisis of political legitimacy.

Considering the history of the presidency in this light, two systemic relationships stand out as especially significant for an analysis of the politics of leadership. The first is the president's affiliation with the political complex of interests, institutions, and ideas that dominated state/society relations before he came to office. The second is the current standing of these governmental arrangements in the nation at large. These relationships are always highly nuanced, but the basic variations are easily discerned, and when it comes to explaining outcomes, they do a good deal of the work. For the sake of simplicity, the leadership problem can be conceptualized by referring to those institutions with which political regimes are invariably identified in America—namely, the political parties. With the use of this shorthand, the leadership problem confronting each president can be framed by the answers to two simple questions: Is the president affiliated with the political party that has defined the government's basic commitments of ideology and interest? Are the governmental commitments of that party vulnerable to direct repudiation as failed and irrelevant responses to the problems of the day?

Answers to these questions specify four typical opportunity structures for the exercise of political leadership by a president. In the first, the basic governmental commitments of the previously dominant political party are vulnerable to direct repudiation, and the president is associated with the opposition to them (the politics of reconstruction). In the second, the basic governmental commitments of the previously dominant political party are again on the line, but this time the president is politically affiliated with them (the politics of disjunction). In the third, the governmental commitments of the previously dominant political party still appear timely and politically resilient, but the president is linked with the political opposition to them (the politics of preemption). In the fourth, the governmental commitments of the previously dominant political party again appear to hold out robust solutions to the problems of the day, and the president is affiliated with them (the politics of articulation).

These four opportunity structures are represented in Table 12-1, with the "previously dominant political party" designated as the "regime party" for easy reference. Each of these structures defines a different institutional relationship between the presidency and the political system; each engages the president in a different type of politics; and each defines a different kind of leadership challenge. These differences are summarized in the four cells of the table. Any discussion of the table must be prefaced, however, by two points of clarification. First, the table is a schematic presentation of pure types that are only more or less closely approximated in history. In the discussion that follows, the presidents that best fit each type are grouped together. The objective is to highlight the distinctive problems and dynamics of political action that adhere to leadership in these situations and, by implication, to reconsider the problems and prospects faced by contemporary presidents. The procedure radically delimits the play of personality and skill in determining leadership outcomes,

Table 12-1

The Political Structures of Presidential Leadership

		Presidents' Political Identity	
		Opposed	*Affiliated*
Regime party commitments	Vulnerable	Politics of reconstruction	Politics of disjunction
	Resilient	Politics of preemption	Politics of articulation

Source: Stephen Skowronek.

but, in doing so, it may allow a more precise determination of their significance. The second point is that this typology does not provide an independent explanation of the historical patterns on which it draws. There is no accounting here for whether a regime affiliate or a regime opponent will actually be elected (or otherwise come into office), nor for when in the course of the nation's development a regime's basic governmental commitments will be called into question. My purpose is to reorganize the analysis of the politics of leadership by cutting into political history at certain typical junctures. It is to suggest the rather blunt ways in which political structure has delimited the political capacities of the presidency and informed the impact of presidential action on the political system as a whole.

Politics of Reconstruction

The *politics of reconstruction* has been most closely approximated in the administrations of Thomas Jefferson, Andrew Jackson, Abraham Lincoln, Franklin D. Roosevelt, and Ronald Reagan. Each led a political insurgency and rose to power on the heels of an electoral upheaval in political control of the institutions of the federal government. More specifically, their victories were driven by a nationwide crisis of political legitimacy—a tide of discontent with the established order of things potent enough to dislodge a long-established majority party from its dominant position in Congress as well as the presidency. With political obligations to the past severed in this way, these presidents were thrust beyond the old regime into a political interregnum in which they were directly engaged in a systemic recasting of the government's basic commitments of ideology and interest. It is in these circumstances, and apparently only in these circumstances, that presidents are free to do what all political leaders seek to do: redefine legitimate national government in their own terms.

These presidents are widely regarded as the most effective of all political leaders in presidential history, but what is less well appreciated is that they shared the same basic relationship to the political system at large. They are all known as great communicators, but this seems to have less to do with any common training or shared skill than with the fact that they all had the same basic message to communicate. Each was able to repudiate received commitments of ideology and interest outright, to indict them forthrightly as failed and illegitimate responses to the problems of the day, and to identify his leadership with a new beginning, with the salvation of the nation from political bankruptcy.

More important, however, is what the performance of leaders in this situation can say about the structured capacities of the presidency as a political institution. Order-shattering elections do not themselves shape the future, but they vastly expand the president's capacities to break prior governmental commitments and to orchestrate a political reordering of state–society relations. It is significant in this regard that none of the presidents who reconstructed the terms and conditions of legitimate national government had much success in actually resolving the tangible problems that gave rise to the nationwide crisis of political legitimacy in the first place. Jefferson's embargo policy proved to be a total failure in dealing with the international crisis of the opening years of the nineteenth century; Jackson's attempt to deal with the long-festering problem of national banking precipitated an economic panic and ultimately exacerbated a devastating depression in the late 1830s; Lincoln's proposed solution to the sectional conflict of the 1850s plunged the nation into a civil war; and Roosevelt's New Deal failed to pull the nation out of the depression of the 1930s. But what these presidents could do, that their predecessors could not, was to define for themselves the significance of the events they oversaw and to secure the legitimacy of the new governing commitments they brought to power. Released from the burden of upholding the integrity of the old regime, these presidents were not restricted in their leadership to mere problem solving. Unaffiliated with the old regime, they reformulated the nation's political agenda as a direct response to the manifest failures of the immediate past, presented their solutions as the only alternative to national ruin, and galvanized political support for a government that eyed an entirely new set of possibilities.

The leadership opportunities afforded by this kind of political breakthrough are duly matched by its characteristic political challenges. In penetrating to the core of the political system and forthrightly reordering relations between state and society, these presidents ultimately found it imperative to try to secure a governmental infrastructure capable of perpetuating their cause. The shape of the new regime came to depend on the way party lines were recast and on how institutional relationships within the government were reorganized. Reconstructive presidents are all great party builders, and each is engaged in rooting out the residual institutional supports for the politics of the past. Court battles, bank wars, a real civil war—great confrontations that dislodged entire frameworks of governing—are the special province of the reconstructive leader, and they can be counted on to forge new forms of opposition as well as support. The reconstructive leader passes to his successor a political system that is not only reconfigured in its basic commitments of ideology and interest, but also newly constricted in its potential for independent action.

Politics of Disjunction

The *politics of disjunction* has been most closely approximated in the administrations of John Adams, John Quincy Adams, Franklin Pierce, James Buchanan, Herbert Hoover, and Jimmy Carter. With due regard for the reputations of these men for political incompetence, it is evident in identifying them as a group that they shared what is an impossible leadership situation. Rather than orchestrating a political breakthrough in state–society relations, these presidents were compelled to cope with the breakdown of those relations. Their affiliation with the old regime at a time when its basic commitments of ideology and interest were being called into question severely limited their ability to control the meaning of their own actions, and this limitation ultimately turned their office into the focal point of a nationwide crisis of political legitimacy. This situation imparts to the president a consuming preoccupation with a political challenge that is really a prerequisite of leadership—that is, establishing political credibility.

Each of the major historical episodes in the politics of disjunction has been foreshadowed by a long-festering identity crisis within the old majority party itself. But the distinctiveness of this juncture goes beyond these simmering tensions within the ranks; it lies in changes within the nation itself that obscure the regime's relevance as an instrument of governance and cloud its legitimacy as caretaker of the national interest. The Adamses, Pierce, Buchanan, Hoover, and Carter are notable for their open recognition of the vulnerabilities of the establishments with which they were affiliated; each promised to solve national problems in a way that would repair and rehabilitate the old order. But solving the nation's problems is a hard test for any president, and in this situation, in which they have little else to offer, they find themselves in especially difficult straits. Actions that challenge established commitments in the name of rehabilitation and repair are likely to leave the president isolated from his most likely political allies, and actions that reach out to allies and affirm established commitments will provide insurgents with proof positive that the president has nothing new to offer, that he really is nothing more than a symptom of the problems of the day.

Invariably, these presidents drive forward the crisis of legitimacy they came into office to forestall. Unable to control the meaning of their own actions, they find their actions defined by others. They become the leading symbols of systemic political failure and regime bankruptcy and provide the reconstructive leader his essential premise. Certainly, it is no accident that the presidents who have set the standard of political incompetence in American political history are succeeded by presidents who set the standards of political mastery. This recurrent coupling of dismal failure with towering success suggests that the contingent political relationship between the presidency and the political system is far more telling of leadership prospects than the contingencies of personality and skill.

Politics of Preemption

The *politics of preemption* has engaged a large number of presidents. Some of the more aggressive leaders among them are John Tyler, Andrew Johnson, Grover Cleveland, Woodrow Wilson, Richard Nixon, and Bill Clinton. The men in this grouping stand out as wild cards in American political history. As their experiences indicate, the politics of leadership in this situation is especially volatile, and perhaps least susceptible to generalization. Tyler was purged from the ranks of the party that elected him; Wilson took a disastrous plunge from the commanding heights of world leadership during World War I into the political abyss; and Andrew Johnson and Nixon were crippled by impeachment proceedings. Of all the presidents who might be grouped in this category, only Dwight D. Eisenhower finished a second term without suffering a precipitous reversal of political fortune, but this exception is itself suggestive, for Eisenhower alone kept whatever intentions he might have had for altering the shape of national politics well hidden.

As leader of the opposition to a regime that still claims formidable political, ideological, and institutional support, the president interrupts the working agenda of national politics and intrudes into the establishment as an alien power. The opportunity for creative political leadership in this situation comes from the independence that the president enjoys by virtue of his opposition stance. However, so long as the incumbent is unable to issue a forthright repudiation of established commitments as bankrupt and illegitimate solutions to the problems of the day, opposition leadership is limited in its reconstructive power. Short of authority to redefine legitimate national government, preemptive leaders exploit their relative freedom from received political definitions.

They disavow orthodoxies of all kinds. They offer hybrid political alternatives. Their attraction lies in their unabashedly mongrel appeal, their free mixing of different, seemingly contradictory political commitments.

As a practical matter, preempting the political discourse of an established regime means simultaneously carrying the support of its stalwart opponents, avoiding a frontal attack on the orthodoxy they oppose, and offering disaffected interests normally affiliated with the dominant coalition a modification of the regime's agenda that they will find more attractive. Floating free of established commitments, preemptive leaders look for and play upon latent interest cleavages and factional discontent within the ranks of the regime's traditional supporters. Though these opportunities are not hard to identify, the political terrain to be negotiated in exploiting them is treacherous. Testing both the tolerance of stalwart opponents and the resilience of establishment allies, preemptive leaders provoke the defenders of regime norms to assault the president's highly personalized, seemingly normless political manipulations.

Compared with presidents caught in a politics of disjunction, preemptive leaders have a much greater opportunity to establish and exploit their political independence; all preemptive leaders who were elected to office in the first instance were reelected to second terms. The danger here is not that the president will get caught in a systemic rejection of regime norms per se, but that he will find himself the object of a relentless campaign of character assassination, the effect of which would be to confirm those norms. Compared with a president engaged in the politics of reconstruction, these leaders do not cut into national politics deeply enough to create durable political alternatives, and personal political isolation is the ever-present danger. Preemptive leadership is, in fact, historically unique in its propensity to provoke impeachment proceedings. Probing alternative lines of political cleavage, these presidents may well anticipate future party-building strategies, but they are more effective at disrupting the established political regime than at replacing it.

Politics of Articulation

The *politics of articulation* has engaged the largest number of presidents; in contemporary politics George Bush and his son George W. Bush both fit the bill. Although it may be no more "normal" a situation than any other, this situation does pinpoint the distinctive problems of political leadership that arise when relations between the incumbent and established regime commitments are the most consonant. Here the presidency is the font of political orthodoxy and the president is the minister to the faithful. The leadership posture is wholly affirmative; the opportunity at hand is to service coalition interests, to deliver on outstanding political commitments on the regime's agenda, and to update these commitments to accord with the times. The corresponding challenge is to uphold definitions, to affirm established norms, to maintain a sense of regime coherence and integrity in changing times, and to mitigate and manage the factional ruptures within the ranks of the regime's traditional supporters that inevitably accompany alternations in the status quo ante. These challenges have been met in various ways, and with varying degrees of skill, but a look at the record suggests that the political effects are pretty much the same.

Consider the most impressive of the bunch. In each of America's major political regimes, there has been one particular episode in orthodox innovation that stands out for its programmatic accomplishments. In the Jeffersonian era, it was the administration of James Monroe; in the Jacksonian era, the administration of James Polk; in the Republican era, the administration of Theodore Roosevelt; in the era of New Deal liberalism, the administration of Lyndon B. Johnson. These administrations were not only pivotal in the course of each regime's development, but also emblematic of the problems this situation poses for presidential leadership. These men exercised power in what were, for all appearances, especially propitious circumstances for orthodox innovation. At the outset of each presidency, a long-established regime party was affirmed in its control of the entire national government, and the national posture was so strong at home and abroad that it left no excuses for not finally delivering on long-heralded regime promises. Each president thus set full sail at a time when it was possible to think about completing the unfinished business of national politics, realizing the regime's vision of America, and finally turning the party of orthodoxy into a consensual party of the nation. To that end, each in fact enacted a full and programmatic policy package.

But just as surely as a leadership project of culmination and completion suggests a great leap into the promised land, it accentuates the underlying problem of definition, of upholding fundamental commitments in some coherent fashion and having old allies see the new arrangements as the legitimate expression of their ideals. Each of America's great orthodox innovators found his administration mired in the dilemmas of reconciling old commitments with the expansive political possibilities at hand. Leading a regime at the apex of its projection of national power and purpose, each was beset by a political implosion of conflicting expectations. By pushing ahead with the received business of national politics and embellishing its commitments, these presidents fomented deep schisms within their own ranks; by making real changes in governing commitments, they undercut their own ability to speak for the party faithful. While most fully articulating his regime as a system of national government, each of these presidents was charged with a betrayal of the faith, and each pulled the regime into an accelerated sectarian struggle over the true meaning of orthodoxy. These presidencies were not undermined by the assaults of their nominal political opponents but by the disaffection of their ostensible allies.

CHARACTER AND SKILL IN CONTEXT

Presidential success, in summary, is determined at least as much by systemic factors as by presidential character, decision-making styles, or political skills. All presidents possess a modicum of political competence, but the political challenges they face shift abruptly from one presidency to the next. If this analysis is correct, any evaluation of the importance of a president's personal attributes and skills in leadership must be rendered with great caution.

Take Bill Clinton. Setting Clinton's experience against that of other preemptive presidents recasts understanding of both the typical and extraordinary aspects of his leadership. Although the convulsive character of the Clinton administration stands out among recent presidencies, it fits a recurrent pattern of extraordinary volatility in pursuit of a third way. Independence is the watchword of preemptive leadership, and in exercising this independence preemptive leaders provoke intense political struggles in which their own personal codes of conduct take center stage. Other presidents may be judged incompetent or misguided; these presidents have been attacked as moral degenerates, congenitally incapable of rising above nihilism and manipulation.

When the attraction of "third-way politics" under Woodrow Wilson and Richard Nixon became evident, opponents labeled them "Shifty Tom" (Wilson's first name was Thomas) and "Tricky Dick." When the same became evident under Clinton, his opponents saddled him with the label "Slick Willy." These characterizations are all of a type—a political type, not a personality type. They are characteristic of the personalization of politics that occurs when an opposition leader seeks to preempt established conceptions of the political alternatives and to substitute a third way. Determined to sustain their contention that Clinton's "New Democratic Party" was really a ploy masking a rearguard defense of liberalism, Republicans deftly transposed the question of ideology into a question of character. Character flaws offered an explanation for Clinton's repeated forays onto conservative ground; they accounted for his use of the presidency to mask his party's true leanings and selectively incorporate his opponents' most attractive positions. As Clinton challenged received definitions of liberal and conservative, of Democrat and Republican, and of left, right, and center, opponents compiled evidence from his personal life to suggest that he really had no standards at all, that he was wholly lacking in principles. By casting Clinton as a man who never cared much for the truth, who had proven incapable of standing by any commitment, and who had no higher purpose than his own self-indulgence, opponents found a way to preserve the truth that they wished to promote—namely, that Democrats remained a desperate party of discredited ideas and debased leadership, while the Republicans remained the only legitimate exponents of national solutions.

Consider, too, the leadership of George W. Bush. As indicated, Bush came to power as an orthodox innovator; his political challenge was to redeem long-standing conservative commitments while at the same time updating the conservative agenda with politically attractive proposals addressed to the changing problems of the day. Plausible counterparts in other periods include James Monroe, James Polk, Theodore Roosevelt, and Lyndon Johnson. The pattern is clear. Each of these presidents moved forward aggressively with their updated versions of the orthodox agenda, and all of them ended up shattering the political foundations on which their accomplishments were to rest. Bush's leadership proved true to form. He advanced simultaneously on a variety of fronts—tax cuts, the turn to Iraq, deregulation, a new prescription drug benefit—and ultimately he left conservative government overextended, at cross-purposes, and tumbling into disarray. Before we dub these results a personal failure or a failure of political skill, we might want to think carefully about whether any president regardless of skill has solved the riddle of orthodox innovation.

Barack Obama is up next. He comes to power as an opposition leader at a time when long-standing commitments of ideology and interest have been exposed as failed and barren of new solutions to the problems of the day. Historically speaking, these have been the most auspicious of circumstances for political leadership in the American presidency. Obama finds himself better positioned politically than any president since Ronald Reagan. It would be absurd to assert that Obama is destined to join the ranks of America's greatest political leaders, but there is no mistaking that the historical context is ripe with that potential. Perhaps it is at these moments that skill becomes most telling, for comparatively speaking there is little else that would predict a shortfall in presidential performance.

RESOLVED, great presidents are agents of democratic change

PRO: Marc Landy

CON: Bruce Miroff

Presidential scholars periodically receive a letter inviting them to rank the presidents. They are asked to separate the "great" presidents from the "above average" presidents, the "failures" from the merely "average." The effort to rank presidents in this fashion dates from 1948, when historian Arthur M. Schlesinger famously asked fifty-five prominent fellow historians to grade past presidents: "A" signified great; "B," near great; "C," average; "D," below average; and "E," failure. The results were published in *Life* magazine. Believing there to be wisdom in numbers, some subsequent surveys dramatically expanded the panel of experts polled. In 1970, for example, sociologist Gary Maranell published a presidential ranking based on a survey of 571 scholars. And in 1982 historians Robert Murray and Tim Blessing released the results of their survey based on the responses of nearly 850 historians.

In the 1990s, the greatness rankings—not for the first time—became enveloped in partisan controversy. Conservatives were incensed at the low ranking that scholars gave to Ronald Reagan. In 1996 Arthur M. Schlesinger Jr. replicated his father's survey and found that his thirty-two experts ranked Reagan twenty-fifth, just above Chester A. Arthur. Reagan fared just as poorly in a poll of 719 political scientists and historians that was published in 1997. Believing (with good reason) that these surveys were tainted by the liberal and Democratic biases of political scientists and historians, conservatives decided to pick their own panel of experts. *Policy Review* selected a panel of more conservative scholars, which placed Reagan squarely in the near-great category. And in 2000 the *Wall Street Journal* and Federalist Society selected an "ideologically balanced group" of 132 scholars who also ranked Reagan as near great.

Although Reagan's standing varied dramatically in these polls, the more striking result was the extent of agreement in all of these surveys, spanning more than a half century and divergent ideologies, about which presidents were great and which were failures. Virtually every survey identified Abraham Lincoln, George Washington, and Franklin D. Roosevelt (usually in that order) as great. The survey respondents also generally agreed on the failures: James Buchanan, Ulysses S. Grant, and Warren G. Harding. Although the stock of particular presidents rose and fell over time—Dwight D. Eisenhower climbed from the lower end of the average category in 1962 to the top ten by 1996, for example—the great presidents stayed great and the mediocre presidents stayed mediocre. Nobody mistook Harding for a great president, and nobody deemed Lincoln a failure.

Although scholars seem to know presidential greatness when they see it, it is harder to say which behaviors or accomplishments qualify as great. Marc Landy's essay offers one way to define presidential greatness. Great presidents, Landy suggests, inspire "conservative revolutions"—that is, great presidents are those who fundamentally alter the political landscape in ways that align the political system more closely with the nation's guiding constitutional principles.

Bruce Miroff's essay asks readers to think hard about the dangers inherent in the concept of presidential greatness. Waiting for great presidents to arrive and act, Miroff warns, may enervate the nation's democracy by creating passive citizens. Miroff reminds readers, too, of the ways in which presidential actions have harmed American democracy. A president granted the power to do great things may also do great harm.

At the heart of the debate between Landy and Miroff lies the question of what citizens want from the presidency. Of course, few Americans would prefer James Buchanan to George Washington or Franklin Pierce to Franklin Roosevelt. No sane person prefers failure to success. But that does not settle the question. One needs to ask as well whether the concept of presidential greatness, and the ratings game that fuels that concept, encourages presidents to do more than is good for the political system. If greatness is defined, at least in part, as transforming the political system, then does the concept encourage presidents to pursue change over stability, recklessness over prudence? And does searching for the grail of greatness encourage presidents to create the kinds of crises that can justify heroic actions? Most of the "greatest" presidents, it is worth remembering, governed in times of war and widespread human misery.

PRO: Marc Landy

Any defense of the proposition that great presidents are agents of democratic change must begin with an explanation of what democratic change is and what it is not. In a democracy the people rule, but ruling is not merely a matter of arithmetic. Indeed, much of the most profound thinking about American democracy, from founder James Madison to French political observer Alexis de Tocqueville to President Abraham Lincoln, has been about coping with the problem of majority tyranny. The principles of republican government embedded in the Constitution represent an effort by the framers to ensure that the inalienable rights of life, liberty, and the pursuit of happiness would not be trampled by majorities. Democratic change, therefore, is not the same thing as change preferred by the majority.

During the last century, state and national constitutional rules, as well as the procedures of the political parties, have been revised in an increasingly majoritarian direction. Majoritarian simply means decision making on the basis of a majority of voters. Today, U.S. senators are directly elected by the voters and not by state legislatures, which was the practice in most states before adoption of the Seventeenth Amendment to the Constitution in 1913 requiring popular election. As a result of new rules adopted by the national political parties in the 1960s and 1970s and by state parties during a similar time span, primaries, not party leaders, now govern the choice of party nominees. Many states also make liberal use of the tools of direct democracy: popular referendums, recalls, and initiatives. In 2003 the voters of California even fired their governor. These majoritarian changes have not proven tyrannical. Instead, they have reflected the debilitating flip side of majority tyranny: majority apathy. The low turnout in most primary and general elections and the meager attendance at town meetings, legislative hearings, and other political forums all demonstrate the people's desire to forgo political participation. For a change to be truly democratic, it must do more than increase the opportunities to have a voice in government. It also must improve the capacity of the citizenry to make use of such opportunities and to do so wisely.

Anyone who has ever sat through an academic committee meeting knows that tyranny and apathy are not the only vices to which democracy is prone. Others include indecision, shortsightedness, wishful thinking, vengefulness, irresponsibility, and selfishness. Luckily, as those who have sat through such committee meetings also know, such vices can be mitigated by the mutual instruction that democratic deliberation makes possible. Compelling arguments by my colleagues have sometimes helped me to overcome my own indolence, pettiness, and narrow-mindedness. But American democracy is a sprawling affair; it cannot be squeezed into a committee meeting room. Because the opportunities for genuine deliberation are few, other means must be found to promote democratic virtues and limit democratic vice.

When the Republic has faced its greatest challenges, the chief agent for promoting true democratic change has been the president. At crucial moments in their history, Americans had to be taught how to behave like real democrats. But they proved to be quite educable. The great American presidents were agents of democratic change, because they were great teachers. They prodded and dared Americans to show courage and compassion. But they also accepted democratic discipline: they did not coerce citizens to change, and they submitted themselves to the people's judgment. However audacious their demands, they never interfered in the people's ability to hold them to account, to defeat them at the next election. High among America's democratic moments are the presidential elections of 1864, 1944, and 2004, when in the midst of war American presidents subjected themselves to the verdict of the electorate.

The character of democratic presidential leadership has been obscured, however, because the leading presidential scholars have either underestimated or overestimated the president's ability to lead. The most celebrated of all presidential scholars, Richard E. Neustadt, understood presidential leadership to be essentially an exercise in manipulation. To be politically effective, a president had to court public opinion assiduously. Obsessed with maintaining popularity, the president could ill afford to teach, which often requires imparting unwelcome truths.[1] At the other extreme, James MacGregor Burns defined great leadership as transformational. "The leader can bring about lasting change ... only by altering ... the channels in which the stream of events takes place."[2] Stephen Skowronek is closer to Burns than to Neustadt, but his understanding of transformation stresses the role that great presidents play in shattering the existing order. "Time and again the lesson is the same: *the power to recreate order hinges on the authority to repudiate it.* ... [T]he American presidency has proven itself most effective politically as an instrument of negation."[3]

All leaders must at times be manipulative and must at times work to undermine previously held beliefs. But great democratic leadership aims in a different direction. It seeks to make citizens more *resistant* to manipulation and more able to recognize what elements of the existing order are worth *preserving*. It is not the business of democratic leaders to transform their followers. If indeed such transformations are possible, they are the province of religion, not politics—and especially not democratic politics. As Abraham Lincoln put it in his first inaugural address in 1861, democratic leaders urge citizens to respond to "the better angels of our nature," not in order to escape human limitations, but rather to realize the best possibilities those limitations permit.

In our book *Presidential Greatness,* Sidney M. Milkis and I coined the term *conservative revolution* to describe the kinds of democratic change that great presidents inspire.[4] Such change is revolutionary because it significantly alters the existing regime. It is conservative because it reconciles those alterations with American constitutional traditions and purposes. Conservative revolutions ensure that political innovations go with the American constitutional grain.

Two tools that figure prominently in conservative revolution are rhetoric and party leadership. Presidential words and deeds shape the quality and character of the citizenry. They can either make the public more submissive and self-regarding or encourage it to be more energetic and public-spirited. Just as parents are held responsible for the moral and practical education of their children, so presidents bear responsibility for the education of citizens. Legal scholar (later Supreme Court justice) Felix Frankfurter said of President Franklin D. Roosevelt that he took the "country to school."[5]

Since George Washington's presidency, all the conservative revolutionary presidents have been founders or re-founders of political parties. Over the course of American history, political parties have been the most important source of democratic accountability. Parties have not only held presidents to account, but also have given them a strong popular base for their conservative revolutionary projects. The rest of this essay describes how great presidents have used rhetoric and party leadership to accomplish democratic change by forging conservative revolutions.

THOMAS JEFFERSON

The election of 1800 was the first popularly contested presidential election. Although often called the "Revolution of 1800," it was an exceedingly lawful and merciful revolution, and presidential rhetoric played a decisive role in keeping it that way. In his first inaugural address, President Jefferson reminded the people, including the vengeful among his followers, that "we are all republicans, we are all federalists." He meant that the principles shared by his supporters and opponents, especially their mutual commitment to the constitutional order, were far more important than their differences. Jefferson followed up this plea for unity with a pledge to preserve the general government in its "whole constitutional vigor."

Jefferson's "revolution" had elements of both style and substance. He made the president look like a democrat. He jettisoned the presidential coach and rode his own horse. He ignored distinctions of rank at official functions. He severed the connection between rank and privilege that the Federalists had sought to establish. He presided over a drastic reduction in the size of the national government. To this day, the United States retains a degree of local self-government, commitment to the rights of individuals, mistrust of elites, and lack of centralized rule that is unique among modern democracies. But these profound changes were wrought in a manner consonant with fundamental constitutional principles. Jefferson steadfastly resisted pressure from his more radical congressional allies to destroy the constitutional system of checks and balances by making the courts and the president subservient to Congress.

Jefferson's conservative revolution could not have occurred without his sustained efforts at party building. As the beloved author of the Declaration of Independence, Jefferson might well have been elected in 1800 in the absence of party. But without party support and party discipline, he would have become either a prisoner of the status quo or a fomenter of schismatic change. Jefferson used his party leadership to keep Republican moderates committed to major reforms of the judiciary, public finance, and administration, and to keep party radicals from undermining the form and substance of the Constitution.

ANDREW JACKSON

Andrew Jackson would seem to be a poor candidate for a conservative revolutionary. As a young lawyer and soldier, he was bold to the point of recklessness. He suffered recurrent illnesses and debilitating pain from the bullets lodged in his body from his many duels. Then-senator Martin Van Buren recognized that only the discipline of party could temper Jackson's imperious nature. He set about to reestablish the interregional alliance of Jeffersonians, anchored by the two largest states, New York and Virginia, and to offer Jackson its support in return for Jackson's pledge to conform to party principles. Jackson accepted the offer. Of course, he could have broken with the party after he was elected in 1828, but, to his own surprise, he found the mutual consultation and loyalty instilled through party to be so positive that he willingly succumbed to its discipline.

Jackson and Van Buren grafted a full-fledged party system onto the existing antipartisan political rootstock. By so doing, they preserved the integrity of the Constitution, while endowing American politics with hybrid democratic vigor. Parties were the bulwarks of decentralization. They were localized political associations that linked the people and the national government, thereby providing meaningful popular control of the executive.

Although rooted in locality, parties were knit together nationally. Initially, this unity was solely for the purpose of winning presidential elections. Over time, however, enduring bonds among party loyalists from different regions were forged in the heat of national partisan combat. Both Whigs and Democrats flourished in the South, West, and North. Indeed, the national party ties that developed provided the strongest political counterweight to the sectionalism that continually threatened to tear the country apart. Party provided the president with a national constituency to which he could be held accountable. The Democrats' great success inspired their opponents to create a similar national confederation of state and local party organizations. President Van Buren's reelection defeat by the Whig Party in 1840 ushered in a truly competitive party system, and the alternation in power between two major parties has helped to safeguard American liberty ever since.

Parties also reflected the concern first expressed by the Anti-Federalists that the Constitution did not adequately cultivate an active and competent citizenry. Because the citizens of a great commercial republic like the United States inevitably were tempted to become obsessed with private concerns, political parties were needed to engage them in civic affairs. Parties forge identities that transcend the candidates and issues of the moment and make it possible for individuals to form bonds of civic affiliation. Party loyalty encourages them to honor their public obligations even as they jealously guard their rights. As conceived by Jackson and Van Buren, party provided the vitality and solidarity necessary to complement the formalities of the Constitution.

Jackson also used rhetoric for critical "conservative revolutionary" purposes. In his memorable Nullification Proclamation of 1832, he expressly denied the Jeffersonian notion that the Union was merely a product of an agreement between the states and of which they were the sole constituents. Jackson claimed that the Union actually predates the Constitution and was formed as a result of the joint decision to declare independence from Great Britain and to fight for that independence as a nation rather than a coalition of states. Directly contradicting Jefferson, Jackson claimed that "the people of the United States formed the Constitution.... Not only did they establish the federal government but they are its citizens."[6] The right to make treaties, declare war, levy taxes, and exercise exclusive judicial and legislative powers were all functions of sovereign power. The states, then, for all these important purposes were no longer sovereign. The allegiance of their citizens was transferred to the government of the United States; they became U.S. citizens and owed obedience to the Constitution of the United States and to laws made in conformity with the powers it vested in Congress.[7]

Presaging Lincoln's later defense of the Constitution, Jackson went beyond rational-legal arguments to declare that "the Constitution is still the object of our reverence. The sages whose memory will always be reverenced have given us a practical and, as they hoped, a permanent constitutional compact."[8] Perhaps nothing so demonstrates Jackson's determination to foster such devotion as his willingness to invoke the name of Washington, "the Father of his Country," in support of it.[9] Such an encomium was a bitter pill indeed to the devout old Republican, who, as a young congressman, had been one of the few members of the House to vote against a congressionally drafted tribute to Washington issued in the wake of Washington's Farewell Address.[10]

The final pages of the Nullification Proclamation contain a hymn to the glories of the American nation-state that verges on the Whitmanesque. Jackson implores South Carolinians to

> consider the Government, uniting in one bond of common interest and general protection so many different States, giving to all their inhabitants the proud title of American citizen, protecting their commerce, securing their literature and their arts, facilitating their intercommunication, defending their frontiers and making their name respected in the remotest parts of the earth. Consider the extent of its territory, its increasing and happy population, its advance in arts which render life agreeable and the sciences which elevate the mind. See education spreading the lights of religion, morality and general information into every cottage in this wide extent of our Territories and States. Behold it as the asylum where the wretched and the oppressed find a refuge and support. Look on this picture of happiness and honor and say, we too are citizens of America.[11]

Jackson hardly needed to indulge in such a rhetorical outpouring if all he had wanted to do was mollify South Carolina. But Jackson had more than tariffs on his mind. Although the specific threat posed by the nullification ordinance could have been defused through compromise, to do so immediately would be to lose a crucial opportunity to educate his friends, Van Buren among them. His opponents Daniel Webster and John Quincy Adams already understood the need to preserve federal supremacy. It was the disciples of Jefferson, susceptible to the nullificatory contagion spread by his Kentucky resolution, who needed to improve their constitutional understanding. Jackson's deepest purpose in issuing the proclamation was to teach Van Buren and other Democrats how to combine their zeal for limited government with an equally strong attachment to the Union.

ABRAHAM LINCOLN

Lincoln wielded Jackson's nationalist precedent in the service of the boldest of all presidentially inspired conservative revolutions. In a series of speeches, he explained to the people why a house divided against itself could not endure—that is, why defense of the Constitution actually required a revolutionary act, the freeing of slaves. This stand was no mean feat, because the Constitution actually contained provisions protecting slavery. Lincoln overcame this anomaly by first invoking the key principles of the Declaration of Independence and then claiming that the basic purpose of the Constitution was to bring those principles to life. Drawing on a biblical verse, "a word fitly spoken is like apples of gold in a picture of silver," Lincoln made the Declaration's principle of "liberty for all" the measure of American political life. "The assertion of that principle at that time," Lincoln wrote, "was the word 'fitly spoken' which has proved an 'apple of gold' to us. The Union, and the Constitution, are the pictures of silver, subsequently framed around it. The picture was made not to conceal or destroy the apple; but to adorn and preserve it."[12] Thus Lincoln incorporated the liberty-loving Declaration into the order-providing Constitution, using the former to infuse meaning into the latter. Seen in this light, the "house" of the Union could not possibly endure "half slave and half free."[13]

Lincoln's success in ending slavery and winning the Civil War was also due to his brilliant use of party to mobilize and sustain public support for that difficult and bloody enterprise. Lincoln did not found the Republican Party. Like the Democratic and Whig Parties, the Republican Party grew out of local protest meetings and political organizations. But Lincoln steered the party to success on a national scale and sustained and nurtured it through its time of testing. The Lincolnian Republicans kept what was best about the existing party system and infused it with a greater sense of moral purpose.

In his famous debates with Illinois senator Stephen A. Douglas, a Democrat, Lincoln clarified the essential difference of principle between Democrats and Republicans. Republicans would not accept Douglas's amoral deference to majority rule as the means for determining whether a federal territory should adopt slavery. Lincoln also organized the Republican Party into a formidable political instrument for opposing slavery. He dispensed patronage with a vengeance, removing Democrats from federal offices and giving those jobs to Republicans from all the competing factions of the party. He displayed the same commitment to party unity in selecting and managing his cabinet, which included both William H. Seward, the party's leading moderate, and Salmon P. Chase, its leading antislavery militant. When the tension between Seward and Chase precipitated a cabinet crisis in 1862, Lincoln managed the dispute masterfully, maintaining the loyalty of both statesmen and the party factions they represented. His responsiveness to the needs of his party enabled him to wield it as a powerful weapon of war.

FRANKLIN D. ROOSEVELT

Roosevelt used both party and rhetoric to lead the New Deal conservative revolution. He infused a moribund Democratic Party with new life. Because he had placed the name of New York governor Alfred E. Smith, a Catholic, in nomination at two previous national party conventions, he was able to appeal to Catholics with far more success than any previous Protestant politician and thus to cement Catholic loyalty to the Democrats. By championing the rights of labor to organize, he established the American labor movement as a central element of the Democratic Party and preserved that attachment even when organized labor's top leader, John L. Lewis, deserted him in 1940. New Deal programs also earned the Democrats the allegiance of two previously Republican-leaning groups, blacks and Jews. FDR's greatest electoral victory, however, the one that confirmed the strength and persistence of the New Deal Democratic coalition, occurred posthumously. In 1948 Roosevelt's successor in office, Harry S. Truman, would never have defeated Republican Thomas E. Dewey on his own. But by wrapping himself in Roosevelt's shroud and emphasizing his credentials as a New Deal Democrat, Truman pulled off the greatest electoral upset of the twentieth century.

FDR's mastery of radio, as displayed in his famous "fireside chats," enabled him to explain the significance of the New Deal to the American people in appealing and comprehensible terms.[14] His most comprehensive explanation of his conservative revolution came in a campaign speech to San Francisco's Commonwealth Club. In it, the president declared it was time to recognize the "new terms of the old social contract" in order to take account of how the economy had been transformed by industrial capitalism and the ensuing concentration of economic power. Just as the founders had created the government on a foundation of political rights, it was now time to re-create the economy on the basis of economic rights. The traditional emphasis on individual self-reliance, he argued, must give way to governmental protection from the harshest vagaries of the marketplace. Basic economic security was to be a new government-guaranteed, self-evident right.[15] Thus Roosevelt sought to free the public from excessive economic uncertainty in a manner consonant with American constitutional principles and tradition.

AFTER FDR

No full-fledged conservative revolutions have occurred since the New Deal. But some modern presidents have promoted democratic changes and defeated antidemocratic challenges. They have used rhetoric and party leadership to fulfill

Lincoln's promise of political equality for African Americans and to mount a successful defense of liberal democracy against Soviet totalitarianism.

Although the Union victory in the Civil War had ostensibly promised legal and political equality to African Americans, the failure of Reconstruction and the passage of "Jim Crow laws" in the South deprived them of equal protection of the law and of the right to vote. Only presidential leadership could make this democratic promise a reality. If President Dwight D. Eisenhower had not sent troops to Little Rock, Arkansas, in 1958 and President John F. Kennedy had not sent federal marshals to Oxford, Mississippi, in 1962, federal court decisions ending racial segregation in education might have appeared unenforceable, making a mockery of African Americans' efforts to obtain justice through the courts. The Voting Rights Act of 1965 put the power of the Justice Department and the federal courts behind African Americans' right to vote, finally giving meaning to the Fifteenth Amendment, enacted almost a century earlier, which declared that the right to vote could not be abridged "on account of race, color, or previous condition of servitude." President Lyndon B. Johnson spearheaded the act's passage by making effective use of party and rhetoric. His bold 1964 election campaign succeeded in electing such a large number of northern Democrats to Congress that he no longer needed to water down potent voting rights provisions for the purpose of garnering southern Democratic support. In his address to Congress on voting rights on March 15, 1965, Johnson indelibly placed the weight and majesty of the presidency behind the cause of civil rights, even adopting the slogan of the civil rights movement—"we shall overcome"—as his own.

In the realm of foreign policy, the Truman administration, faced with the threat of Soviet domination of Europe and Asia, adopted a strategy of "containment" that committed the United States to wage a "cold war." To wage a cold war, Truman had to commit all the resources necessary to wage real war and deploy them in a fashion that would deter the enemy from instigating major hostilities. Although this strategy promised to keep casualties to a minimum, it required the American people to engage in sustained financial sacrifice and to endure the frustrations and anxieties that decades of continual confrontation with a powerful enemy engendered. From Truman to Reagan, over the course of more than forty years, presidents explained to the American people why such sacrifices and difficulties were necessary and why the patient firmness that containment required was better than either preemptive attack or appeasement.

Terrible mistakes were made prosecuting the cold war. On the home front, Eisenhower failed to confront Joseph R. McCarthy, thereby allowing the reckless Republican senator from Wisconsin, in his pursuit of domestic communist threats, to threaten the very freedoms the cold war was being fought to preserve. The failure of Johnson's strategy for fighting the Vietnam War came close to undermining public support for containment. But these mistakes did not prove fatal. The Senate censure of McCarthy precipitated his downfall and a renewed commitment to avoiding the excesses of McCarthyism. By electing Ronald Reagan, who opposed a nuclear freeze and supported a massive military buildup, the American people in 1980 demonstrated their continued support for the cold war. The inability of the Soviet Union to match this buildup undermined its morale and contributed to its implosion in 1991 and to the earlier toppling of the Berlin Wall in 1989.

Victory in the cold war, which owed so much to the presidential leadership exercised over more than four decades, heralded great democratic change. East Germans became citizens of a democratic Germany, and democratic governments were established in Poland, Hungary, the Czech Republic, and the Baltic states. Since Reagan, every president has sought to forge a foreign policy dedicated to human rights and democratization. These principles were at the heart of the coalition President George H. W. Bush assembled to drive Iraq from Kuwait in 1991. They were the rationale behind President Bill Clinton's decision to wage war against Serbia in Kosovo in 1999 and to immerse himself in the negotiations that sought to establish a broad-based government in Northern Ireland culminating in the Good Friday Agreement of 1998. They were also central to President George W. Bush's efforts to establish free government in Iraq as part of the broader war on global terror. Indeed, Bush was convinced that the only way to defeat terrorism is to bring democracy to places where it does not currently exist—most notably Egypt, Iran, and Saudi Arabia.[16] Barack Obama has adopted a different tone in his discussion of the war on terror, but it remains unclear to what extent, if at all, he is deviating from the commitments of his predecessors.

This identification of the American president with global democracy is not new; it dates back at least to Woodrow Wilson. But not since Wilson tried to use the post–World War I peace treaty to democratize Europe has a president committed himself so deeply to reforming the politics of foreign nations. In recognition of the profound importance of this development, this essay ends where it began, praising the president as an agent of democratic change while recognizing the dangers inherent in unfettered majoritarianism. To serve the cause of democracy, the president must pair exuberance with caution. He must use the bully pulpit not only to exhort those suffering under dictatorships to throw off their fetters, but also to help them understand that self-government requires self-control, not just self-expression. To find inspiration for this extraordinarily difficult assignment, the president can turn to predecessors in office. Every president can look to Thomas Jefferson, who, even as he was launching his "Revolution of 1800," reminded both his partisan allies and his opponents that when it came to fundamental questions "we are all Republicans, we are all Federalists." Every president can look to Abraham Lincoln, who, even as he was demanding that the South acknowledge African Americans as free persons and citizens, insisted that North and South reconcile in a spirit of "malice towards none and charity for all." Thus presidents promote democracy in large part by encouraging citizens to embody the great virtues that democracy can promote.

CON: Bruce Miroff

In the storybook history of the American presidency, great presidents are the champions and promoters of democratic change. Most Americans, especially those who were educated before the recent rise of a more revisionist-minded historical profession, are familiar with the landmarks of presidential service to democracy. Andrew Jackson combated elite privilege and opened government to the common man. Abraham Lincoln emancipated the slaves. Theodore Roosevelt castigated the "malefactors of great wealth" and committed the federal government to a "Square Deal" for all citizens. Franklin D. Roosevelt built a strong national state that offered both opportunity and security to working people. John F. Kennedy and Lyndon B. Johnson placed the weight of the federal government behind the civil rights of black Americans.[1]

Like most such stories that a people tell themselves to inspire pride and instill patriotism, there is enough truth in these tales to make the proposition that great presidents are agents of democratic change plausible. American history includes numerous episodes in which democratic values and practices have been advanced, and in many of these episodes the president's role has been necessary, even indispensable. Where structures of hierarchy and privilege have been deep-rooted and encrusted, the energy and force that presidents uniquely bring to the American political system have played a key part in democratic breakthroughs.

As Barack Obama begins his administration, hopes for a new era of presidential greatness are widespread. The very fact of electing an African American to the nation's highest office surely counts as a breakthrough for racial equality. Coming into the White House at a time of great economic distress, and pledging to rectify long-standing national failures in the areas of health care, energy, and education, Obama bids for a record of democratic achievements that will rank with the most acclaimed of his predecessors. If he is perceived as successful in meeting the enormous challenges he has outlined, a new chapter will be added to the storybook history of the presidency.

GREAT PRESIDENTS AS AGENTS OF DEMOCRATIC CHANGE

The presidents conventionally accorded the status of "greatness" have acted as agents of democratic change in famous episodes, whereas other individuals who might have occupied the executive office at the time would probably not have rendered the same democratic services. Rooted in the republican credo and lineage of the nation's founders, Andrew Jackson's predecessor, John Quincy Adams, favored government by gentry; it took the rough-hewn Jackson to sponsor and symbolize governance by self-made men from modest backgrounds. Harboring a deep revulsion toward the South's "peculiar institution," Abraham Lincoln moved gradually, but ultimately with boldness, to free the slaves; his chief rival for the presidency, Democratic senator Stephen A. Douglas of Illinois, had proclaimed that he did not care whether America embraced or rejected slavery. Theodore Roosevelt thundered and roared against business abuses that did not disturb his predecessor, William McKinley. If President-elect Franklin D. Roosevelt had been struck early in 1933 by the assassin's bullet that missed its target and instead killed Chicago's mayor, Anton J. Cermak, it is unlikely that Vice President-elect John Nance Garner, a conservative Texan, would have inaugurated a New Deal. Barry Goldwater, the very conservative Republican challenger that Kennedy anticipated and Johnson faced in 1964, was opposed to new civil rights legislation.

In advancing democratic values and practices, these presidents had to engage in fierce battles. First, they identified and named the powers and forces that impeded democracy. Second, they mustered the resources and mobilized the allies required to overcome antidemocratic resistance. Third, they institutionalized democratic change in legal forms, whether through legislation, executive orders, or constitutional amendments. Fourth, and perhaps most critically, they established the democratic meaning of the changes they promoted, educating Americans to a fuller and more expansive understanding of the democratic faith.

In light of these contributions to democratic change by great presidents, why is the resolution to which these arguments are directed more wrong than right? Why is the view of great presidents as agents of democratic change a flawed and even misleading way of understanding the history of the presidency?

Although the agency, or instrumental role, of great presidents has often been required for democratic advances, it has seldom been sufficient. Treating great presidents as agents of democratic change promotes the belief that great presidents are the *principal* agents of democratic change. Presidents thus become the heroes of democracy's story, and the agency of other democratic actors, which has been at least as indispensable, is obscured or neglected. When the great episodes of democratic change just described are revisited and examined more closely, it becomes clear that other agents initiated the changes that presidents later sponsored. In fact, at times it has taken the persistent and determined efforts of other actors to overcome presidents' initial reluctance and transform them into the democratic champions that they did not set out to be.

All presidents, even the great ones, operate within a larger field of forces. Andrew Jackson rode a wave of democratization in an expanding nation, and it was the rise of a mass electorate and the supplanting of gentry leadership by plebian politicians that encouraged Jackson to wage war on political and economic privilege. In Lincoln's case, antislavery instincts had to be balanced precariously with political caution and constitutional scruples; it was only the ability of abolitionist educators to prepare northern public opinion for a change that made it possible for Lincoln to come down decisively against slavery with the Emancipation Proclamation. Theodore Roosevelt's break with Republican orthodoxy about the country's gigantic trusts built on public outrage generated by Progressive "muckrakers" and reflected Roosevelt's anxiety that government inaction in the face of corporate abuses might spur the dreaded growth of a socialist movement. Franklin Roosevelt shifted in a more radical direction, toward the "Second New Deal" of social security and union rights, in response to the mobilization of workers and small farmers, and as a way to steal the limelight from populist demagogues. John Kennedy and Lyndon Johnson were compelled by the dramatic mass demonstrations of the civil rights movement to side with the cause of racial justice despite their prescient fears of alienating the white South.

In each case, the capacity of these great presidents to advance democratic causes depended on the groundwork laid by other agents of democratization. Without this groundwork, these presidents would not have conceived of the democratic projects associated with their names, nor would they have had the political muscle and momentum to bring these projects to a successful conclusion. Put differently, without pressure from the bottom up, presidents would not have championed democracy from the top down. Presidents, great or not, can accomplish some things on their own, but major democratic change is not one of them.

Some people might ask: what harm is there in offering presidents too much praise, or in overestimating the role of presidents and underestimating the role of others in producing democratic change?

The harm is partly intellectual: when great presidents are portrayed as the principal agents of democratic change and the contributions of others are overshadowed, Americans develop a distorted understanding of how change happens in the United States. Misunderstanding their past as having been driven by the deeds of a few great men, they fail to appreciate the sources and possibilities of change in their own time. The intellectual harm feeds a political and moral harm: a limitation in the public's sense of democratic responsibility. If great presidents have been the principal agents of democratic change in American history, the goal of citizens today should be to vote for and rally behind potentially great presidents. Dependence on presidential greatness, and not citizen activism, then becomes the recipe for democratic progress. Unfortunately, this is a recipe for a passive citizenry and a diminished democracy.

Yet the problem of looking to great presidents as agents of democratic change lies deeper than the distortion in understanding that it fosters. The transformative ambitions that drive great presidents to aim at democratic breakthroughs may also drive them to oversee breakdowns in democracy. The presidents associated with striking the greatest blows for democracy have, in most cases, been presidents who also struck blows against democracy. Presidential scholar Stephen Skowronek has written that the presidency is a blunt disruptive force, a "battering ram."[2] Battering rams open enemy fortresses, but they also wreak destruction. Great presidents have been paradoxical agents of change in American history, and the gains for democracy that they have secured must be measured against the restrictions of democracy that they have imposed. And so it is a good idea to revisit the stories of some great presidents one more time, and in somewhat greater detail, because the undemocratic features of the records of the great presidents are less familiar than their democratic accomplishments.

GREAT PRESIDENTS REVISITED

Andrew Jackson was an authentic champion of democratic equality—but only for white men. For Americans of color, his brand of democracy was a disaster. As president, Jackson, the "old Indian fighter," took the initiative to force the tribes residing in the southeastern states to move west across the Mississippi River, opening vast new acreage to land-hungry white settlers and speculators. As biographer Robert V. Remini observes, "Jackson ... took it upon himself to expel the Indians from their ancient haunts and decree that they must reside outside the company of civilized white men."[3] Endorsed by most whites, Jackson's removal policy meant dispossession and death for many Native Americans.

Jacksonian democracy was no more hospitable to African Americans. A supporter of slavery, Jackson was the first chief executive to face the emergence of antislavery agitation. His response was to attempt to stifle the dissemination of antislavery ideas. When angry southern mobs destroyed abolitionist pamphlets impounded by the post office, the president made no effort to enforce the postal laws; instead, he proposed new legislation authorizing the post office to prohibit mailing inflammatory writings to the slave states. When antislavery activists flooded Congress with petitions calling for the abolition of slavery in the District of Columbia, Jackson's legislative supporters backed a "gag rule" whereby the petitions were tabled and ignored. Ironically, it was the "elitist" president Jackson had defeated, John Quincy Adams, who, as a member of the House of Representatives, took the lead in fighting the gag rule and defending the First Amendment.

The supreme character in the story of the presidency and democracy, Abraham Lincoln, was also the president who most fully tested the constitutional limits to executive power over the liberties of Americans. Acting in the face of the gravest crisis to the survival of the Republic, Lincoln claimed for himself several powers that the Constitution assigned to Congress, sparking furious accusations from opponents that he was a dictator and a tyrant. In perhaps his most controversial move, the president set aside the writ of habeas corpus, a cornerstone of personal liberty whose suspension in times of rebellion or invasion is listed among the powers of Congress in Article I. Under this suspension, Lincoln's military commanders imposed martial law, and many citizens were arbitrarily arrested and imprisoned without charges. As historian Mark Neely Jr. has shown, Lincoln was responding to a very real threat from Confederate spies, agents, and sympathizers, especially in the border states, but he was careful to protect political dissent against his policies in the North.[4] Indeed, compared with later presidents, from Woodrow Wilson to George W. Bush, who would use crises, real or contrived, to expand their powers over the lives and liberties of Americans, Lincoln's curtailment of civil liberties seems the most justifiable expansion of presidential power, as well as the one most tempered by leniency. Nevertheless, he set the essential precedent for the emergency claims of presidents to supersede rights by executive fiat—a precedent all the more dangerous because it was the nation's most revered president who set it.

When Theodore Roosevelt donned the mantle of the people's champion against the "malefactors of great wealth," he assumed for himself the personal discretion to decide whether great wealth had been legitimately or illegitimately accumulated. Appearing before the public as the scourge of avaricious capitalists, Roosevelt would actually become cozy in private with some of the most powerful capitalists in the land. Thus his campaign against the trusts posed less of a challenge to corporate concentration in the economy than his colorful pronouncements suggested. Roosevelt developed a working relationship with the most powerful firm on Wall Street, the financial house of

J. P. Morgan. When Morgan executives exploited the financial Panic of 1907 to acquire the largest southern steel company for the Morgan-dominated United States Steel Corporation, thereby extending its near-monopolistic control over a basic industry, Roosevelt, trusting in the executives' misleading claims of selfless motives, assured them that he had no objections. Roosevelt's deference to the Morgan interests has been mirrored in the tendency of many later presidents to placate those who hold great power in the corporate economy to the great detriment of the power of workers, consumers, and small businesses.

For Franklin D. Roosevelt, building a strong state to serve democratic ends justified strong and sometimes high-handed methods against adversaries who stood in the way. As FDR established the presidency as the dominant force in the federal government, he set it on a road to secrecy and covert action that would lead toward the abuses of the Vietnam War and the Watergate scandal that brought the Nixon presidency to an end. Roosevelt developed an alliance with his director of the Federal Bureau of Investigation (FBI), J. Edgar Hoover, that was constrained by neither law nor democratic norms. The president expected the FBI director to obtain any information he sought, and Hoover, in turn, regaled FDR with political dirt about his enemies and even his friends. In the same spirit, Roosevelt's aides hunted for financial improprieties that might bring down a prominent right-wing critic, Father Charles Coughlin, and prodded the Immigration and Naturalization Service to ascertain whether the Canadian-born priest was residing in the United States illegally. Nor was Roosevelt scrupulous about civil liberties amid the crisis of World War II, especially for nonwhites. The greatest twentieth-century presidential champion of democratic advancement for ordinary people also ordered the century's greatest abuse of American liberty: the wartime internment of Japanese Americans. Fighting fascism, FDR dispatched 110,000 Americans who were not charged with any violations of law or acts of disloyalty to prison camps.

The accelerating political and moral force of the civil rights movement led John Kennedy and Lyndon Johnson to endorse the cause of racial equality. But presidents tend to be cautious and calculating politicians, and so both men tried to slow the movement down and regain some degree of White House control. Fearful that civil rights leaders might press for radical change, Kennedy and Johnson ordered their activities to be secretly monitored, which allowed FDR's old ally, J. Edgar Hoover, to pursue covert measures against a movement that he personally despised. Attorney General Robert F. Kennedy, the president's brother, authorized the wiretapping of Martin Luther King Jr.'s home and office phones in 1963 because of FBI information that King was receiving advice from a New York lawyer who had been associated with the Communist Party. Hoover seized on the order to bug and place wiretaps on

King everywhere he went, and then the FBI director used the fruits of this surveillance, especially information on King's sexual activities, in a bitter crusade to destroy the civil rights leader.

During Johnson's presidency, the covert FBI war against the civil rights movement was expanded beyond King. In 1967 the FBI began a secret program, known as COINTELPRO, to disrupt and weaken a wide variety of black organizations—from King's Southern Christian Leadership Conference to the Student Nonviolent Coordinating Committee and the Black Panther Party—on the grounds that militant blacks were propagating hate and violence. When Americans today hail the civil rights movement for its democratic victories of the 1960s, few realize how much its leaders were hounded and defamed by federal agents at the same time that they were targeted by violent racists.

Thus even in the hands of the greatest chief executives, the American presidency is an ambiguous agent of democratic change. American democracy often requires the great force of the presidency to break through barriers to democratic advancement. Yet American democracy has also been endangered by that same force, wielded by those same hands. Sometimes, the great presidents have operated on the familiar premise that noble ends legitimize ruthless means. At other times, the rationale for undemocratic actions has been even less defensible. Democratic gains for the majority have been paid for by a despised minority, especially persons of color. Checks upon the powerful have been mitigated by covert cooperation with the powerful. Presidential ambition, aiming at history-making transformation, has been easily converted into presidential arrogance. There is, it seems, an enduring tension between democracy and the institution of the presidency: vested with the authority of the state, occupying a position of unique eminence that is a holdover from the days of monarchy, presidents are set too far above the people to be at one with them.

This ambiguity in presidential greatness has been present since the beginning. Among the founders, Alexander Hamilton was the leading exponent of presidential power. Although Hamilton was a harsh critic of democracy, it appears that the executive energy the great Federalist promised has sometimes been enlisted during the later course of American history on the side of democratic change. But executive energy poses dangers to democracy as well—a point made by Hamilton's Anti-Federalist adversaries. Patrick Henry warned that the proposed executive was a monarchical figure whose "mighty" powers would prove a perennial threat to republican liberty.[5] George Mason argued that more vital to the survival and success of the new republic than executive energy was the commitment of citizens "to their laws, to their freedom, and to their country."[6]

It would be petty of democratic citizens to deny praise to great presidents when they perform historic services to democracy. But it would be debilitating to democratic citizenship if this praise were not qualified by a reckoning with these presidents' undemocratic undertakings. Americans ought to keep in mind the conclusion that George Mason's words suggest: democratic change, in the end, depends more on the quality of the nation's citizens than on the greatness of its presidents.

NOTES

PREFACE

1. Aaron Wildavsky, ed., *The Presidency* (Boston: Little, Brown, 1969), ix.

CHAPTER 1: The Framers of the Constitution Would Approve of the Modern Presidency

1. *The Federalist Papers* were originally published as a series of eighty-five newspaper articles (under the pseudonym "Publius") intended to explain the thinking that led to the Constitution and to persuade Americans to adopt it as the cornerstone of the new nation. The essays were written by James Madison, Alexander Hamilton, and John Jay.
2. Michael Walzer, *Politics and Passion: Toward a More Egalitarian Liberalism* (New Haven, Conn.: Yale University Press, 2004), 96.

PRO

1. For the classic description of the modern presidency, see Fred I. Greenstein, "Change and Continuity in the Modern Presidency," in *The New American Political System*, ed. Anthony King (Washington, D.C.: American Enterprise Institute, 1978), 243–244.
2. Max Farrand, ed., *The Records of the Federal Convention of 1787*, 4 vols. (New Haven, Conn.: Yale University Press, 1966), 1:21.
3. Ibid., 1:65–66.
4. Ibid., 2:342.
5. Ibid., 1:68–69.
6. Charles Thach, *The Creation of the Presidency, 1775–1789* (Baltimore: Johns Hopkins University Press, 1969), 101–103.
7. Farrand, *Records of the Federal Convention of 1787*, 2:31.
8. Ibid., 2:29, 230.
9. Ibid., 1:111.
10. See Donald L. Robinson, *"To the Best of My Ability": The Presidency and the Constitution* (New York: Norton, 1987), 82–83.
11. Farrand, *Records of the Federal Convention of 1787*, 2:52.

CON

1. Samuel Kernell, *Going Public: New Strategies of Leadership*, 3rd ed. (Washington, D.C.: CQ Press, 1997).
2. *The Federalist Papers*, No. 51 (New York: Penguin Books, 1961), 322.
3. North Carolina and Rhode Island had not ratified the Constitution by the time of the first presidential election and could not participate. See *Selecting the President: From 1789 to 1996* (Washington, D.C.: Congressional Quarterly, 1997), 4.
4. Max Farrand, ed., *The Records of the Federal Convention of 1787*, 4 vols. (New Haven, Conn.: Yale University Press, 1966), 2:52.
5. Jonathan Elliot, ed., *The Debates in the Several State Conventions on the Adoption of the Federal Constitution* (New York: Burt Franklin, 1888), 2:448.
6. *Federalist Papers*, No. 71, 432.
7. *Federalist Papers*, No. 10, 82.
8. *Federalist Papers*, No. 71, 432.
9. Jack N. Rakove, *Original Meanings: Politics and Ideas in the Making of the Constitution* (New York: Knopf, 1996), 267.
10. *Federalist Papers*, No. 51, 323.
11. Rakove, *Original Meanings*, 281.
12. Ralph Ketcham, *Presidents above Party: The First American Presidency, 1789–1829* (Chapel Hill: University of North Carolina Press, 1984), 4.
13. In addition to these two tours, President Washington visited Rhode Island upon its admittance to statehood.
14. As described in Stanley Elkins and Eric McKitrick, *The Age of Federalism* (New York: Oxford University Press, 1993), 49–50.
15. George Washington, "Farewell Address," September 17, 1796, in *A Compilation of the Messages and Papers of the Presidents* (New York: Bureau of National Literature, 1897), 214.
16. Elkins and McKitrick, *Age of Federalism*, 494.
17. Garry Wills, *Cincinnatus: George Washington and the Enlightenment* (Garden City, N.Y.: Doubleday, 1984), 88–89.
18. Fred I. Greenstein, *The Hidden-Hand Presidency: Eisenhower as Leader* (New York: Basic Books, 1982); Robert M. Johnstone Jr., *Jefferson and the Presidency: Leadership in the Young Republic* (Ithaca, N.Y.: Cornell University Press, 1978).
19. James Sterling Young, *The Washington Community, 1800–1828* (New York: Columbia University Press, 1966), 162–163; Mel Laracey, *Presidents and the People: The Partisan Story of Going Public* (College Station: Texas A&M Press, 2002).
20. John Quincy Adams, "Inaugural Address," March 4, 1825, http://www.bartleby.com/124/pres22.html (accessed March 12, 2005).
21. Terry Moe, "The Politicized Presidency," in *The New Direction in American Politics*, ed. John E. Chubb and Paul E. Peterson (Washington, D.C.: Brookings, 1985), 235–271.

CHAPTER 2: Political Parties Should Nominate Candidates for the Presidency through a National Primary

PRO

1. Barry C. Burden, "The Nominations: Technology, Money, and Transferable Momentum," in *The Elections of 2004*, ed. Michael Nelson (Washington, D.C.: CQ Press, 2005), 19.
2. States receive more attention from the candidates and the media when they advance the dates of their primaries. See Andrew E. Busch and William G. Mayer, "The Front-Loading Problem," in *The Making of the Presidential Candidates, 2004*, ed. William G. Mayer (Lanham, Md.: Rowman & Littlefield, 2004), 11–12.
3. Ibid., 9.
4. Barry C. Burden, "The Nominations: Rules, Strategies, and Uncertainty," in *The Elections of 2008*, ed. Michael Nelson (Washington, D.C.: CQ Press, 2010), 25.
5. Broder and Kirkpatrick are quoted in Michael Nelson, "The Presidential Nominating System: Problems and Prescriptions," in *What Role for Government? Lessons from Policy Research*, ed. Richard J. Zeckhauser and Derek Leebaert (Durham, N.C.: Duke University Press, 1983), 42–43.
6. James Bryce, *The American Commonwealth* (New York: Putnam's, 1959), 28–29.
7. James David Barber, *The Presidential Character: Predicting Performance in the White House* (Englewood Cliffs, N.J.: Prentice-Hall, 1972).
8. The phrase is from Richard E. Neustadt, *Presidential Power* (New York: Wiley, 1960).
9. Henry Mayo, *Introduction to Democratic Theory* (New York: Oxford University Press, 1960), 73.
10. Busch and Mayer, "Front-Loading Problem," 33.
11. Nelson, "Presidential Nominating System," 50; Stephen J. Wayne, *The Road to the White House 2004: The Politics of Presidential Elections*, 7th ed. (Belmont, Calif.: Wadsworth, 2004), 311–312.
12. Busch and Mayer, "Front-Loading Problem," 23.
13. The Supreme Court, which has already confirmed Congress's authority to govern campaign finance through legislation, would hardly blanch at a national primary law. As for the national parties, the Court has regularly endorsed their authority to establish their own rules.

CON

1. Donald Bruce Johnson and Kirk H. Porter, *National Party Platforms: 1840–1972* (Urbana: University of Illinois Press, 1975), 176.
2. Arthur S. Link, ed., *The Papers of Woodrow Wilson*, vol. 29 (Princeton: Princeton University Press, 1979), 7.
3. See Stephen G. Wright, "Voter Turnout in Runoff Elections," *Journal of Politics* 51 (May 1989): 385–396; and Charles S. Bullock III and Loch K. Johnson, *Runoff Elections in the United States* (Chapel Hill: University of North Carolina Press, 1992), chap. 6.

4. For a detailed critique of front-loading, see William G. Mayer and Andrew E. Busch, *The Front-Loading Problem in Presidential Nominations* (Washington, D.C.: Brookings, 2004), esp. chap. 4.

5. See Emily Goodin, "Enough Blame to Share," *National Journal,* December 4, 2004, 3630.

6. See, for example, *Cousins v. Wigoda* (1975); *Republican Party of Connecticut v. Tashjian* (1986); and *March Fong Eu v. San Francisco County Democratic Central Committee* (1989).

7. See *New York v. United States* (1992); *United States v. Lopez* (1995); *Printz v. United States* (1997); and *United States v. Morrison* (2000). The enumerated powers of Congress are those listed in Article I, Section 8, of the Constitution defining the extent and limits of congressional authority. The Tenth Amendment specifies that "[t]he powers not delegated to the United States by the Constitution, nor prohibited by it to the States, are reserved to the States respectively or to the people."

8. See William G. Mayer and Andrew E. Busch, "Can the Federal Government Reform the Presidential Nomination Process?" *Election Law Journal* 3, no. 4 (2004): 613–625.

9. Democrats initially voted to deny delegates to Florida and Michigan when the two states scheduled their primaries earlier than party rules allowed, although the delegates were ultimately restored at the convention in a gesture of party unity. For the same reason, Republicans refused to seat half of the delegates from Florida, Michigan, and three other states.

CHAPTER 3: The President Should Be Elected Directly by the People

PRO

1. John P. Roche, "The Founding Fathers: A Reform Caucus in Action," *American Political Science Review* 55 (September 1961).

2. George C. Edwards III, *Why the Electoral College Is Bad for America* (New Haven: Yale University Press, 2004), 81.

3. Ibid., 80.

4. The importance of battleground states was nicely captured by Nate Silver in his blog, fivethirtyeight.com, in which he offered daily updates on which states were most likely to swing the election and which had the biggest electoral payoffs for the candidates' "investment" of their funds.

5. Some think that a true count of the votes in the 1960 election would have given Richard Nixon more popular votes than John F. Kennedy, but the only count available shows Kennedy receiving more popular votes than Nixon. See Edwards, *Why the Electoral College Is Bad for America,* chap. 3.

6. In 2004 the Harris Poll conducted a survey with the extremely large sample size of almost seven thousand voters. In the survey, 64 percent of respondents expressed

support for a popular vote to choose the president, while just 22 percent expressed opposition. See http://harrisinteractive.com (accessed April 12, 2005).

7. William Ross, "'Faithless Electors': The Wild Card," http://www.jurist.law.pitt.edu/election/electionross4.htm (accessed April 15, 2005).

CON

1. Since electors themselves have become subject to the popular vote, the electoral college has never denied the presidency to a candidate with a majority vote. The sole exception is the election of 1876, when a corrupt bargain among elites determined the outcome.

2. In the same way—a wonderful ultimate irony—it is possible to argue that in the absence of the electoral college, those Gore voters who preferred Nader would have voted for him, such that George W. Bush would have won a plurality of the popular vote. But this leads on to a kind of analytic madness.

CHAPTER 4: The Twenty-second Amendment Should Be Repealed

PRO

1. For a useful summary, see Robert A. Dahl, *How Democratic Is the American Constitution?* (New Haven: Yale University Press, 2001). Calling presidential elections "majoritarian" and "democratic" requires acknowledgment that owing to the electoral college—another problematic aspect of the Constitution—the candidate with the most popular support may not be elected. Yet this has rarely happened.

2. Even the Twelfth Amendment may be seen as a democratizing move, because in cases when no candidate secured a majority of electoral votes Congress was henceforth required to hew more closely to the people's wishes by choosing from among the top three finishers, rather than the top five candidates.

3. "Notes on the Debates in the Federal Convention of 1787": Madison Debates, September 4, 1787, Avalon Project, Yale Law School, http://avalon.law.yale.edu/18th_century/debates_904.asp (accessed May 25, 2009).

4. "Notes on the Debates": Madison Debates, July 17, 1787, and July 19, 1787.

5. Bruce G. Peabody, "George Washington, Presidential Term Limits, and the Problem of Reluctant Political Leadership," *Presidential Studies Quarterly* 31 (2001): 439–453.

6. Ibid.

7. Ibid.

8. Kenneth D. Ackerman, *The Dark Horse: The Surprise Election and Political Murder of President James A. Garfield* (Cambridge, Mass.: Da Capo Press, 2003).

9. Ronald W. Reagan, "Restoring the Presidency," in *Restoring the Presidency: Reconsidering the Twenty-second Amendment* (Washington, D.C.: National Legal Center for the Public Interest, 1990), 4.

10. Gordon Silverstein, *Imbalance of Powers: Constitutional Interpretation and the Making of American Foreign Policy* (New York: Oxford University Press, 1996).

11. France has recently established term limits for its presidents, but they are much less severe than the American version. A French president may now serve two five-year terms in succession and then is again eligible after sitting out five years.

12. See *The Book of the States 2007* (Lexington, Ky.: Council of State Governments, 2007), Table 4.9, "Constitutional and Statutory Provisions for the Number of Consecutive Terms of Elected State Officials."

13. James E. Alt and David Dreyer Lassen, "The Political Economy of Institutions and Corruption in American States," *Journal of Theoretical Politics* 15 (2003): 341–365.

14. Andrew W. Barrett and Matthew Eshbaugh-Soha, "Presidential Success on the Substance of Legislation," *Political Research Quarterly* 60 (2007): 100–112.

15. Matthew J. Dickinson and Kathryn Dunn Tenpas, "Explaining Increasing Turnover Rates among Presidential Advisers, 1929–1997," *Journal of Politics* 64 (2002): 434–448.

16. Sidney M. Milkis and Michael Nelson, *The American Presidency: Origins and Development, 1776–2007,* 5th ed. (Washington, D.C.: CQ Press, 2008).

17. Thomas E. Cronin, "Two Cheers for the Twenty-Second Amendment," *Christian Science Monitor,* February 23, 1987.

18. For three studies decades apart illustrating this point see V. O. Key Jr., *The Responsible Electorate: Rationality in Presidential Voting* (Cambridge: Harvard University Press, 1966); Morris P. Fiorina, *Retrospective Voting in American National Elections* (New Haven: Yale University Press, 1981); and Douglas A. Hibbs Jr., "Bread and Peace Voting in U.S. Presidential Elections," *Public Choice* 104 (2000): 149–180.

19. *The Federalist Papers,* No. 72 (Alexander Hamilton).

CON

1. Robert M. La Follette, quoted in *The Congressional Digest,* January 1947, 16.

2. I have borrowed here from previous writings on this topic, especially from my essay "Presidential Term, Tenure and Reeligibility," in *Inventing the American Presidency,* ed. Thomas E. Cronin (Lawrence: University Press of Kansas, 1989) and from my general entry on this amendment in the *Encyclopedia of the American Presidency,* ed. Leonard W. Levy and Louis Fisher (New York: Simon and Schuster, 1994).

3. Calvin Coolidge, *The Autobiography of Calvin Coolidge* (New York: Cosmopolitan Book Corporation, 1929), 241.

4. See the argument in Charles W. Stein, *The Third Term Tradition: Its Rise and Collapse in American Politics* (New York: Columbia University Press, 1943).

5. See, on this debate, Steven G. Calabresi and Christopher S. Yoo, *The Unitary Executive: Presidential Power from Washington to Bush* (New Haven: Yale University Press, 2008); and Louis Fisher, *The Constitution and 9/11* (Lawrence: University Press of Kansas, 2008).

6. *The Federalist Papers,* No. 72 (Alexander Hamilton).

7. Larry J. Sabato, *A More Perfect Constitution* (New York: Walker, 2007), 87.

8. I do not favor term limits for state and national legislators for reasons I have explained elsewhere. I do not believe that favoring the Twenty-second Amendment and opposing legislative term limits is at all inconsistent. See Thomas E. Cronin, "Term Limits—A Symptom Not a Cure," *New York Times,* December 23, 1990, sec. E.

CHAPTER 5: The Media Are Too Hard on Presidents

PRO

1. See Thomas E. Patterson, *Out of Order* (New York: Knopf, 1993); and Matthew R. Kerbel, *Remote and Controlled: Media Politics in a Cynical Age* (Boulder, Colo.: Westview Press, 1999).
2. Kerbel, *Remote and Controlled.*
3. Shanto Iyengar and Donald Kinder, *News That Matters* (Chicago: University of Chicago Press, 1987).
4. Richard E. Neustadt, *Presidential Power* (New York: Wiley, 1960).
5. Tim Groeling and Samuel Kernell, "Is Network News Coverage of the President Biased?" *Journal of Politics* 60 (1998): 1063–1087.
6. Ibid.
7. Center for Media and Public Affairs, "Kerry Gets Best Press Ever," November 1, 2004.
8. Larry J. Sabato, *Feeding Frenzy: How Attack Journalism Has Transformed American Politics* (New York: Free Press, 1991). These figures are derived by adding Sabato's list of feeding frenzies from presidential politics to his list of feeding frenzies from presidential governance.
9. Sidney Blumenthal, *The Permanent Campaign: Inside the World of Elite Political Operatives* (Boston: Beacon Press, 1980).
10. Michael B. Grossman and Martha Joynt Kumar, *Portraying the President: The White House and the News Media* (Baltimore: Johns Hopkins University Press, 1981).
11. Neustadt, *Presidential Power,* 101–102.
12. Ibid., 90, 95.
13. Robert M. Eisinger, *Evolution of Presidential Polling* (New York: Cambridge University Press, 2003).
14. Bruce Altschuler, "Lyndon Johnson and Public Polls," *Public Opinion Quarterly* 50 (1986): 285–299.
15. Seymour Sudman, "The Presidents and the Polls," *Public Opinion Quarterly* 46 (1982): 303.
16. Ibid., 302–310.
17. Altschuler, "Lyndon Johnson and Public Polls."
18. Sudman, "Presidents and the Polls."
19. Theodore J. Lowi, *The Personal President: Power Invested, Promise Unfulfilled* (Ithaca, N.Y.: Cornell University Press, 1985).
20. Altschuler, "Lyndon Johnson and Public Polls."

21. George C. Edwards III, *The Public Presidency: The Pursuit of Popular Support* (New York: St. Martin's Press, 1983).
22. James A. Stimson, "Public Support for American Presidents: A Cyclical Model," *Public Opinion Quarterly* 40 (1976): 1–21.
23. George C. Edwards, *Presidential Approval: A Source Book* (Baltimore: Johns Hopkins University Press, 1990).
24. Center for Media and Public Affairs, "Kerry Gets Best Press Ever."
25. Matthew R. Kerbel, *Netroots: Online Progressives and the Transformation of American Politics* (Boulder, Colo.: Paradigm Publishers, 2009).

CON

1. Doris Graber, *Mass Media and American Politics*, 6th ed. (Washington, D.C.: CQ Press, 2002), 272.
2. Richard Davis, *The Press and American Politics: The New Mediator*, 3rd ed. (Upper Saddle River, N.J.: Prentice-Hall, 2001), 249.
3. Stephen Lukes, *Power: A Radical View* (New York: Macmillan, 1974).
4. Bartholomew H. Sparrow, *Uncertain Guardians* (Baltimore: Johns Hopkins University Press, 1999), 123–124; Gaye Tuchman, *Making News: A Study in the Construction of Reality* (New York: Free Press, 1978); Shanto Iyengar and Donald Kinder, *News That Matters* (Chicago: University of Chicago Press, 1997); Robert Entman, *Projections of Power: Framing News, Public Opinion, and U.S. Foreign Policy* (Chicago: University of Chicago Press, 2004).
5. Martin P. Wattenberg, "The Changing Presidential Media Environment," *Presidential Studies Quarterly* 34 (September 2004): 557–572.
6. eBizMBA, "20 Most Popular Political Web Sites," March 29, 2009, www.ebizmba.com/articles/politics.
7. Frank Rich, "Laura Bush's Mission Accomplished," *New York Times*, May 8, 2005, sec. A.
8. W. Lance Bennett, Regina Lawrence, and Steven Livingston, *When the Press Fails* (Chicago: University of Chicago Press, 2007).
9. Megan Thee-Brennan, "Poll Finds Disapproval of Bush Unwavering," *New York Times*, January 17, 2009, sec. A, www.nytimes.com/2009/01/17/us/politics/17poll.html.
10. W. Lance Bennett, "Toward a Theory of Press-State Relations in the United States," *Journal of Communication* 40, no. 2 (1990): 103–127; Entman, *Projections of Power.*
11. Nate Silver, "Yes, Obama's Approval Ratings Are Declining. What Did You Expect?" Politics Done Right, March 13, 2009, www.fivethirtyeight.com/2009/03/yes-obamas-approval-ratings-are.html; Mark Murray, "Poll: Obama's Ratings at All-time High," MSNBC, March 3, 2009, www.msnbc.msn.com/id/29493021/.
12. Wattenberg, "Changing Presidential Media Environment"; Jeffrey E. Cohen, "If the News Is So Bad, Why Are Presidential Polls So High? Presidents, the News Media, and the Mass Public in an Era of New Media," *Presidential Studies Quarterly* 34 (September 2004): 493–515; Stephen J. Farnsworth and S. Robert Lichter, "Source Material: New Presidents and Network News," *Presidential Studies*

Quarterly 34 (September 2004): 674–690; Jeffrey S. Peake, "Presidential Agenda Setting in Foreign Policy," *Political Research Quarterly* 54 (March 2001): 69–86.

13. Martha Joynt Kumar, "Presidential Press Conferences: The Importance and Evolution of an Enduring Forum," *Presidential Studies Quarterly* 35 (March 2005): 188, 191.

14. Jeffrey D. Mayer, "The Presidency and Image Management: Discipline in Pursuit of Illusion," *Presidential Studies Quarterly* 34 (September 2004): 620–631.

15. Sean Aday, Steven Livingston, and Maeve Hebert, "Embedding the Truth: A Cross-Cultural Analysis of Objectivity and Television Coverage of the Iraq War," *Press/Politics* 10 (Winter 2005): 3–21; also see David Domke, *God Willing: Political Fundamentalism in the White House, the "War on Terror," and the Echoing Press* (Ann Arbor, Mich.: Pluto Press, 2004).

16. Narasimhan Ravi, "Looking beyond Flawed Journalism," *Press/Politics* 10 (Winter 2005): 45–62; John Hutcheson et al., "U.S. National Identity, Political Elites, and a Patriotic Press following September 11," *Political Communication* 21 (January 2004): 27–50.

17. David Zarefsky, "Presidential Rhetoric and the Powers of Definition," *Presidential Studies Quarterly* 34 (September 2004): 607–619; also see Mark Fishman, *Manufacturing the News* (Austin: University of Texas Press, 1980).

18. The phrase is from Mayer, "Presidency and Image Management," 629.

CHAPTER 6: The President Is a More Authentic Representative of the American People Than Is Congress

CON

1. This dynamic has deep roots in American history. Writing at the end of the nineteenth century, James Bryce, for example, noted that "the nation, which has often good grounds for distrusting Congress, a body liable to be moved by sinister private influences or to defer to the clamor of some noisy section outside, looks to the man of its choice [the president] to keep Congress in order" (*The American Commonwealth*, 2 vols. [Indianapolis: Liberty Fund, 1995], 1:53).

2. Martin P. Wattenberg, "Tax Cut versus Lockbox: Did the Voters Grasp the Tradeoff in 2000?" *Presidential Studies Quarterly* 34 (December 2004): 845.

3. Justin Lewis, Michael Morgan, and Sut Jhally, "Libertine or Liberal? The Real Scandal of What People Know about President Clinton," University of Massachusetts/Amherst, February 10, 1998, www-unix.oit.umass.edu/~mmorgan/commstudy.html (accessed November 13, 2005).

4. Raymond E. Wolfinger, "Dealignment, Realignment, and Mandates in the 1984 Election," in *The American Elections of 1984*, ed. Austin Ranney (Durham, N.C.: Duke University Press, 1985), 293.

5. On presidents' use of polling, see Diane J. Heith, *Polling to Govern: Public Opinion and Presidential Leadership* (Stanford: Stanford University Press, 2004).

6. Edmund S. Morgan, *Inventing the People: The Rise of Popular Sovereignty in England and America* (New York: Norton, 1988), 13.

7. Clinton Rossiter, *The American Presidency,* 2nd ed. (New York: Harcourt, Brace, 1960), 18.

8. Ibid., 34.

CHAPTER 7: Presidents Have Usurped the War Power That Rightfully Belongs to Congress

1. Alexis de Tocqueville, *Democracy in America,* trans. Arthur Goldhammer (New York: Library of America, 1966).

PRO

1. Edward S. Corwin, *The President: Office and Powers* (New York: New York University Press, 1957), 201.

2. Alexander Hamilton, James Madison, and John Jay, *The Federalist Papers* (New York: New American Library, 1961), 418 (emphasis in original).

3. Ibid., 417.

4. Max Farrand, ed., *The Records of the Federal Convention of 1787,* 4 vols. (New Haven, Conn.: Yale University Press, 1937), 1:292.

5. That same concept was included in an early federal court case, *U.S. v. Smith* (27 Fed. Cas. 1192 [No. 16,342] [C.C.N.Y. 1806] at 1230), in which the court said that "it is the exclusive province of congress to change a state of peace into a state of war."

6. Louis Henkin, *Foreign Affairs and the Constitution* (Mineola, N.Y.: Foundation Press, 1972), 50–51.

7. Farrand, *Records of the Federal Convention of 1787,* 2:318.

8. The April 1952 executive order was declared unconstitutional by the Supreme Court in *Youngstown Sheet & Tube Co. v. Sawyer,* 343 U.S. 579 (1952). For an analysis of Truman's decision to send U.S. forces to Korea in 1950, see Louis Fisher, *Presidential War Power* (Lawrence: University Press of Kansas, 1995), 84–90; Louis Fisher, "The Korean War: On What Legal Basis Did Truman Act?" *American Journal of International Law* 89 (1995): 21; and Glenn D. Paige, *The Korean Decision: June 24–30, 1950* (New York: Free Press, 1968).

9. Senate Committee on Foreign Relations, 91st Cong., 1st sess., 1969, S. Rep. 129, as reprinted in Peter M. Shane and Harold H. Bruff, *Separation of Powers Law: Cases and Materials* (Durham, N.C.: Carolina Academic Press, 1996), 777–791.

10. Arthur M. Schlesinger Jr., *The Imperial Presidency* (Boston: Houghton Mifflin, 1973), 108. Congress effectively ratified the bases deal retroactively in April 1941.

11. Ibid., 113.

12. There is no better description of this circumstance than Justice Robert Jackson's pointed as well as prescient warning to Congress in his *Youngstown* concurrence: "We may say that power to legislate for emergencies belongs in the hands of Congress, but only Congress itself can prevent power from slipping through its fingers" (343 U.S. at 654).

13. Leonard Meeker, "The Legality of United States Participation in the Defense of Viet-Nam," *Department of State Bulletin* 54 (1966): 474, as reprinted in Shane and Bruff, *Separation of Powers Law: Cases and Materials*, 771–776.

14. Ibid., 772.

15. Ibid.

16. S. Res. 85, 91st Cong., 1st sess., *Congressional Record* 115 (June 25, 1969): S 7153.

17. Senate Committee, S. Rep. 129, 781.

18. Ibid., 781–782.

19. Public Law 93-148, *U.S. Statutes at Large* 555 (1973).

20. Some scholars, such as Louis Fisher and David Gray Adler, would go further, arguing that the existence of the resolution has actually lulled Congress into even greater complacency by discouraging it from using the constitutional tools it already—and always—had, such as the appropriations power, the legislative power, and, ultimately, the impeachment power. See Louis Fisher and David Gray Adler, "The War Powers Resolution: Time to Say Goodbye," *Political Science Quarterly* 113 (Spring 1998): 1.

21. The judicial record is, indeed, a mixed one, ranging from *United States v. Curtiss-Wright Export Corporation* (299 U.S. 304 [1936]), the most expansive interpretation (and an incorrect one, at that) of executive power in foreign policy, to *Youngstown Sheet & Tube Co. v. Sawyer* (343 U.S. 579 [1952]) and *Dellums v. Bush* (752 F. Supp. 1141 [D.D.C. 1990]), decisions that rest on a traditional understanding of the scope of powers allotted to each branch. *Youngstown*, though technically a decision that addressed domestic powers, is clearly applicable to war powers issues, because it includes as a vital part of its consideration the reach of the president's commander in chief power. The record of cases challenging the constitutionality of the Vietnam War that the federal courts refused to decide on the merits demonstrates just how unwilling the judiciary is to counter a sitting president during wartime. See, for example, *Mora v. McNamara* (386 U.S. 934 [1967]); *Mitchell v. Laird* (488 F.2d 611 [D.C. Cir. 1973]); *Orlando v. Laird* (443 F.2d 1039 [2d Cir. 1971]); and *Berk v. Laird* (429 F.2d 302 [2d Cir. 1970]). The judicial response to the war on terrorism under President George W. Bush is a work in progress, although the Supreme Court in its June 2004 decisions in *Hamdi v. Rumsfeld* (124 S. Ct. 2633 [2004]) and *Rasul v. Bush* (124 S. Ct. 2686 [2004]) was more critical of the president's claims than might have been expected during wartime, and it rejected the government's narrow view in those cases of a very limited scope of judicial power to review habeas corpus claims from enemy combatants. Similarly, in the most recent cases of *Hamdan v. Rumsfeld* (548 U.S. 557 [2006]) and *Boumediene v. Bush* (128 S. Ct. 2229 [2008]), the Court also ruled against the government, declaring unconstitutional in *Hamdan* the military commissions that President Bush authorized in his November 2001 military order, and deciding in *Boumediene* that the CSRT regime for determining whether Guantanamo detainees were illegal enemy combatants was an insufficient substitute for the traditional privilege of habeas corpus.

22. *Dellums v. Bush* (752 F. Supp. 1141 (D.D.C. 1990).

23. Ibid.

24. Ibid.

25. See, for example, John C. Yoo, "Memorandum Opinion for the Deputy Counsel to the President: The President's Constitutional Authority to Conduct Military Operations Against Terrorists and Nations Supporting Them," U.S. Department of Justice, Washington, D.C., September 25, 2001, www.usdoj.gov/olc/warpowers925.htm.

26. Ibid.

27. See www.usdoj.gov/opa/documents/olc-memos.htm for links to Office of Legal Counsel memos from 2001 and 2002 that rested on the president's unlimited power to act in wartime.

28. Public release of some opinions occurred in June 2004; see Jay S. Bybee, "Standards of Conduct for Interrogation under 18 U.S.C. §2340-2340A," Memo from the Office of Legal Counsel, U.S. Department of Justice, to Alberto R. Gonzales, Counsel to the President, August 1, 2002, www.pbs.org/wgbh/pages/frontline/torture/paper/cron.html. Seven more opinions issued during 2001–2002 were released and repudiated by the Department of Justice in March 2009; see www.usdoj.gov/opa/documents/olc-memos.htm for links to these seven opinions.

29. See Walter E. Dellinger et al., "Principles to Guide the Office of Legal Counsel," U.S. Department of Justice, December 21, 2004, www.acslaw.org/files/2004%20programs_OLC%20principles_white%20paper.pdf.

30. Stephen G. Bradbury, "Memorandum for the Files Re: October 23, 2001 OLC Opinion Addressing the Domestic Use of Military Force to Combat Terrorist Activities," Office of Legal Counsel, U.S. Department of Justice, October 6, 2008, www.usdoj.gov/opa/documents/memoolcopiniondomesticusemilitaryforce10062008.pdf.

31. Barack Obama, "Executive Order: Ensuring Lawful Interrogations," The White House, January 22, 2009, www.whitehouse.gov/the_press_office/Ensuring_Lawful_Interrogations.

32. David Mervin, "The Demise of the War Clause," *Presidential Studies Quarterly* 30 (December 2000): 767–773.

33. David Gray Adler, "The Virtues of the War Clause," *Presidential Studies Quarterly* 30 (December 2000): 777–782.

CON

1. All quotations are taken from *Notes of Debates on the Federal Convention of 1787* (Athens: Ohio University Press, 1966), 475–477.

2. *Prize Cases*, 67 U.S. 635 (1863).

3. *Luftig v. McNamara*, 373 F.2d 664 (1967).

4. *Berk v. Laird*, 429 F.2d 302 (Calif. 2 1970).

5. *Orlando v. Laird*, 443 F.2d 1039 (2d Cir. 1971).

6. *Massachusetts v. Laird*, 451 F.2d 26 (1st Cir. 1971).

7. *Da Costa v. Laird I*, 448 F.2d 368 (2d Cir. 1971).

8. *Da Costa v. Laird II*, 471 F.2d 1146 (2d Cir. 1973).

9. *Dellums v. Bush*, 752 F. Supp. 1141 (D.D.C. 1990).

10. *Campbell v. Clinton*, 52 F. Supp.2d 34 (D.D.C. 1999).

11. *Doe v. Bush*, 322 F.3d 109 (2003).

CHAPTER 8: Fighting the War on Terrorism Requires Relaxing Checks on Presidential Power

PRO

1. The quotations are from Edwin Borchard, a Yale law professor, criticizing President Franklin D. Roosevelt's decision in 1940 to trade American destroyers for British bases in the Western Hemisphere. See Edwin Borchard, "The Attorney General's Opinion on the Exchange of Destroyers for Naval Bases," *American Journal of International Law* 34 (1940): 690, 691.
2. Edward S. Corwin, "Executive Authority Held Exceeded in Destroyer Deal," *New York Times,* October 13, 1940.
3. To Erastus Corning and Others, 12 June 1863, in *The Collected Works of Abraham Lincoln,* ed. Roy P. Basler (New Brunswick, N.J.: Rutgers University Press, 1953), 6: 261.
4. See "President's Military Order of November 13, 2001, Detention, Treatment, and Trial of Certain Non-Citizens in the War Against Terrorism," *Federal Register* 66, no. 222 (November 16, 2001): 57,833, sec. 1(a); *Authorization for Use of Military Force,* Public Law 107-40, *U.S. Statutes at Large* 115 (2001): 224.
5. *The Federalist Papers,* No. 70 (Alexander Hamilton).
6. *The Federalist Papers,* No. 74 (Alexander Hamilton).
7. *The Federalist Papers,* No. 70 (Alexander Hamilton).
8. Alexis de Tocqueville, *Democracy in America,* trans. Henry Reeve (London: Saunders and Otley, 1835), vol. 1, chap. 8.
9. *Youngstown Sheet & Tube Co. v. Sawyer,* 343 U.S. 579 (1952).
10. Ibid., 637 (Jackson concurring).
11. See, for example, Mark E. Neely Jr., *The Fate of Liberty: Abraham Lincoln and Civil Liberties* (New York: Oxford University Press, 1991); J. G. Randall, *Constitutional Problems under Lincoln,* rev. ed. (Urbana: University of Illinois Press, 1951).
12. *Ex parte Vallandigham,* 68 U.S. 243 (1863).
13. *Ex parte Quirin,* 317 U.S. 1 (1942).
14. See, for example, *Hamdan v. Rumsfeld,* 548 U.S. 557 (2006); *Rasul v. Bush,* 542 U.S. 466 (2004); *Detainee Treatment Act of 2005,* Public Law 109-148, *U.S. Statutes at Large* 119 (2005): 2739; *Military Commission Act of 2006,* Public Law 109-366, *U.S. Statutes at Large* 120 (2006): 2600. For discussion, see Jesse Choper and John Yoo, "Wartime Process: A Dialogue on Congressional Power to Remove Issues From the Federal Courts," *California Law Review* 95 (2007): 1243.
15. *Boumediene v. Bush,* 128 S. Ct. 2229 (2008).
16. For discussion of the program, see John Yoo, *War by Other Means: An Insider's Account of the War on Terror* (New York: Atlantic Monthly Press, 2006), 99–127.
17. *In re* Sealed Case, 310 F.3d 717, 742 (FISA Ct. Rev. 2002) (footnote omitted).
18. Ibid.
19. See House Committee on Intelligence, Subcommittee on Legislation, *Foreign Intelligence Surveillance Act of 1978: Hearings on H.R. 5794, H.R. 9745, H.R. 7308,*

and H.R. 5632, 95th Cong., 2d Sess., (1978), 14 (statement of Attorney General Griffin Bell).

20. Robert H. Jackson, *That Man: An Insider's Portrait of Franklin D. Roosevelt* (New York: Oxford University Press, 2003), 68–69. See also *United States v. United States District Court*, 444 F.2d 651 (6th Cir., 1971).

21. National Commission on Terrorist Attacks upon the United States, *The 9/11 Commission Report: Final Report of the National Commission on Terrorist Attacks upon the United States* (Washington, D.C.: National Commission on Terrorist Attacks Upon the United States, 2004), 266–271.

22. Ibid., 273.

23. See Yoo, *War by Other Means*, 79–80.

CON

1. *Ex parte Jackson*, 263 F.100, 113 (D. Mont. 1920).

2. Christopher M. Finan, *From the Palmer Raids to the Patriot Act: A History of the Fight for Free Speech in America* (Boston: Beacon Press, 2007), 303.

3. *Schenck v. United States*, 249 U.S. 47 (1919).

4. Zechariah Chafee Jr., "Freedom of Speech in Wartime," *Harvard Law Review* 32, no. 8 (1919): 932–973.

5. *Whitney v. California*, 274 U.S. 357 (1927).

6. Louis Fisher, "Justifying War against Iraq," in *Rivals for Power: Presidential-Congressional Relations*, 3rd ed., ed. James A. Thurber (Lanham, Md.: Rowman & Littlefield, 2006), 289–313.

7. U.S. Department of State, "Illustrative Example of Omissions From the Iraqi Declaration to the United Nations Security Council," Fact Sheet, December 19, 2002.

8. Robert J. Hanyok, "Skunks, Bogies, Silent Hounds, and the Flying Fish: The Gulf of Tonkin Mystery, 2–4 August 1964," *Cryptologic Quarterly*, declassified by the NSA on November 3, 2005. See also Scott Shane, "Doubts Cast on Vietnam Incident, But Secret Study Stays Classified," *New York Times*, October 31, 2005, sec. A.

9. Errol Morris (filmmaker), *The Fog of War*, Dunvagen Music, 2003.

CHAPTER 9: Presidential Signing Statements Threaten to Undermine the Rule of Law and the Separation of Powers

PRO

1. Portions of this essay are excerpted from Peter M. Shane, *Madison's Nightmare: How Executive Power Threatens American Democracy* (Chicago: University of Chicago Press, 2009), © 2009 Peter M. Shane, and are reprinted with permission. All rights reserved.

2. U.S. Const., Art. I, sec. 7, par. 2.

3. Christopher N. May, *Presidential Defiance of "Unconstitutional" Laws: Reviving the Royal Prerogative* (Westport, Conn.: Greenwood Press, 1998), 76.

4. American Bar Association, "Report of the American Bar Association Task Force on Presidential Signing Statements and the Separation of Powers Doctrine," August 2006, 10, www.abanet.org/op/signingstatements/aba_final_signing_statements_recommendation-report_7-24-06.pdf.

5. T. J. Halstead, "Presidential Signing Statements: Constitutional and Institutional Implications," CRS Report for Congress (Washington, D.C.: Congressional Research Service, Sept. 26, 2006), 3, https://www.policyarchive.org/bitstream/handle/10207/2986/RL33667_20060920.pdf?sequence=1. The 2006 Halstead report relies on a count of signing statements provided by Christopher S. Kelley in his doctoral research, "The Unitary Executive and the Presidential Signing Statement" (PhD dissertation, Miami University, Oxford, Ohio, 2003), 192, app. 3.1. A later version of the Halstead paper reports somewhat different numbers, relying instead on a count by law professors Curtis A. Bradley and Eric Posner. The numbers Bradley and Posner found for Reagan, George H. W. Bush, and Clinton signing statements objecting to statutory provisions were 86, 107, and 70, respectively, which would make Clinton, not Reagan, the most modest of this trio and Bush the most constitutionally adventurous; see T. J. Halstead, "Presidential Signing Statements: Constitutional and Institutional Implications," CRS Report for Congress (Washington, D.C.: Congressional Research Service, September 17, 2007), 3, 5, 6, www.fas.org/sgp/crs/natsec/RL33667.pdf.

6. Halstead, "Presidential Signing Statements" (2006), 5.

7. Ibid., 6.

8. Neil Kinkopf and Peter M. Shane, "Signed under Protest: A Database of Presidential Signing Statements, 2001–2006," Social Science Research Network, 2007, http://papers.ssrn.com/sol3/papers.cfm?abstract_id=1022202#.

9. "Presidential Memorandum for the Heads of Executive Departments and Agencies Re: Presidential Signing Statements," *Federal Register* 74, no. 46 (March 11, 2009): 10669.

10. "Statement by the President on Signing H.R. 1105, The Omnibus Appropriations Act of 2009," March 11, 2009, www.whitehouse.gov/the_press_office/Statement-from-the-President-on-the-signing-of-HR-1105/.

11. *Postal Accountability and Enhancement Act,* Public Law 109-435, *U.S. Statutes at Large* 120 (2006): 3198.

12. *U.S. Code,* title 39, sec. 502.

13. "Statement on Signing the Postal Accountability and Enhancement Act," *Weekly Compilation of Press Documents* 42 (2006): 2196.

14. Ibid.

15. Kinkopf and Shane, "Signed under Protest," 7.

16. *Department of Defense Appropriations Act, 2002,* Public Law 107-117, sec. 8098, *U.S. Statutes at Large* 115 (2002): 2230, 2268.

17. "Statement on Signing the Department of Defense and Emergency Supplemental Appropriations for Recovery from and Response to Terrorist Attacks on the United States Act, 2002," *Weekly Compilation of Press Documents* 38 (2002): 46.
18. Kinkopf and Shane, "Signed under Protest."
19. Gerhard Casper, "An Essay in Separation of Powers: Some Early Versions and Practices," *William and Mary Law Review* 30 (211, 240–242; Jerry L. Mashaw, "Recovering American Administrative Law: Federalist Foundations," *Yale Law Journal* 115 (2006): 1256, 1284–1287.
20. Kinkopf and Shane, "Signed under Protest."
21. "Statement on Signing Legislation to Provide for Improvement of Federal Education Research, Statistics, Evaluation, Information, Dissemination and for Other Purposes," *Weekly Compilation of Press Documents* 38 (2002): 1995.
22. *Specialty Crops Competitiveness Act of 2004,* Public Law 108-465, sec. 1408A(d), *U.S. Statutes at Large* 118 (2004): 3882, 3886.
23. "Statement by President George W. Bush upon Signing H.R. 3242," *Weekly Compilation of Press Documents* 40 (2004): 3009.

CON

1. A more detailed version of the argument presented here can be found in Nelson Lund, "Signing Statements in Perspective," *William & Mary Bill of Rights Journal* 16 (2007): 95, http://papers.ssrn.com/sol3/papers.cfm?abstract_id=995930.
2. American Bar Association, "Report of the American Bar Association Task Force on Presidential Signing Statements and the Separation of Powers Doctrine," August 2006, www.abanet.org/op/signingstatements/aba_final_signing_statements_recommendation-report_7-24-06.pdf.
3. See "Presidential Signing Statements Accompanying the Fiscal Year 2006 Appropriations Acts" (memo no. B-308603 from the U.S. Government Accountability Office to Sen. Robert C. Byrd and Representative John Conyers Jr., June 18, 2007), www.gao.gov/decisions/appro/308603.pdf. For my analysis of the memo's findings, see Lund, "Signing Statements in Perspective," 107–110.

CHAPTER 10: The President Has Too Much Power in the Selection of Judges

PRO

1. Senator Thurmond apparently told this story to various law school audiences. The author was present on one such occasion when Thurmond spoke to students at the University of Virginia Law School during the spring of 1988.
2. By all accounts, President Barack Obama—the first chief executive with Senate experience in thirty-five years—bucked this trend by phoning every member of the Senate Judiciary Committee for committee members' personal advice prior to choosing Sonia Sotomayor as his first Supreme Court nominee in May 2009.

According to Sen. Charles Grassley, R-Iowa, a longtime member of the committee, it was "the first time I've ever been called by a president on a Supreme Court nomination, be it a Republican or a Democrat." If anything, Grassley's sentiment only serves to confirm just how alienated senators of both parties have been from actual judicial selections in recent decades.

3. That threesome does not include Abe Fortas, whose ill-fated bid for chief justice in 1968 was technically filibustered by the Senate, thereby preventing a formal vote on the merits of his nomination.

4. John O. McGinnis, "The President, the Senate, the Constitution, and the Confirmation Process: A Reply to Professors Strauss and Sunstein," *Texas Law Review* 71 (February 1993): 638–639.

5. Alexander Hamilton, James Madison, and John Jay, *The Federalist Papers* (New York: New American Library, 1961).

6. See Sheldon Goldman, *Picking Federal Judges: Lower Court Selection from Roosevelt through Reagan* (New Haven: Yale University Press, 1997), 210.

7. Michael Gerhardt, *The Federal Appointments Process: A Constitutional and Historical Analysis* (Durham, N.C.: Duke University Press, 2000), 145.

8. John Anthony Maltese, *The Selling of Supreme Court Nominees* (Baltimore: Johns Hopkins University Press, 1995), 7.

9. Mark Silverstein, *Judicious Choices: The New Politics of Supreme Court Confirmations* (New York: Norton, 1994), 4.

10. Maltese, *Selling of Supreme Court Nominees*, 93–109.

11. Ibid., 110.

CON

1. Alexander Hamilton, James Madison, and John Jay, *The Federalist Papers* (New York: New American Library, 1961), 454–459.

2. Ibid., 457.

3. Ibid., 456.

4. George Mason to James Monroe, January 30, 1792, quoted in Michael J. Gerhardt, *The Federal Appointments Process: A Constitutional and Historical Analysis* (Durham, N.C.: Duke University Press, 2000), 346, 92n. James Wilson of Pennsylvania likewise argued that presidential nomination "should be … unfettered and unsheltered by counselors" (quoted in ibid., 31).

5. Hamilton, Madison, and Jay, *Federalist Papers*, 457.

6. Ibid., 455.

7. This sentence appeared in the original publication of *Federalist* No. 76 in the *New-York Packet,* but was omitted in the so-called McLean edition (the first collected edition), which serves as the basis of the New American Library edition cited above. The McLean edition was published in 1788 and was corrected and edited by Hamilton and Jay, but not by Madison. Most online sources of *Federalist* No. 76, however, include this sentence, including those based on the McLean edition. See, for example, http://usinfo.state.gov/usa/infousa/facts/funddocs/fed/federa00.htm. That cite draws its text "primarily from the McLean edition," but

notes that "glaring errors—mainly printer's lapses—have been corrected." That suggests that this sentence may have been omitted in error by the printer.

8. Gerhardt, *Federal Appointments Process*, 21. Other positions were taken by different members of the convention. Some, such as John Rutledge of South Carolina, remained fearful of too much executive power.

9. Quoted in ibid., 22.

10. Quoted in ibid., 24. The convention originally rejected the compromise (which required a two-thirds vote of the Senate to confirm) and voted 6-3 in July to vest the appointment power in the Senate alone. In September, however, the Convention unanimously agreed to the "advice and consent" language for federal judges that ended up in the Constitution (see ibid., 24–25).

11. For an articulation of this view, see, for example, David A. Strauss and Cass R. Sunstein, "The Senate, the Constitution, and the Confirmation Process," *Yale Law Journal* 101 (1992): 1491ff.

12. John O. McGinnis, "The President, the Senate, the Constitution, and the Confirmation Process: A Reply to Professors Strauss and Sunstein," *Texas Law Review* 71 (February 1993): 638–639 (footnotes omitted).

13. Hamilton, Madison, and Jay, *Federalist Papers*, 457.

14. James E. Gauch, "The Intended Role of the Senate in Supreme Court Appointments," *University of Chicago Law Review* 56 (1989): 347–348.

15. These numbers do not include Lyndon B. Johnson's nomination or withdrawal of Homer Thornberry in 1968 or George W. Bush's withdrawal of the nomination of John G. Roberts Jr. to fill Sandra Day O'Connor's associate justice seat in 2005. Thornberry's name was withdrawn only because the anticipated vacancy in Abe Fortas's associate justice seat failed to materialize. Roberts was withdrawn so that he could be nominated to fill the vacancy left by the death of Chief Justice William H. Rehnquist. The numbers do include Ronald Reagan's nomination and withdrawal of Douglas H. Ginsburg in 1987, even though his nomination was never formally submitted to the Senate. Harriet Miers's nomination was submitted to the Senate in 2005 but was withdrawn before her confirmation hearings.

16. President John Tyler renominated three "failed" nominees in 1844: John C. Spencer (after Senate rejection), Edward King (after the Senate blocked his confirmation by postponement), and Reuben H. Walworth (twice renominated—first after a Senate vote to postpone and then again after no action was taken by the Senate).

The 123 total nominations before 1968 do not include consecutive resubmissions of the same nominee by the same president for the same vacancy, nor do they include the seven nominees who declined. They do include Edwin M. Stanton (who was confirmed in 1869 but died before taking office) and Stanley Matthews (who was consecutively renominated by two different presidents in 1881). Confusion over how to count renominations has led to some disagreement about the precise number of Supreme Court nominees. The official U.S. Senate Web site lists eight consecutive resubmissions of nominations of the same person by the same president for the same seat (usually for merely technical reasons).

17. Fund-raising letter for the Free Congress Foundation's Judicial Selection Monitoring Project signed by Robert Bork and quoted in Henry Weinstein, "Drive Seeks to Block Clinton Judicial Nominees," *Los Angeles Times,* October 26, 1997, sec. A. One could quibble with this claim. Studies of the voting behavior of Clinton's judges—even those appointed when his fellow Democrats controlled the Senate in 1993–1994—suggest a moderate voting record. See, for example, Ronald Stidham, Robert A. Carp, and Donald Songer, "The Voting Behavior of President Clinton's Judicial Appointees," *Judicature* 80 (July–August 1996): 16; Sheldon Goldman and Elliot Slotnick, "Picking Judges under Fire," *Judicature* 82 (May–June 1999): 265; Nancy Scherer, "Are Clinton's Judges 'Old' Democrats or 'New' Democrats?" *Judicature* 84 (November–December 2000): 151.

    Until conservative interest groups mobilized in 1997, Republican senators had generally been deferential to Clinton. He had gone out of his way to seek their advice after they took control of the Senate after the 1994 midterm elections. Overall, the Senate confirmed 99 percent of Clinton's first-term judicial nominations.

18. Free Congress Foundation Judicial Selection Monitoring Project, press release, January 23, 1997.

19. Quoted in Michael Kelly, "Judge Dread," *New Republic,* March 31, 1997, 6.

20. Quoted in Ronald Brownstein, "GOP Stall Tactics Damage Judiciary, President Charges," *Los Angeles Times,* September 28, 1997, A1.

21. William H. Rehnquist, "1997 Year-End Report on the Federal Judiciary," Administrative Office of the United States Courts, Washington, D.C., 1998, 7.

22. Sheldon Goldman, Elliot Slotnick, Gerard Gryski, and Gary Zuk, "Clinton's Judges: Summing Up the Legacy," *Judicature* 84 (March–April 2001): tables 3 and 6.

23. Statistics for Franklin D. Roosevelt through George W. Bush can be found in a chart accompanying Neil A. Lewis, "Bitter Senators Divided Anew on Judgeships," *New York Times,* November 15, 2003, sec. A. The Senate did reject two of Nixon's Supreme Court nominees.

24. See George W. Bush, "Remarks after Meeting with Members of Congress on Federal Judicial Nominations," May 9, 2002; transcript and audio available at www.whitehouse.gov/news/releases/2002/05/20020509-6.html (accessed December 12, 2005).

25. Because Senator Hatch had, as chair of the Senate Judiciary Committee in the 1990s, allowed Republicans to block hearings of Clinton's nominees, some Democrats cried foul and accused Hatch of manipulating the rules for partisan reasons.

26. Sarah A. Binder and Steven S. Smith, *Politics or Principle? Filibustering in the United States Senate* (Washington, D.C.: Brookings, 1997), 5.

27. Ibid., 33, 37.

28. Martin B. Gold and Dimple Gupta, "The Constitutional Option to Change Senate Rules and Procedures: A Majoritarian Means to Overcome the Filibuster," *Harvard Journal of Law and Public Policy* 28 (Fall 2004): 216. Gold served as floor adviser to Senate majority leader Bill Frist in 2003–2004; Gold served in the George W. Bush Justice Department.

29. See Figure 2-5 in Binder and Smith, *Politics or Principle?* 48.

30. John Anthony Maltese, *The Selling of Supreme Court Nominees* (Baltimore: Johns Hopkins University Press, 1995), 55.

31. Ibid., 71.

32. Stephen Carter, *The Confirmation Mess: Cleaning Up the Federal Appointments Process* (New York: Basic Books, 1994), 187.

33. *Judicial Roulette: Report of the Twentieth Century Fund Task Force on Judicial Selection* (New York: Priority Press, 1988), 4, 9.

34. Neil A. Lewis, "Moderate Is Said to Be Pick for Court," *New York Times,* March 17, 2009, sec. A.

CHAPTER 11: The Vice Presidency Should Be Abolished

PRO

1. Cato IV, *New York Journal,* November 8, 1787, in *Founding the American Presidency,* ed. Richard J. Ellis (Lanham, Md.: Rowman & Littlefield, 1999), 263. Scholars have long attributed the Cato letters to Clinton; however, some scholars now argue that Clinton's political ally Abraham Yates may have penned the letters.

2. Sidney Blumenthal, "The Imperial Vice Presidency," Salon, June 28, 2007, www. salon.com/opinion/blumenthal/2007/06/28/cheney/.

3. George Mason, "Virginia Ratification Debate," in *Federalists and Antifederalists: The Debate over the Ratification of the Constitution,* 2nd ed., ed. John Kaminski and Richard Leffler (Madison, Wis.: Madison House, 1998).

4. "The close intimacy that must subsist between the president & vice president," Gerry went on to argue, "makes it absolutely improper." See Mark O. Hatfield et al., Wendy Wolff, ed., *Vice Presidents of the United States, 1789–1993* (Washington, D.C.: U.S. Government Printing Office, 1997).

5. Richard Neustadt, *Presidential Power and the Modern Presidents* (New York: Free Press, 1990).

6. Mason, "Virginia Ratification Debate."

7. Adams wrote: "[The vice presidency] is totally detached from the executive authority and confined to the legislative." Hatfield et al., *Vice Presidents of the United States, 1789–1993,* 3–11.

8. See *Cheney v. United States District Court,* 542 U.S. 367 (2004). To clarify, the initial request by the National Archives to inspect the vice presidential records was made in 2004. A June 2006 memo presented Cheney's justification for his office's repeated refusals to comply with Executive Order 12958. For a timeline and overview of the issues involved, see Henry A. Waxman, chairman, Committee on Oversight and Government Reform, U.S. House of Representatives (letter to Vice President Cheney, June 21, 2007), http://oversight.house.gov/documents/20070621093952.pdf.

9. For *United States Government Policy and Supporting Positions,* the so-called "Plum Book," with alternate issues published by the Senate and the House of Representatives, see www.gpoaccess.gov/plumbook/2004/p226_appendix5.pdf. For Cheney's efforts to use this doctrine to avoid both executive and legislative oversight, see Barton Gellman and Jo Becker, "A Different Understanding with the President," *Washington Post,* June 24, 2007, sec. A.

10. Imtiyaz Delawala and Z. Byron Wolf, "Palin Says Vice President 'In Charge of' Senate," ABC News.com, October 22, 2008, http://blogs.abcnews.com/ politicalradar/2008/10/palin-says-vice.html.

11. James Madison, "Virginia Ratification Debate," in *Federalists and Antifederalists,* 95.

12. Indeed, this was a major concern raised by opponents of the Twelfth Amendment who claimed that it would make the vice presidency nothing more than a political bargaining chip.

13. See Lee Sigelman and Paul J. Wahlbeck, "The 'Veepstakes': Strategic Choice in Presidential Running Mate Selection," *American Political Science Review* 91 (December 1997): 855–864. Disaggregating vice presidential selection into pre- and post-primary reform eras, Mark Hiller and I find that state size was only a significant predictor of a candidate's prospects of winning the vice presidential nomination before the McGovern-Fraser reforms. Since the early 1970s, a potential vice presidential nominee's prior level of governing experience does appear to be a significant predictor of likelihood of selection. However, the emergence of the modern primary period brought along its own consequences for vice presidential selection mechanisms. See Mark Hiller and Douglas Kriner, "Dynamics of Vice Presidential Selection," *Presidential Studies Quarterly* 38 (2008): 401–421.

14. See E. E. Schattschneider, *Party Government: American Government in Action* (New Brunswick, N.H.: Transaction Publishers, 2004 [1942]).

15. Inter alia see Thomas Holbrook, "The Behavioral Consequences of Vice Presidential Debates: Does the Undercard Have Any Punch?" *American Politics Quarterly* 22 (1994): 469–487; David Romero, "Requiem for a Lightweight: Vice Presidential Candidate Evaluations and the Presidential Vote," *Presidential Studies Quarterly* 31 (2001): 454–463. For a contrasting argument, see Martin Wattenberg, *The Decline of American Political Parties, 1952–1980* (Cambridge: Harvard University Press, 1984); Martin Wattenberg, "The Role of Vice-Presidential Candidate Ratings in Presidential Voting Behavior," *American Politics Quarterly* 23 (1995): 504–514.

16. Cato IV, *New York Journal,* November 8, 1787, in Ellis, *Founding the American Presidency,* 263.

17. Richard Nixon in 1960, Hubert Humphrey in 1968, Walter Mondale in 1984, George H. W. Bush in 1988, and Al Gore in 2000 won their parties' nominations. Only Dan Quayle, who ended his 2000 run before the first primary ballot was cast, failed to become his party's nominee.

18. For the classic political science treatment of momentum in presidential primaries, see Larry Bartels, *Presidential Primaries and the Dynamics of Public Choice* (Princeton: Princeton University Press, 1988).

19. Of course, it could be argued that the vice presidency is most dangerous precisely when the current occupant of the office has *no* intention of seeking the presidency. Such an incumbent is freed from the constraint of seeking the presidency and is empowered to expand aggressively the office's power base.

20. For an insightful and thorough analysis of the emergence of the modern vice presidency, see Joel Goldstein, *The Modern American Vice Presidency: The Transformation of a Political Institution* (Princeton: Princeton University Press, 1982); Joel Goldstein, "The Rising Power of the Modern Vice Presidency," *Presidential Studies Quarterly* 38 (2008): 374–389.

21. "Military Order of November 13, 2001," *Federal Register* 66, no. 222 (November 16, 2001): 57833–57836.

22. For a thorough overview of Cheney's remarkably powerful tenure as vice president, see Barton Gellman, *Angler: The Cheney Vice Presidency* (New York: Penguin Press, 2008); see also James Pfiffner, *Power Play: The Bush Presidency and the Constitution* (Washington, D.C.: Brookings, 2008).

23. Most White House staff officials, including the chief of staff, do not require Senate confirmation.

24. Moreover, the Cheney years are not as anomalous as some protest. Previous vice presidents, most notably Walter Mondale and Al Gore, exerted considerable power and authority in office. Admittedly, they did so to a lesser extent than Cheney; however, these additional precedents speak to the potential for powerful vice presidents to arise again in the future.

CON

1. The argument in this section is developed in greater detail in Joel K. Goldstein, *The Modern American Vice Presidency: The Transformation of a Political Institution* (Princeton: Princeton University Press, 1982).

2. See, generally, Joel K. Goldstein, "The Rising Power of the Modern Vice Presidency," *Presidential Studies Quarterly* 38 (September 2008): 374–389; Richard Moe, "The Making of the Modern Vice Presidency: A Personal Reflection," *Presidential Studies Quarterly* 38 (September 2008): 390–400.

3. Michael Nelson, "Background Paper" in *A Heartbeat Away,* Report of the Twentieth Century Fund Task Force on the Vice Presidency (New York: Priority Press, 1988), 22.

4. U.S. Constitution, Twenty-fifth Amendment. The Twenty-fifth Amendment supplanted in part and also supplemented Article II, Section 1, Clause 6.

5. See, generally, John D. Feerick, *From Failing Hands: The Story of Presidential Succession* (New York: Fordham University Press 1966); John D. Feerick, *The Twenty-Fifth Amendment: Its Complete History and Earliest Applications,* 2nd ed. (New York: Fordham University Press, 1992); Robert E. Gilbert, ed., *Managing*

Crisis: Presidential Disability and the 25th Amendment (New York: Fordham University Press, 2000).

6. For an argument that since the 1970s able people are chosen to run for vice president, see Mark Hiller and Douglas Kriner, "Institutional Change and the Dynamics of Vice Presidential Selection," *Presidential Studies Quarterly* 38 (September 2008): 401–421.

7. I would include on the list of "clearly presidential" Nixon, Johnson, Humphrey, Ford, Rockefeller, Mondale, George H. W. Bush, Al Gore, Dick Cheney, and Joe Biden. Agnew and Dan Quayle are the other two. Quayle has been underestimated, in my view, but he had not been considered a leading presidential candidate when Bush chose him in 1988 and never later had success at that level.

8. Nixon (1968), Johnson, Ford, and Bush became president; Nixon (1960), Humphrey, Ford, and Gore lost four of the closest elections of the twentieth century.

9. Nixon (1960, 1968, 1972), Johnson (1964), Humphrey (1968), Ford (1976), Mondale (1984), Bush (1988, 1992), Gore (2000).

10. These leaders were Johnson (Senate majority leader), Humphrey (Senate majority whip), Ford (House minority leader), Cheney (House minority whip), Biden (chairman of the Senate Judiciary Committee and chairman of the Senate Foreign Relations Committee).

11. Joel K. Goldstein, "Why the Sarah Palin Gamble Didn't Pay Off," History News Service, November 12, 2008, www.h-net.org/~hns/articles/2008/111208a.html.

12. Carter, Reagan, Clinton, and George W. Bush had been governors and had never held office in the national government. Barack Obama had been a senator but for fewer than four years. Of presidents elected since 1976, only George H. W. Bush had had considerable experience in national government when first elected president.

CHAPTER 12: A President's Personal Attributes Are the Best Predictors of Performance in the White House

1. James David Barber, *The Presidential Character: Predicting Performance in the White House* (Englewood Cliffs, N.J.: Prentice-Hall, 1972).
2. Stephen Skowronek, *The Politics Presidents Make: Leadership from John Adams to George Bush* (Cambridge: Belknap Harvard Press, 1993).
3. Fred I. Greenstein, *The Presidential Difference: Leadership Style from FDR to George W. Bush,* 2nd ed. (Princeton: Princeton University Press, 2004).

PRO

1. This article is based on Fred I. Greenstein, *Inventing the Job of President: Leadership Style from George Washington to Andrew Jackson* (Princeton: Princeton University Press, 2009).

CHAPTER 13: Great Presidents Are Agents of Democratic Change

PRO

1. Richard E. Neustadt, *Presidential Power and the Modern Presidents: The Politics of Leadership from Roosevelt to Reagan* (New York: Free Press, 1991), 3–10, 73–90.

2. James MacGregor Burns, *Roosevelt: The Lion and the Fox* (New York: Harcourt, Brace, Jovanovich, 1960), 487.

3. Stephen Skowronek, *The Politics Presidents Make: Leadership from John Adams to Bill Clinton* (Cambridge, Mass.: Belknap Press of Harvard University Press, 1993), 27 (emphasis in original).

4. Marc Landy and Sidney M. Milkis, *Presidential Greatness* (Lawrence: University Press of Kansas, 2000).

5. Felix Frankfurter to Franklin D. Roosevelt, August 9, 1937, Box 210, Papers of Thomas Corcoran, Manuscript Division, Library of Congress, Washington, D.C.

6. James D. Richardson, ed., *A Compilation of the Messages and Papers of the Presidents, Prepared under the Direction of the Joint Committee on Printing, of the House and Senate, Pursuant to an Act of the Fifty-second Congress of the United States (with Additions and Encyclopedic Index by Private Enterprise)*, 20 vols. (New York: Bureau of National Literature, 1917), 1211.

7. Ibid., 1213.

8. Ibid., 1208.

9. Ibid.

10. Robert V. Remini, *Life of Andrew Jackson* (New York: Harper and Row, 1988), 36.

11. Richardson, *Messages and Papers*, 1217.

12. Undated fragment written in late 1860 or early 1861, in Paul N. Angle, ed., *New Letters and Papers of Lincoln* (Boston: Houghton Mifflin, 1930), 241–242. Lincoln's reference is to Proverbs 25:11.

13. Abraham Lincoln, "House Divided Speech," Springfield, Illinois, June 16, 1858, http://www.lincolnbicentennial.gov/about/speeches/housedivided.php (accessed December 16, 2005).

14. Transcripts of these radio addresses have been compiled in Russell D. Buhite and David W Levy, eds., *FDR's Fireside Chats* (Norman: University of Oklahoma Press, 1992).

15. Franklin Delano Roosevelt, "The Commonwealth Club Address," in *Public Papers and Addresses of Franklin D. Roosevelt*, ed. Samuel Rosenman, 13 vols. (New York: Random House, 1938–1950), 1:751–752.

16. See especially Bush's second inaugural address, January 20, 2005, http://www.whitehouse.gov/inaugural/index.html (accessed December 12, 2005).

CON

1. Although Kennedy and Johnson may not fit into the category of great presidents as a general matter, they are often placed in that company in the area of civil rights.

2. Stephen Skowronek, *The Politics Presidents Make: Leadership from John Adams to Bill Clinton* (Cambridge: Belknap Press of Harvard University Press, 1997).

3. Robert V. Remini, "Andrew Jackson and Indian Removal," http://edweb.tusd.k12. az.us (accessed December 16, 2005).

4. Mark E. Neely Jr., *The Fate of Liberty: Abraham Lincoln and Civil Liberties* (New York: Oxford University Press, 1991).

5. Henry quoted in Ralph Ketcham, ed., *The Anti-Federalist Papers* (New York: New American Library, 1986), 211.

6. Max Farrand, ed., *The Records of the Federal Convention of 1787*, 4 vols. (New Haven: Yale University Press, 1937), 1:112.